Conclave

Conclave

THE POLITICS, PERSONALITIES, AND PROCESS OF THE NEXT PAPAL ELECTION

John L. Allen, Jr.

Image

DOUBLEDAY

New York   London   Toronto   Sydney   Auckland

AN IMAGE BOOK
PUBLISHED BY DOUBLEDAY
a division of Random House, Inc.
1540 Broadway, New York, New York 10036

IMAGE, DOUBLEDAY, and the portrayal of a deer drinking from a stream
are trademarks of Doubleday, a division of Random House, Inc.

Book design by Jennifer Ann Daddio

Library of Congress Cataloging-in-Publication Data
Allen, John L., 1965–
   Conclave: the politics, personalities, and process of the next
papal election / by John L. Allen, Jr.
   p. cm.
   1. Popes—Election.   I. Title.
BX1805 .A54 2002
262'.135—dc21

                         2001047607

ISBN 0-385-50453-5
Copyright © 2002 by John L. Allen
All Rights Reserved

PRINTED IN THE UNITED STATES OF AMERICA

July 2002
First Image Books Edition

10 9 8 7 6 5 4 3 2 1

To Shannon . . . as promised.

Ti amo sempre, la mia
dolce ciambella.

Contents

Preface

 FOR ABOUT eight centuries, the Roman Catholic Church has used a strange process called a *conclave* to select its pope. The term comes from two Latin words meaning *with a key* and refers to the practice of putting electors in a locked room and refusing to let them come out until they choose someone. A conclave is an event surrounded by legend, one that uniquely blends theater with mystery, politics with prayer. Oddly enough, the best vantage point to see just how strong a grip the conclave has on the popular religious imagination may not be Rome, with Saint Peter's Square and the Sistine Chapel, but a stretch of rural Highway 24 in northeastern Kansas. Following the road about twelve miles to the north and west of the state capital of Topeka leads one to the small town of Delia, population 172, and a nondescript thrift shop called the Question Mark.

Few realize that the most recent conclave on the record (and there may be others we don't know about) happened not on October 16, 1978, with the election of the archbishop of Krakow, Karol Wojtyla, as John Paul II. Instead it took place in Delia on July 16, 1990, in a tiny chapel inside the Question Mark, space for which had been created by shoving aside the shop's soda machine and laying some shag carpet. Six ultra-right-wing

Catholics gathered to elect the person they regard as the first valid pope since 1958, when Pius XII died. The pope who followed, John XXIII, launched an era of modernization that some traditionalists have never accepted, including the electors in Delia that hot Kansas summer day. They included Clara "Tickie" Bawden, her husband, Kenneth (owner and operator of the Question Mark), a couple from Michigan, a Colorado spiritualist, and the Bawdens' son, David. All are former members of the Society of Saint Pius X, a movement launched by a right-wing French archbishop who disapproved of the liberalizing trends in the Catholic Church after the Second Vatican Council (1962–65). The six who assembled in the Question Mark not only had rejected the mainstream of the Roman Catholic Church but had also abandoned the Pius X movement, alleging that it too had been corrupted by modern secular civilization. (The fact that the society had kicked David out of one of its seminaries was also acknowledged to be a factor. David had later signed up with another traditionalist Catholic group, in Saint Marys, Kansas, only to grow disenchanted there too and eventually cooperate in an exposé published in the *Kansas City Star*.)

As conscientious Catholics, the six electors followed the outlines of the church's process for selecting a pope. They secluded themselves in a chapel, prayed for the guidance of the Holy Spirit, and proceeded to election by secret ballot. They swore before God to discharge their duties faithfully and to elect the person they considered best suited to lead the Roman Catholic Church. In short, they held a conclave. Some incidentals proved impossible to reproduce; no white smoke, for example, appeared above the roof of the Question Mark. For all that, the essentials of the conclave were there. It was a watershed day for the Bawdens, since the new pontiff who emerged from the one-ballot conclave was their son, David. In keeping with a papal custom that dates from the sixth century, he took a new name: Pope Michael I, after Saint Michael the archangel.

Little else changed, however, for the would-be pope. He still lives at home, still takes out the garbage at night. He reigns from his version of a papal throne—an old armchair with orange cushions that sits on the porch of the family house overlooking Highway 24. He insists that his obscurity leaves him untroubled. He takes comfort from Saint Athanasius, whose opposition to the Arian heresy once made him, too, a minority inside the church. Today it's Athanasius that Catholics remember as a saint, while the Arians languish in the dustbin of history. Pope Michael keeps in touch with his flock, estimated at thirty, by answering e-mail and maintaining his Web site (www.homestead.com/POPEMICHAEL/index.html). His biggest problem is that he is not a priest, and thus he cannot celebrate a papal high mass. He wants to find a dissident bishop somewhere in the world willing to impose hands in the sacramentally prescribed fashion, but until that happens, the pews with leopard-print cushions in his private chapel remain empty.

Catholic history offers several cases of popes elected under odd circumstances who later came to be recognized as legitimate. Yet it seems highly unlikely the future holds such validation in store for Michael I. And although the headquarters of the Catholic papacy did once relocate from Rome to Avignon, in France, for sixty-eight years, 1309 to 1377, it's equally doubtful Catholics around the world will ever learn to look to Delia, Kansas, as their spiritual center. Delia is just outside Topeka (which in the Shawnee Indian language means *a good place to dig for potatoes),* and despite its rustic charm, it is difficult to envision the small town as the see of the vast papal bureaucracy. "All roads lead to Delia" does not have quite the right ring.

Yet the image of Pope Michael sitting by a sleepy Kansas highway, musing on his next papal bull, which will be released via the Internet to an audience of a few dozen, nevertheless illustrates the psychological punch the conclave packs. The six people who chose Pope Michael might just as well have drawn straws, played rocks-and-scissors, or simply pointed to David Bawden and said, "It's him." (Indeed, for much of church history, Catholics chose their leader in a variety of ways, and if Saint Peter were somehow to show up at a modern conclave, he would have absolutely no idea of what was going on.) Yet without even discussing the point, the electors in the Question Mark knew that today, after centuries of accumulated tradition, if you want to have a pope, you have to have a conclave—and somehow, the fact of having had a conclave lends legitimacy to their pope. It's a quasimagical chain of causation: because they cast the right spell, the frog turned into a prince—in this case, the successor of the prince of the apostles.

The next time a conclave unfolds in Rome, it will, of course, be a much bigger show than what happened in Delia. Some six thousand journalists are expected to descend on the Eternal City to cover the death of John Paul II and the election of his successor. Roman rooftop space is being snatched up by TV networks hustling to find the just-right shot of the crowd in Saint Peter's Square and the white smoke. CBS, for example, has paid $180,000 for the right to use the five-thousand-square-foot terrace atop the Atlante Star Hotel, beating out CNN and a Japanese network in a fierce bidding war. The terrace offers such a spectacular view of Saint Peter's Square that with a pair of binoculars, one can actually see inside the papal apartments. Cable television networks will be offering virtually round-the-clock coverage, parading a series of talking heads offering commentary in order to fill the long spaces between pieces of real news. (I, too, will be on parade, offering whatever news and insight I can find on the Fox News Channel as their expert analyst.) The world's newspapers will be filled every day with reams of reporting, analysis, and commentary, and the Internet will be abuzz with the wildest possible gossip and speculation—which will then be dutifully reported by many in the press corps.

At least in terms of public interest, the difference between the election of John Paul's successor and the election of Pope Michael is simple: the man who comes out of the Sistine Chapel wearing white really does become head of the Roman Catholic Church. Automatically he becomes one of the most important figures on earth, a man (and it *will* be a man) who commands a unique combination of political and spiritual power. Depending on how he chooses to exercise that power, governments and political systems may rise or fall, religious wars may heat up or abate, and the church may relax or rigidify its stance on issues such as women, sexuality, and the role of the papacy itself. Hence the conclave in Rome shares the element of the numinous with what happened in Delia—the sense of contact with the mysteries of the faith—but it adds the ingredient of very real political consequences. That's what makes the conclave special: it is the Roman Catholic Church in microcosm, a cocktail of ritual, romance, and realpolitik. It is, as both the Bawdens and CNN realize, the greatest show on earth.

This is a book about the conclave, and hence about the election of the next pope. I discuss the issues, the parties, and the people that will be at the heart of the matter when the world's cardinals next gather to elect a successor to Saint Peter. I offer my own top twenty list of front-runners, though the book is not intended as a handicapper's guide to the papal sweepstakes. (I realize some people will use it as such anyway, and if you're one of them, read on; I'll even suggest a couple of Web sites where you can plunk down your bets.) My aim is to help interested people who don't know much about the inner workings of the Catholic Church to understand what the big deal is about a papal election. I explain why it matters who becomes the pope, by looking at what popes in the modern world actually do. I examine the tough issues facing the Catholic Church today that will form the agenda of the next pope. Then I move step by step through the election process, beginning with the first word that the current pope is ill and continuing through the early days of the new pope's reign. I offer my own classification system for the informal political parties that currently exist within the College of Cardinals, the body of 120-plus men who will elect the next pope. Finally I offer a critical, independent look at each of those cardinals, since the new pope is certainly among them. The book is, so to speak, everything you need to know about the next conclave, under one roof.

There are many other very good books that offer bits and pieces of this story, and I have drawn on them liberally. In English, *Inside the*

Vatican: The Politics and Organization of the Catholic Church by Father Thomas J. Reese, S.J., is a good guide to the basics of the conclave process and to the nature of the pope's job. Father Richard P. McBrien's *Lives of the Popes* is a fascinating tour through papal history, including snippets from conclaves past. Peter Hebblethwaite, my predecessor as Vatican correspondent for the *National Catholic Reporter,* offered a readable overview of the conclave process and some of the candidates in *The Next Pope.* The book has been capably updated by Peter's widow and collaborator, Margaret Hebblethwaite. In Italian, no one could enter into this territory without drawing on two masterworks by Giancarlo Zizola: *Il conclave: Storia e segreti: L'elezione papale da San Pietro a Giovanni Paolo II* and *Il Successore.* Alberto Melloni's *Storia del conclave nel Novecento* was also extremely helpful. In the German language, I am indebted to Heiner Boberski, editor of the Austrian Catholic weekly *Die Furche,* for his fine book *Der Nächste Papst,* the only other work I know of that offers critical biographical sketches of all the candidates. I have not only drawn on these books but know the authors personally, and hence am blessed to be able to express my gratitude not just to sources but to valued friends and colleagues. At the same time, what makes this book unique is that it brings together in one place all the information needed to understand the conclave—the process, the personalities, the issues, the parties, and what's at stake.

Before turning to the pope's job, I need to thank certain other individuals without whose assistance the book would have been impossible. My gratitude goes first of all to my colleagues Robert Blair Kaiser and Gerald O'Connell, who each read the entire manuscript and offered constructive criticism. Of course, its flaws are my own, but many of its stronger sentences reflect their input. I also wish to acknowledge Cardinal Franz König of Vienna, the only current cardinal who has participated in three conclaves—that of 1963 and the two of 1978. Without violating his oath of secrecy, König offered invaluable perspectives during an interview at his residence. The editorial staff at the *National Catholic Reporter,* especially editor Tom

Roberts and managing editor Pamela Schaeffer, were indulgent in allowing me time to work on this project. I also want to thank the staff of the Weber Ambassador Hotel on the island of Capri, in whose company much of this book was written. They live in paradise and have not lost their work ethic. *Bravi!* Finally, I need to thank my wife, Shannon, whose support is beyond the poor power of words to describe.

1.

What Does the Pope Do?

 TO UNDERSTAND why the election of a pope is important, we first need to grasp what the pope does. Unfortunately, there is no job description for the head of the Roman Catholic Church. Lots of titles go with the job, but they are of little immediate help: supreme pontiff (*pontifex maximus*), servant of the servants of God, vicar of Christ, successor of Peter, bishop of Rome, patriarch of the West. Catholics sometimes say the pope steps into "the shoes of the fisherman," meaning that he follows Saint Peter, who was a fisherman before being called by Jesus Christ to lead the church. That phrase, unfortunately, is more metaphorical than informative. A twentieth-century way to describe the pope might be to say that he is the legal and spiritual head of the Roman Catholic Church, at 1 billion members the largest Christian denomination in the world, and certainly the most vertically integrated. One way of putting the point: the pope can push a button in Rome and see something happen in Singapore in ways that the archbishop of Canterbury or the Dalai Lama cannot.

In reality, however, the demands of the position are far more vast. A modern pope is called upon to be an intellectual, a politician, a pastor, a media superstar, and a *Fortune* 500 CEO. He must produce complex documents setting out the thinking of the Catholic Church on the most vexing problems that confront humanity. While he has a staff and as many advisers as he wants to help with writing and research, ultimately the message is for him to determine. He must oversee the work of the oldest diplomatic corps on earth, involved in mediating conflicts and protecting the institutional interests of the Catholic Church in dozens of global hot spots. On any given day, the pope may be briefed about the latest violence in the Middle East, about Muslim-Christian slaughter in Indonesia, and about the role of Western commercial interests in sustaining the civil war in the Congo. Then he will be expected to make decisions. If he does too little, he will be accused of indifference; if he does too much, he will be accused of meddling. The pope must be a skilled public figure who knows how to use, rather than be used by, the global communications industry. If he shrinks from publicity, they will say he is weak; if he courts it, they will say he's an egomaniac. Finally, the pope must manage the personnel and financial resources of an enormous multinational religious organization. Since to govern is to choose, as de Gaulle once said, some of those choices are bound to make people unhappy.

Many of these burdens are similar to demands imposed on other world leaders, such as the president of the United States or the secretary general of the United Nations. One key difference is that the pope, in addition to being a politician and administrator, is also expected to be extraordinarily holy. People might forgive a president all sorts of moral failings, but they have higher standards for pontiffs. Another is that being elected pope is, in effect, a life sentence—there's no retirement to anticipate, no comfortable years as an elder statesman writing memoirs and giving lucrative speeches at foreign policy seminars. Popes carry the burden of their office until they die. (We can't follow the idea here, but it's worth noting that if they wanted to, popes *could* retire. There's a provision for it in canon 332 of the Code of Canon Law, the supreme law of the Catholic Church. Some reform-minded Catholics wish popes would do so, in effect building term limits into the system. For now, however, the papacy remains a lifetime occupation.)

For all these reasons, being pope is an impossible job, and despite what you may hear, few church leaders actually want it. Mastering any one of its elements is a life's work. Inevitably, popes emphasize some aspects of the job at the expense of others. Beloved, roly-poly, off-the-cuff John XXIII was a magnificent pastor, but he was never accused of worrying about details. He once summoned Cardinal Franz König of Vienna and told him to go to Budapest to visit Hungarian cardinal József Mindszenty, who had taken refuge from his country's Communist government in the American embassy. A flabbergasted König reminded the pope that it was not simple to get in and out of Iron Curtain countries, especially to visit a man the local authorities regarded as a public menace. Pope John smiled and said, "Find a way." König was irritated by such an offhand dismissal of the problems generated by the request. Then, of course, he found a way to carry it out. Globe-trotting John Paul II strikes an imposing figure for the news producers at CNN, but he too leaves many day-to-day details to others—more, some say, than the CEO of any multinational corporation could without being asked to step down by his board of directors. (The pope, of course, has no board of directors, just a corps of advisers, called cardinals.) He once signed three different criticisms of the work of a major Catholic theologian, Belgian Jesuit Jacques Dupuis, each one changed in important respects, even though each one was supposedly an expression of the pope's quasi-infallible ordinary teaching authority. John Paul was simply signing what was put in front of him without noting the fine print.

Despite the naturally unequal distribution of gifts, the fact remains that popes are called upon to fulfill all of these roles. Inattention to any one of them leads to problems; excellence in any one of them can change the world.

Priest and Bishop

To get a better grip on the job, let's start with the word itself. *Pope* is an English equivalent of the Italian term *papa*, which is the word for *father* (though with a different accent). The idea is that the pope is a spiritual father for the Catholic family, which in some sense includes all the 1 billion members of the Roman Catholic Church worldwide. Popes take this notion very seriously; Paul VI, for example, who served as pope from 1963 to 1978, once said that he could not resign his office because it is not possible to give up "spiritual paternity." A father of a family can't lay down that burden just because he's tired of carrying it, Paul reasoned, and in the same way a pope can't renounce being a spiritual father to his children. (Some Catholic theologians point out, however, that Paul VI decreed a retirement age of seventy-five for bishops, who are also supposed to be spiritual fathers of the Catholics in their care. In this case Paul's logic stopped at the papal doorstep.)

A pope, like any priest, is first and foremost a pastor, someone who offers spiritual guidance, who preaches the word of God, who celebrates the sacraments of the Catholic Church, and whose job it is to help Catholics live holy lives and prepare for communion with God in the next world. John Paul II takes his priesthood to heart, sending out annual letters on Holy Thursday to all the priests of the world, giving advice and offering encouragement. The celebration of his fiftieth anniversary of priestly ordination, in 1996, was one of the biggest events in Rome during his tenure.

The pope is also a bishop. He is the chief shepherd of the archdiocese of Rome, and whenever Catholics in Rome celebrate mass, they pray for "John Paul, our bishop." In fact, theologically speaking, every other function of the papacy is rooted in his status as the bishop of Rome. His claim to primacy comes from the fact that Rome was one of the pillars of the primitive Christian church, the place where both Peter, the leader of the twelve apostles, and Paul, the great missionary, were imprisoned and executed. As the Roman empire was divided into Eastern and Western halves, the bishop of Rome became the leader of the churches in Europe. The sees of Constantinople (modern Istanbul, in Turkey), Alexandria, Antioch, and Jerusalem continued to be, at least in theory, on the same level with Rome. After the division of Christianity between West and East in 1054, the bishop of Rome became the recognized primate over all of the Western church. The Eastern patriarchs, meanwhile, could never agree on which one among them was most important, which helps explain why there are fifteen independent branches of the Eastern Orthodox Church today.

As a matter of fact, however, the pope's status as a local bishop is more symbolic than real. He appoints another cleric to do the administrative work of running the archdiocese of Rome, such as meeting with priests, overseeing budgets, approving building projects, and commenting on the local and national political scene. This post, of *vicar* of Rome, is currently held by Italian cardinal Camillo Ruini, a powerful figure sometimes considered a candidate to become pope himself. John Paul has so far visited 297 of Rome's 330 parishes, but in the end, his responsibilities as pope, especially his trips abroad, mean that his work as a local bishop remains largely nominal.

It is thus the presidential aspect of the pope's work, the nature of his job as Roman Catholicism's chief executive officer, that makes the papacy an object of concern in newsrooms and foreign ministries. The world takes note of John Paul II not primarily because he is a caring priest or talented bishop but because as the leader of the Catholic Church he contributes to shaping the destiny of nations, cultures, and social movements. The next pope could, of course, change this. But if he follows the model set by the popes of the modern age, he will play three core roles:

- a political and diplomatic actor
- the most influential religious leader in the world
- the governor of the Catholic Church

Political Leader

Before 1870, the pope's status as a political figure was much more obvious, since he was a monarch who ruled over the middle third of

Italy, a sizable piece of real estate known as the Papal States. Popes considered this territory essential to the independence of the Catholic Church. Pius IX, who was the last pope to control the Papal States, once compared them to "the robe of Jesus Christ." Borders varied over the years as the political and military fortunes of the papacy waxed and waned, but for centuries, this territory was subject to both the civil as well as the religious laws of the papal bureaucracy. Popes issued ordinances, signed treaties, commanded armies, and even had a few dissidents beheaded. Today's Swiss Guards represent the vestigial remains of the papal military. One can still walk down Roman streets and find Latin inscriptions threatening excommunication and other ecclesiastical penalties for throwing garbage in the streets, a reminder of the days when Rome was the capital of a thriving theocracy.

On September 20, 1870, after the French army abandoned Rome in order to fight Prussia, Italian revolutionaries entered Rome and declared Vittorio Emmanuele the first king of a unified Italy. The pope locked himself up inside the Apostolic Palace, refusing to recognize the new Italian state and declaring himself "prisoner of the Vatican." Some people thought the political role of the papacy was finished forever. In fact, however, the loss of territory freed the pope to be a player on the world stage in a way he never could have been before. At his best, the pope no longer appears as a monarch looking out for his own interests but as a voice of conscience for the world. Moreover, a supranational pope can, at least in theory, rely on support from hundreds of millions of Catholics worldwide, which gives him a capacity to mobilize public opinion that no government can afford to ignore.

The twentieth century offers examples of popes who either changed the course of world history or narrowly missed the opportunity to do so by the way they chose to exercise their political clout. We'll look at three examples that illustrate the nature of the Roman Catholic pope as a political player.

John XXIII and the Opening to the East

The avuncular "Good Pope John," who reigned from October 1958 to June 1963, was the first pope to soften the Vatican's steely line against Communism. In part, the Catholic Church's uncompromising stand was based on ideology, since classical Marxism is atheistic. In part, it reflected the bitter experience of Christians in Marxist states, where priests had been executed, churches looted and burned, and believers packed off to gulags. In part, too, it was rooted in the politics of Italy, which had the strongest Communist party in the West after World War II. Italian Catholics were threatened with excommunication for voting for Communists or any party allied with them, even for reading a Communist newspaper. Cardinal Alfredo Ottaviani, the former head of the Vatican's doctrinal congregation, the Holy Office (the modern successor of the Inquisition), once declared, "People can say whatever they want about the Trinity, but if they vote Communist their excommunication will show up in the mail the next day." Pius XII, pope from 1939 to 1958, was referred to as "the chaplain of NATO" for his pro-Western political stance.

John XXIII, however, felt that the polarization of the world into armed camps, especially in the nuclear age, was unacceptable. Cautiously but firmly, he reoriented the Vatican's foreign policy, sending signals to Marxist governments that he wanted improved relations. The shift came to be known as the Vatican's *Ostpolitik,* or Eastern policy. John XXIII's first encyclical on social questions, entitled *Mater et Magister (Mother and Teacher)* appeared in 1961, and his second, *Pacem in Terris (Peace on Earth)* shortly before his death on June 3, 1963. In the first he endorsed state intervention in sociopolitical matters, a prized principle of socialism, and called for respect for both individual and social rights. *Pacem in Terris* maintained that peace could be reached only by collaboration between all people of upright conscience, which meant even those involved in movements inspired by ideologies that Catholics considered erroneous.

He encouraged Catholics to look beyond political labels, at what public figures actually do, since they may contain "good and commendable elements."

Pope John sent another signal of openness when he decided to receive Nikita Khrushchev's son-in-law, Alexei Adjubei, and his family in a private audience, to the shock and scandal of hard-line anti-Communists. Later, when the pope received John McCone, head of the CIA, in April 1963, he made clear he was not playing favorites. "I bless all the peoples and do not subtract my faith from some of them," the pope said. When Khrushchev sent a greeting for the pope's eightieth birthday, many in the Vatican thought he should ignore it, but John sat down and wrote a reply: "Thank you for the thought," he wrote. "And I will pray for the people of Russia."

The policy paid off during the Cuban missile crisis of October 1962, when, in a little-known chapter of papal diplomacy, Pope John helped ease the tension between Kennedy and Khrushchev. The standoff triggered by the discovery of Soviet missiles in Cuba brought the world as close as it has ever been to nuclear war. Pope John was not directly engaged in the exchanges between the superpowers, but he sent messages, both publicly and privately, urging a solution and offering both sides his support. Khrushchev used the pope's messages to convince hard-liners in the Politburo that not all Western leaders were hostile to the Soviet Union's interests. Khrushchev said: "What the pope has done for peace will go down in history. The pope's message was the only gleam of hope." Kennedy echoed these sentiments, awarding the pope in 1963 a posthumous Presidential Medal of Freedom.

When John XXIII was beatified in September 2000, Romano Prodi, former Italian prime minister and current head of the European Union, said he felt Pope John should receive some of the credit generally assigned to John Paul II for the fall of Communism. Through his policy of *Ostpolitik,* Prodi argued on Italian national television, Pope John challenged the logic of the Cold War. He helped convince the Communist world that the West was not bent on its destruction, and likewise suggested to the West that Russia (and all of Eastern Europe) could change if given a chance to join the world community. Hence, when the internal problems of socialist economies became unsustainable, the peoples of Eastern Europe, including most of their leaders, did not think the only option was conflict. They felt they could bring down the walls because they saw a degree of sympathy on the other side. Prodi may be overvaluing the role of a pope he obviously cherished, but he is not the only one who has underlined the global political significance of John XXIII's initiatives.

PAUL VI AND VIETNAM

The political clout of the papacy can also be glimpsed from its failures, such as Paul VI's efforts to end the Vietnam War. The brilliant, brooding Paul VI was elected to succeed John XXIII in June 1963, and he continued his *Ostpolitik*. Given the Vatican's effort to address itself to all nations and ideological systems, Western leaders came to see it as uniquely positioned to mediate in situations of conflict. Recently declassified documents from the U.S. State Department show that President Lyndon Johnson repeatedly sought Paul VI's help from 1965 to 1968 in trying to find a way out of the war. Those efforts included two personal meetings between the president and the pope—one in New York's Waldorf-Astoria Hotel—as well as three personal letters from Johnson to Pope Paul and a meeting between the pope and Vice President Hubert Humphrey.

In part, Johnson hoped to exploit Paul VI to advance U.S. war aims. Johnson requested papal declarations critical of North Vietnam, for example, as well as Vatican intervention with Hanoi over the treatment of American prisoners of war. He also hoped Paul would lean on Catholic officials in Saigon to open a dialogue with Communist sympathizers in South Vietnam, trying to bring them over to the American cause. Paul refused these requests and insisted on preserving Vatican neutrality, but signaled his desire to do what he could to bring a just peace. On February 10, 1965, he had a cable sent to Johnson expressing this aim. "His Holiness is deeply worried over developments in Southeast Asia," the cable read. "He appreciates the gravity and delicacy of the situation and is gravely concerned lest it lead to general war."

In early 1967, Pope Paul met Vice President Hubert Humphrey in Florence. The pope offered suggestions on how to improve the U.S. image in Vietnam and "repeatedly volunteered his services," Humphrey said. The pontiff suggested using South Vietnamese officials as military spokesmen instead of Americans because it appeared to the average person that "big, strong America is being brutal and cruel" with its overwhelming public presence in Saigon, Humphrey wrote. Shortly before Christmas 1967, Johnson, returning to the United States from Australia, stopped at the Vatican for a second meeting with Pope Paul. "I must differentiate my position from yours although I very clearly understand your good intentions and your good hopes," the pope said, according to a transcript of the conversation. "I want to further the solidarity of my agreement with your intentions but you must understand I can never agree to war," he said, asking if he could tell Hanoi's Soviet sponsors that Washington truly wanted peace.

Paul VI hoped to celebrate Christmas mass in Saigon in 1968 and then to visit North Vietnam. His request was refused by Hanoi in the wake of the Tet offensive. The Johnson administration eventually abandoned the idea of using Paul as a mediator, choosing instead to pursue the Paris peace talks. The war dragged on for almost five more years. Paul's initiative was, measured against his own hopes, a failure. Nevertheless, the three-year effort of the president of the United States to enlist the pope in the most critical foreign policy crisis of the time is an eloquent testimony to the political importance of the papacy. Johnson rightly perceived that no other world leader had Pope Paul's capacity to appear credible to both sides. Moreover, the Vatican's centuries of diplomatic experience meant that the United States could count on the pope not to muddle his good intentions through poor statecraft. Vatican diplomacy is, in that sense, a unique combination of appeals to conscience and time-tested realism.

JOHN PAUL II AND THE BEAGLE ISLANDS

John Paul's role in helping to bring about the fall of Communism in Eastern Europe is so well documented that it hardly needs repeating. The pope's influence on the political reunification of Europe was such a stunning event that it has in some ways obscured other political victories of his pontificate. To illustrate the way in which this pope has been a political force, it will be helpful to take a less-known example, that of the Vatican's role in avoiding a war between Argentina and Chile in 1979 over control of the Beagle Islands.

The Beagle Islands, which lie just off the southern tip of Latin America, are named after the British ship in which Charles Darwin explored the area between 1831 and 1836. The argument between Argentina and Chile over who owns these three small islands (named Picton, Lennox, and Nueva) dates back to the nineteenth century. At stake was not just control of the islands but also thirty thousand square miles of fishing and mineral rights. The case ended up before the International Court of Justice in 1971, which pondered it for six years before ruling for Chile on May 2, 1977. Argentina disputed the decision and sought a new round of negotiations. Preparations for war began in July, an alarming development since both nations were then ruled by military dictators. General Augusto Pinochet had seized power from socialist Salvador Allende in Chile in 1973, and in 1977, a military junta had taken control in Argentina. On December 9, 1978, Argentina sent a naval squadron to the Beagle Channel region. The country's military leaders apparently did not believe that Chile would actually fight to defend the islands, and thus they gave the order to seize them. Argentina drafted a declaration of war to legitimize the occupation. The weather intervened, and a storm prevented Argentine troops from landing. Both sides understood they were on the brink of a devastating war.

On December 11, Pope John Paul II sent a personal message to both presidents urging a peaceful solution. The pope pointed out that both nations were overwhelmingly Catholic, with long-standing good relations with the Holy See, and he offered to help mediate the conflict. Preparations for a war continued on both sides. Argentina complained to the United Nations, while Chile asked the Organization of American States to convene to hear its case. Neither organization was able to move negotiations forward. John Paul then offered to send Vatican officials to arbitrate the dispute. On December 21, 1978, Chile accepted the pope's mediation, and Argentina did so the next day. The results were dramatic. On January 9, 1979, the Act of Montevideo was signed, pledging both sides to finding a peaceful solution and to a return to the military situation of early 1977, before the mobilizations. War was averted, although the tensions were not completely eliminated until the democratic government of Raul Alfonsin took office in Argentina in December 1983.

On January 23, 1984, Argentina and Chile signed a Treaty of Peace and Friendship. In a telling tribute to the pope's role, the treaty was signed at the Vatican. It specified maritime boundaries, called for increased physical integration and economic cooperation, and established a binational commission to promote these goals. It set up conflict resolution procedures to deal with future disputes and addressed navigational issues. Both sides ended up with rights of access to the islands and the adjacent territorial waters. After 80 percent of the Argentine electorate voted to accept the Vatican-mediated compromise, a protocol of agreement was signed on October 18. It was ratified by Argentina on March 14, 1985, and by Chile on April 12, 1985.

The point to be gleaned from these three examples—John XXIII, Paul VI, and John Paul II—is that the personal background and interests of the man who becomes pope can, under the right circumstances, change history. John's desire to be pope not just for Catholics but for all men and women led to his historic opening to the East, which helped make coexistence in the nuclear age possible. Paul VI did not succeed in ending the war in Vietnam, but he tried. Who knows how many lives were saved by the pope's insistent pressure for peace? John Paul's willingness to get involved wherever Catholic interests are at stake has also revitalized the political capital of the papacy.

Religious Leader

While religion is still a powerful force in shaping culture, it no longer controls the culture in the West. The dominant realities of the modern period are secularization and pluralism. Institutions such as the media, education, social services, and the courts operate independently of ecclesiastical control. Governments no longer compel membership in a particular religion. The days of *cuius regio, eius religio*—"whoever the ruler, his the religion"—are over. Where spiritual leaders could once take the option for *religion itself* as a given, and argue over *which one,* today they have to propose the very idea of religion to a culture that often finds it alien.

Several figures in the world community today have a high media profile and the capacity to articulate a religious message—the Dalai Lama, for example, and Archbishop Desmond Tutu of South Africa. But if one were to ask a sample of randomly selected persons, at least in the West, what word they associate with *religious leader,* most would come up with *pope.* For better or worse, the Roman Catholic pontiff is the most recognizable spiritual leader in the world, with the strongest bully pulpit and the most significant presence in the mass media. Hence the pope plays a unique, if undeclared and sometimes controversial, role as a spokesperson for the religious community. How he chooses to exercise that role can have enormous impact.

One example came on October 27, 1986, when John Paul II

hosted a one-day summit of religious leaders from around the world in Assisi, Italy, to pray for peace. The group that assembled in Assisi in 1986 was unique. It included rabbis wearing yarmulkes and Sikhs in turbans, Muslims praying on thick carpets and a Zoroastrian kindling a sacred fire. Robert Runcie, the Anglican archbishop of Canterbury, exchanged pleasantries with the Dalai Lama. Orthodox bishops chatted with Allan Boesak, the South African antiapartheid activist and president of the World Alliance of Reformed Churches. The leaders came to Assisi not to "pray together"—according to the pope's advisers, that would be theologically problematic, since prayer presupposes doctrinal agreement—but "to be together and pray."

Despite strong pressure from the conservative wing of the Catholic Church to abandon the idea, John Paul saw this gathering as an expression of his mission of promoting unity. At one point, each of the faiths was assigned a church to hold services. Buddhists chanted and beat drums, while Shintoists played haunting melodies on thin bamboo reed instruments. Afterward they all assembled with the pope and formed a circle to offer their own prayers. Two animists from Africa prayed: "Almighty God, the Great Thumb we cannot avoid in tying any knot, the Roaring Thunder that splits mighty trees, the All-Seeing Lord up on high who sees even the footprints of an antelope on a rock here on earth . . . you are the cornerstone of peace." John Pretty-on-Top, a Crow medicine man from Montana in full headgear and smoking a peace pipe, offered: "O Great Spirit, I raise my pipe to you, to your messengers the four winds, and to mother earth, who provides for your children. . . . I pray that you bring peace to all my brothers and sisters of this world." After the prayers were finished the spiritual leaders gathered at a Franciscan monastery for a meal of bread, pizza, vegetables, Coke, and water (in a rare concession for Italians, no wine was served, so as not to offend believers for whom alcohol is off limits).

John Paul has pressed the cause of interreligious harmony beyond the gathering in Assisi, becoming the first pope to visit a Jewish synagogue (in Rome in 1986) and the first pope to enter an Islamic mosque (in Damascus in 2001). It is difficult to establish what sort of impact these gestures generate, but most observers agree that at a symbolic level, they are enormously important. When the pope and a rabbi, or the pope and an imam, embrace in public and wish each other well, it sends a signal. Those who wish to commit violence in the name of religion or to hate in the name of religion are marginalized. They can no longer present themselves as allies of their own leadership.

In addition to his interreligious role, the pope is also the most visible Christian figure in the world, and hence has another special role as the informal leader of the Christian community. (Christians call relations between themselves *ecumenical;* relations with non-Christian groups are known as *interreligious dialogue.*) Despite the prayer of Jesus that his followers "may all be one," Christians are badly divided into a staggering variety of denominations and splinter groups. Worldwide, there are more than 2 billion Christians, roughly one-third of the planet's population. Roman Catholics constitute the largest group, with slightly more than 1 billion members, followed by mainline Protestants (such as Methodists, Lutherans, and Baptists), with 321 million. The world's Orthodox Churches have 222 million believers. Anglicans, whom most people classify separately, report 74.5 million. In addition, there are almost 450 million Christians around the world who belong to a local church community that has no strong affiliation with any larger group. Many are so-called *pentecostal* and *charismatic* communities, which stress the gifts of the Holy Spirit, such as spiritual healings and speaking in tongues. It is a bewildering cacophony of theologies and styles of prayer and practice.

There are places where members of the different branches of Christianity live in near-perfect solidarity. In ancient Christian villages in the mountains of Syria, for example, one can find Orthodox and Catholic believers who have been living side by side for centuries, who attend one another's sacraments and feasts, who make practically no distinction between members of one church and the other. When one asks Syrian Christians whether they are Orthodox or Catholic, the question often elicits a puzzled expression indicating this is not something they think about very much. It is a charming example of peaceful coexistence. Yet in other places, relations are hardly so pacific. Divisions between Christians have caused much bloodshed over the years. Think of Europe's wars of religion or of Northern Ireland's ongoing battles between Catholics and Protestants. If Christians can't get together, how can they preach unity to the wider world?

Under the impact of globalization, the followers of the world's religions are rubbing up against one another as never before. Religious diversity is a fact of modern life and is, at present, a mixed blessing. There are places where cultures have been enriched and strengthened by a reciprocal exchange between different religions, but religion (along with language, ethnicity, culture, and geography) is fast becoming one of the principal factors in the social equation that ends in violence. In the Sudan, for example, where a long-running civil war pits Muslims in the north against Christians in the south, more than 1.9 million people have died since 1983, and another 4 million have been displaced. In Kashmir, a disputed province on the border between India and Pakistan, religion (Hindus versus Muslims) is a main bone of contention. In the 1990s, 24,000 people died, by the Indian government's official count. Others say 40,000; still others, 70,000. In the Balkans, where Orthodox Serbs battled the Western Christian nations of NATO as well as Muslim Kosovar Albanians, the Serbs took 5,000 military casualties and 2,000 civilian deaths. The Kosovars lost an estimated 10,000 lives, and more than 800,000 people at one time or another found themselves refugees. NATO believes that mass murders took place in at least sixty-five villages. The NATO-led bombing campaign against Serbia also claimed a number of civilian casualties, and there are voices in the Orthodox world that see that result as part of a Western, largely Catholic, anti-Orthodox campaign. In East Timor, horrific slaughter seemed to stem from enmity between Christians and Muslims. Of course, the tragic events of September 11, 2001, also had strong religious undertones.

In a world threatened ever more by tribalism, religion has a remarkable capacity to stir the dark side of the human soul. Spiritual leaders are called upon to reject violence hallowed by religious conviction. Cooperation, whether between Christians or between the followers of all the world's religions, will require a sustained commitment to dialogue. The pope is in a position, institutionally and because of his media profile, to chair that dialogue. It is a role that John Paul II's successor will have to play in an ever more sustained and complex fashion.

Governor of the Catholic Church

According to the Code of Canon Law, the body of law that regulates the internal life of the Catholic Church, the pope is the *supreme legislator*. At least in theory, his is the last word on every question. Before anything else—before he involves himself in secular politics or reaches out to members of other religions or other Christian churches—the pope is responsible for the internal life of the Catholic Church. Of course, Catholicism is a sprawling, 1 billion–strong international church, and no pope can possibly make all its decisions. Even if he tried, experience suggests that many Catholics might not listen. Since the Second Vatican Council (1962–65), an increasing number of Western Catholics have tended to minimize the pope's authority, seeing him as a symbol of unity but not necessarily someone to be obeyed in every particular. *Dissent* has entered the Catholic vocabulary as a legitimate option, at least in some people's minds. Thus for both practical and political reasons, the vast majority of judgment calls in the Catholic Church are made on the local level. Yet Catholicism remains a tenaciously hierarchical body compared to mainline Protestantism or Hinduism. How any given pope chooses to exercise this power is one of the central hallmarks of his reign.

TEACHING

The pope is the ultimate voice on the doctrine, or the teaching, of the Catholic Church. This power is not unlimited, since popes are bound by precedent. They cannot decide that the Catholic Church no longer believes in the Trinity, or in life after death. Nevertheless, new questions constantly arise, and applications of old teaching are always needed. To this end, popes issue many documents, some of them long and complex, some short and to the point. They have exotic-sounding names: apostolic exhortations, documents *motu proprio,* encyclicals. It is an open question exactly how many Catholics actually read these documents, but they nevertheless can have serious repercussions. In them, popes mark out the limits of Catholic faith, challenge opinions they find erroneous, encourage some kinds of development in the church and retard others, and mark out their priorities.

Today the most important type of papal document is an *encyclical,* a lengthy meditation on some topic of high importance. The word comes from the Greek *kyklos,* which means *circle,* and hence an encyclical is a letter meant to circulate widely in the church. Under John Paul II, the argument has been made that encyclicals are part of the *ordinary and universal magisterium*—in other words, the normal teaching activity of the church. Over time, this ordinary magisterium may acquire a kind of infallibility, even if its content is never officially declared infallible. Encyclicals express the most important points a pope wishes to make to the church and to the world; a pope's first encyclical is usually considered programmatic for the rest of his pontificate.

John Paul II has so far issued these thirteen encyclicals, their Latin titles coming from the opening words of the documents:

Redemptor Hominis (March 4, 1979), on salvation in Jesus Christ

Dives in Misericordia (November 30, 1980), on the mercy of God the Father

Laborem Exercens (September 14, 1981), on the value of human work

Slavorum Apostoli (June 2, 1985), on the churches of Eastern Europe

Dominum et Vivificantem (May 18, 1986), on the Holy Spirit

Redemptoris Mater (March 25, 1987), on the Virgin Mary

Sollicitudo Rei Socialis (December 30, 1987), on economic justice

Redemptoris Missio (December 7, 1990), on missionary work

Centesimus Annus (May 1, 1991), on Catholic social teaching

Veritatis Splendor (August 6, 1993), on the challenge of relativism

Evangelium Vitae (March 25, 1995), on sexuality and bioethics

Ut Unum Sint (May 25, 1995), on ecumenism and Christian unity

Fides et Ratio (September 14, 1998), on harmony between human reason and faith

Some of these documents were forgotten as soon as they appeared, though others had enormous consequences and continue to be touchstones for Catholic debate. *Veritatis Splendor,* for example, rejected many forms of dissent from papal teaching and has led to crackdowns on theologians, especially in the area of moral theology and ethics. In mid-2000, Spanish moral theologian Marciano Vidal was the object of a denunciation from the Vatican's Congregation for the Doctrine of the Faith, the chief theological watchdog agency in the church, for alleged deviations from the line spelled out in *Veritatis*

Splendor. (He had suggested that under certain narrowly defined circumstances one could justify masturbation, homosexuality, abortion, or artificial birth control.) Another encyclical, *Ut Unum Sint,* is an important point of reference in the ecumenical field. In it, John Paul called for reflection on how papal primacy might be reinterpreted in ways that would make it more acceptable to other Christian groups. This invitation displeased some lieutenants in the Roman Curia, who saw it as a threat to their own authority.

Another type of papal document, an *apostolic constitution,* can be important in creating new policies or laws. Under John Paul, one of the most debated has been *Ex Corde Ecclesiae,* of August 15, 1990, which asserted new controls over Catholic colleges and universities. Most controversially, it required a theologian wanting to teach at a Catholic university to receive a *mandatum,* or license, from the local bishop. The idea was to give bishops more direct control over the way in which theology is taught in Catholic universities. The document has proved difficult to implement in the United States, where the country's tradition of academic freedom makes such external controls problematic (though the pope hardly sees episcopal authority at a Catholic university as *external*). Another important apostolic constitution is *Universi Dominici Gregis,* of February 22, 1996, setting the rules for the next papal conclave.

Popes also issue a type of document called a *motu proprio,* a term that signifies the provisions were decided on by the pope personally, that is, not on the advice of the cardinals or others but for reasons that he himself deemed sufficient. It's meant to indicate that the force of the conclusion does not depend upon the reasoning but upon the pope's exercise of his personal authority. Two controversial examples under John Paul are *Apostolos Suos,* of May 21, 1998, restricting the authority of national bishops' conferences, and *Ad Tuendam Fidem,* of May 18, 1998, writing penalties for theological dissent into canon law.

Given the enormous volume of literature churned out under the pope's name, it is impossible to imagine that the pope writes every

word himself. With encyclicals, John Paul has often used a drafting
committee, while reserving control over the finished product to himself. With other types of documents, the pope's involvement is sometimes restricted to reading it or having it explained to him, and then
affixing his name. When a new document appears, seasoned Vatican
watchers often try to figure out who actually wrote it. Officials rarely
reveal the names of people who worked on a document because they
do not want to undercut its authority as a papal text. No matter who
wrote the document, they say, it always reflects the authority of the
Holy See. That, of course, does not stop some from trying to peer behind the curtain. Acquiring a reputation for having helped shape papal documents can often be a help to an ecclesiastical career.
Cardinal Dionigi Tettamanzi of Genoa, for example, is regarded as a
serious *papabile,* or candidate to be the next pope, in part because he
contributed to several Vatican documents on moral theology, most especially the 1995 encyclical *Evangelium Vitae.*

ORGANIZATIONAL MANAGEMENT

The pope is the supreme head of the Catholic Church, but he is
more immediately the boss of the Roman Curia, the bureaucracy inside the Vatican. More than three thousand people are employed in
the Vatican, although the number of decision makers is much
smaller. Given that the number-one and number-two officials (the
prefects and the *secretaries)* of the various congregations, councils,
and tribunals hold ultimate authority on most questions, one could
say that approximately fifty men actually run the Catholic Church.
Theoretically, the curia exists to be of service to the pope in performing his tasks as bishop of Rome and head of the church. In fact,
the curia functions as a kind of federal branch of government, exercising oversight over the other levels of authority, such as national
conferences of bishops, dioceses, even individual parishes and
schools. Of course, the curia has no police force, and a few bishops

say they just ignore edicts not to their liking. (A good example came in the summer of 2001, when the curial office for worship ordered Archbishop Rembert Weakland of Milwaukee not to destroy the baldachino, or spiral canopy, over the main altar of his cathedral. Weakland said he felt he had complied with the spirit of the curia's concerns, and he demolished the baldachino anyway.) Most often, however, the curia eventually gets its way.

The pope keeps track of the curia largely through regular meetings with the cardinals who act as prefects, or heads, of the various agencies. Hence he meets with Cardinal Joseph Ratzinger, head of the Congregation for the Doctrine of the Faith, every Friday afternoon. He sees Cardinal Giovanni Battista Re, head of the Congregation for Bishops, on Saturdays. The secretary of state, Cardinal Angelo Sodano, and the number-two official at the Secretariat of State, Archbishop Leonardo Sandri, see the pope more regularly, sometimes almost daily, as the world situation demands. During these meetings the pope will review decisions, sign documents, give direction on policy matters, and listen to updates about ongoing projects. Sometimes the pope will also participate in interdicasterial meetings (offices in the curia are referred to as *dicasteries*), which involve the prefects of several Vatican offices, to discuss major policy questions. In March 2001, for example, an interdicasterial meeting was held to discuss the reintegration of the followers of the late French archbishop Marcel Lefebvre. The pope heard various opinions and decided the time was not yet right to take action.

How is curial authority exercised? An example will help. A few years ago an American bishop of a major city had agreed to sponsor an ecumenical service in his cathedral. The service called for liturgical dancers to perform as part of the ritual. Knowing that liturgical dance has been a controversial subject in the curia, the bishop asked his liturgical expert to contact Rome and make sure that their plans would not run into any opposition. The official called, faxed, and sent e-mails to the office for liturgy, without any response. The bishop then instructed him to go ahead with plans for the event. Less than twenty-four hours after the program was published, a fax arrived from the Vatican office on liturgy instructing the bishop to drop the liturgical dance. Though angry, the bishop complied.

The incident illustrates three points. First, modern telecommunications have extended the reach of the curia, like that of other centralized bureaucracies. One hundred years ago the service would have been over before Rome received a letter informing them of what was happening. Today, busybodies use e-mail. Second, curial officials often concern themselves with even the smallest details of local affairs when they feel a matter of principle is at stake. This can infuriate bishops and other local Catholics, who object that curial officials cannot possibly understand the dynamics of their situation. From a curial point of view, on the other hand, it would be unfair to demand that Catholics in one place observe a certain norm and not to expect others to do the same. Moreover, curial officials believe distance from the local situation allows them to make judgments that are more serene and objective, untainted by local pressures. Third, the story also illustrates the tricky question of who has the curia's ear. In the case cited above, the bishop's own expert couldn't get a response from Rome, but a grump with the right fax number obviously could. (It is possible that a wise curial official did not want to take official notice, but once the plans became public, felt forced to do so. But curial offices rarely reveal the history behind their decisions.)

A pope must strike a delicate balance in dealing with the curia. On the one hand, he is dependent upon the curia in implementing his policies, and hence must be cooperative. Many curial officials are dedicated servants of the church whom any pope would feel obliged and pleased to support. Yet the pope also cannot allow the curia to get out of control, antagonizing bishops and local communities and thus dividing the church. Pope Paul VI had attempted a sort of reform of the curia by depriving cardinals of their right to vote in papal elections at age eighty and setting a retirement age of seventy-five, but in the process he badly antagonized some of his own lieutenants. John Paul II, on the other hand, has taken a hands-off approach, concerning himself with big-picture concerns and otherwise leaving his appointees to figure out the details. Every pope has to figure out how to back his closest associates, while also making sure the rest of the church does not feel suffocated.

APPOINTING BISHOPS

Teaching means very little if people aren't inclined to listen to the teacher. In order to keep the world's Catholics moving in the same direction, a pope has to rely upon his bishops, the men who lead local church communities across the world. Today there are more than four thousand bishops in the Catholic Church. The majority of them head local churches (called *dioceses*). Larger churches are *archdioceses,* headed by an archbishop, who is often assisted by auxiliary bishops. Virtually all of them are appointed by the pope, though few Catholics realize that this central control is quite recent. In the early church, bishops were selected by the people of a diocese, in some cases by simple acclamation, in others by voting. Sometimes this worked well, and in other cases bribery, force, and demagoguery produced spectacularly bad results. Yet local election of bishops, at least as a principle, lived on in the church for centuries. The first bishop in the United States, John Carroll of Baltimore, was elected to the post by the priests of the thirteen states. As late as 1829, when Pope Leo XII died, there were 646 diocesan Latin-rite bishops outside the Papal States, and only twenty-four had been appointed by the pope. Over the nineteenth century, popes gradually won (or seized) the right to name bishops, arguing that doing so would help protect local churches from being unduly pressured by secular authorities. The 1917 Code of Canon Law made this official by saying the pope has the exclusive power to appoint bishops in the Latin rite, or Western church.

No pope can possibly make informed appointments all over the world by himself. Hence he relies primarily on the *nuncios,* papal ambassadors to the various nations, who have the job of collecting information about prospective candidates and passing it on to Rome. In making his assessment the nuncio can rely upon input from the current bishop and others in the local church, but he has no obligation to do so. Normally the nuncio is looking for someone who is a mix of good pastor and good administrator, and a man who toes the line on matters of church doctrine and practice. In Rome the nuncio's report is evaluated by the Congregation for Bishops, and eventually three names (the list is known as a *terna*) are given to the pope for a final decision. If the bishop is to serve in what has traditionally been considered a mission territory, such as Africa or Asia, the nomination will go through the Congregation for the Evangelization of Peoples. The Congregation for Bishops handles about 135 appointments every year, the Congregation for Evangelization fifty or so.

Usually the pope simply accepts the top recommendation put before him; one cardinal has said the pope accepts "the overwhelming majority" of these recommendations. On occasion, however, John Paul has been known to send lists back for further consideration or simply to appoint other people he prefers to key posts. When New York's powerful Cardinal John O'Connor died in 2000, for example, the pope rejected the *terna* given to him and insisted on naming Edward Michael Egan to the post. Egan had been a close associate of the pope when he worked in Rome, having advised him on the 1983 revision of the Code of Canon Law.

The process has been heavily criticized for lacking any formal guarantee that the people of the diocese, including the clergy, have a say in the selection of the bishop. Others argue that popes, especially John Paul, use their monopoly to ensure that bishops are like-minded papal loyalists, restricting the diversity that should characterize the church. They point to a few ultraconservative John Paul nominees who have badly divided local churches or national bishops' conferences: Hans Hermann Groër and Kurt Krenn in Austria, Wolfgang Haas in Switzerland, George Pell in Australia, Fabian Bruskewitz in the United States. Defenders argue that papal appointment means the selection of bishops is protected from ideological pressures on the local level. Moreover, they say, a few flops should not obscure the vast majority of appointees who turn out to be decent, competent men.

There are few papal prerogative more decisive in exercising control over the church than the appointment of bishops. In Austria, for example, under the leadership of Cardinal Franz König, the Catholic Church in the 1960s and 1970s had acquired a reputation as open, moderate, and committed to dialogue and social justice. Critics believed internal discipline under König was lax, however, and John Paul agreed. He appointed ultraconservative Krenn as an auxiliary in Vienna, then gave him his own diocese in Sankt Pölten. The pope named Groër to replace König in Vienna, then tapped Dominican theologian Christoph Schönborn when Groër had to resign in the wake of allegations that he had been making sexual advances to young monks. The effect has been to reorient the bishops' conference in Austria sharply to the right. Similarly, in the United States, John Paul has appointed a string of papal loyalists to key posts, such as Bernard Law in Boston, Francis George in Chicago, Charles Chaput in Denver, William Levada in San Francisco, and Justin Rigali in Saint Louis. The U.S. bishops' conference, which during the 1980s issued widely praised documents on peace and economic justice that reflected overwhelming consensus, is now much more divided, and in the eyes of some, subservient to Rome.

MAINTAINING DISCIPLINE

Part of what it means to be the boss is dealing with personnel. Every pope has to confront this kind of headache: defiant bishops who threaten the unity of the church; dissident theologians who question every papal pronouncement; clerical embarrassments who marry, steal from church coffers, or spill secrets revealed to them in confessionals. How a pope manages this part of the job, especially the balance he strikes between being firm and also being compassionate, is critically important. In part, the pope sets a tone for lower levels of management in his selection of which problems he handles and how he approaches them. In a larger sense, he sends signals to the world about what Catholicism is really like when confronting the hard questions of real life.

Two cases from John Paul's tenure make the point. French archbishop Marcel Lefebvre, who died in 1991, was a fierce critic of the changes unleashed in the Catholic Church by the Second Vatican Council, especially translation of the mass from Latin into the vernacular languages. Without authorization, Lefebvre set up his own seminary in Switzerland and ordained his own priests in order to keep alive the pre–Vatican II Latin mass, which he regarded as the only valid mass. Up to a point the Vatican was willing to tolerate his actions, but when Lefebvre ordained four bishops in 1988 in order to ensure that his movement would continue after his own death, John Paul II declared a formal schism and excommunicated Lefebvre and his bishops. Today Lefebvre's Society of Saint Pius X claims 150,000 followers in thirty-seven nations with 401 priests, 200 seminarians, 55 brothers, and two religious communities with a total of 198 members.

In the years since the schism, John Paul II has repeatedly signaled his interest in bringing the Lefebvrites, as they are popularly known, back into the fold. Formal negotiations began anew in the summer of 1999, when the head of the Vatican's Ecclesia Dei Commission, created by the pope to heal the schism, wrote to each of the four bishops ordained by Lefebvre. Colombian cardinal Dario Castrillón Hoyos addressed the bishops as "my dear brothers" and said that the pope's arms were open wide to embrace them. A meeting between three of the bishops and Castrillón took place on August 14, 2000, in Castrillón's Rome apartment. One public signal of progress came on August 8, 2000, when more than a thousand members of the society entered Saint Peter's Basilica for a prayer service to mark the Jubilee Year. Though the event had not been on the Vatican calendar, officials acknowledged it had taken place with the approval of the Holy See. Though talks are currently stalled, the Vatican continues to express its interest in reconciliation.

That kind of pastoral interest, some critics would say, has not been present in cases in which the troublemaker was on the left rather than the right. An example is Edward Schillebeeckx, a Dominican theologian who has long been regarded as a thorn in the side of John Paul and the curia. One of the world's best-known Catholic theologians, Schillebeeckx has faced three different Vatican investigations for his progressive views. Though he has never been silenced, nor have his works ever been condemned, some Catholics see him as disloyal to the papacy. Two of the three investigations came under John Paul's papacy. In 1979 Schillebeeckx was compelled to answer questions about his book *Jesus: An Experiment in Christology.* The issues ranged from whether Jesus was conscious of his mission as Messiah to whether Jesus' tomb really was empty. In the mid-1980s, Schillebeeckx was interrogated for his views on ministry. Based on his historical study, Schillebeeckx concluded that the church always gives itself the ministers it needs, hence the ordination of married men and women "cannot be excluded."

No sign of rapprochement has been forthcoming from the Vatican. In 2000, under pressure from the Roman curia, the University of Nijmegen, in Holland, dropped plans to name an academic chair for Schillebeeckx in honor of his eighty-fifth birthday. The gesture seemed petty to some observers, who felt the pope and his advisers could have left the aging Schillebeeckx alone. A similar moment came in 1999, when Catholic and Lutheran leaders signed a joint statement declaring their old debates on the doctrine of justification closed. Swiss Catholic writer Hans Küng, whose work on justification in the 1960s blazed the trail for the agreement, was supposed to be on the guest list for the signing ceremony in Augsburg, Germany. But because his license to teach as a Catholic theologian had been lifted by Rome in 1979 due to his views on papal infallibility, the Vatican insisted his name be crossed out. Many observers wondered if a twenty-year-old dispute over an unrelated issue really required such a punitive gesture. Others, however, see such actions as part of John Paul's iron determination that the faith handed down by the apostles not be squandered by theologians who are either seeking popular approval or in love with their own daring new ideas.

TRAVEL

Paul VI was the first modern pope to take his show on the road, making twenty-three foreign trips. Before Paul, the Vatican attitude on travel was still basically imperial: the pope doesn't go to the people, they come to him. Paul, however, believed that this regal posture was preventing the papacy from bringing its message to the world. John Paul II followed Paul's lead with high enthusiasm. He has so far made ninety-five trips outside Italy, visiting more than 121 nations, logging some 650,000 miles in the process. Some trips left indelible images, such as that of the pope placing a note inside the Wailing Wall in Jerusalem, asking pardon for mistreatment of Jews by Christians over the centuries. On the other hand, many were largely forgettable, and some imposed large debts on local churches that took years to pay off.

In some cases, according to critics, the trips were little more than exercises in "papolatry," a demonstration of the pope's command of the masses that had more value as propaganda than as pastoral work. Certainly the trips were hits with the media, which followed John Paul in great numbers. When the pope went to Syria in May 2001, for example, local organizers said some six hundred foreign journalists followed him. Most experts believe that John Paul's successor will travel less, if only because few leaders could keep up the same pace (spokesperson Joaquín Navarro-Valls once jokingly suggested that somebody should explain to the pope what the word *weekend* means). Given the precedents set by Paul VI and John Paul, however, the next pope will have to be a pilgrim.

2.

Voting Issues

 POPE JOHN Paul II has appointed virtually all of the cardinals who will elect his successor. As of this writing, he has named 116 of the 123 cardinals eligible to vote. It seems common sense to assume these cardinals will choose someone like the current pope. Media commentators routinely use phrases such as *stacking the deck* to express the idea that John Paul II has influenced the outcome of the next papal election by creating cardinals in his own image and likeness. History, however, suggests a different view. Conclaves full of cardinals appointed by the deceased pope do not elect photocopies of the man who named them. More often the opposite holds true: they elect popes who pursue different policies. This tendency, amply documented by students of papal history such as Italian journalist Giancarlo Zizola and American theologian Richard McBrien, is sometimes called the *pendulum law* of conclave psychology.

In 1903, for example, the cardinals met to pick a successor to Leo XIII, who had reigned for twenty-five years. He had been pope so long one of his own cardinals had famously groaned, "We elected a Holy Father, not an Eternal Father." Leo XIII's pontificate was enormously important. He opened the Catholic Church to the modern age, encouraged scientific biblical studies, launched

Catholic social teaching, and moved the church beyond its nostalgic desire to revive a "sacred alliance" of Catholic monarchies by engaging in a cautious détente with secular democracies. The obvious candidate to carry forward his modernizing project was Cardinal Mariano Rampolla, Leo's secretary of state. In fact, however, the conclave chose Giuseppe Sarto, the patriarch of Venice, whom the Italian government had defined as "the most intransigent of the intransigents." As Pius X, Sarto launched a vast crackdown against what he called *modernism*—that is, virtually every attempt to reconcile Catholic thought with the new century. He silenced some theologians, excommunicated others, and set up a network of informants to identify those entertaining unacceptable ideas. Why did the conclave pick Sarto? It wasn't only that the Austrian emperor vetoed Rampolla's candidacy. The move toward Rampolla had already stalled by the time the emperor's wishes became known. A majority of electors simply felt it was time to slow down the pace of change.

Another clear illustration of the pendulum principle came again in 1958, when Angelo Roncalli succeeded Pius XII. The cerebral, almost ethereal Pius had promoted a thinking church during his early years as pope, but during his last decade in office, he had become suspicious of change. He had theologians such as Yves Congar in France and John Courtney Murray in the United States silenced. Where Pius XII had become pessimistic and fearful, Roncalli was bold and optimistic. He called an ecumenical council, a move that Pius XII had considered and rejected, to bring the church up to date. At Vatican II, some of the very theologians Pius XII had suspended came out of their deep freeze to lead a thorough reform of the church. Few of the fifty-five cardinals in that conclave of 1958 imagined exactly what they were getting with Roncalli. But the pattern held up nonetheless: a group of men appointed by one pope produced a successor of a very different sort.

What explains this pendulum law? To begin with, in most pontificates there is a creative period that does not last much more than a decade, after which ossification sets in. Dynamic energies are replaced by repetition, and new ideas are put on hold as papal bureau-crats follow patterns already set. People routinely say about unre-solved problems, "It will have to wait for a new pope." Hence there is always a degree of frustration toward the end of a long regime. Even though John Paul II is still breaking new ground in many areas after twenty-three years, this sense of suspended animation is nonetheless widespread. Many Catholics believe that on some of the most pressing issues—the role of women in the church, the need for the church to decentralize, new challenges in the area of bioethics—John Paul has already given the only answers he can. More far-reaching solutions have to wait.

Beyond impatience, there are two other realities that help explain the pendulum dynamic. One is that many cardinals, in the grand Roman tradition, have long memories and know how to wait to win an argument. The side that lost in the last conclave never really goes away. Thus the supporters of Rampolla were defeated in 1903, but many of the same cardinals regrouped to elect Giacomo della Chiesa—Pope Benedict XV—in 1914. Could something similar hap-pen in the conclave that will select the successor to John Paul II? It's possible. There are still cardinals who remember the man who was the main alternative to Karol Wojtyla in 1978, Cardinal Giovanni Benelli of Florence, who would likely have steered a moderate course closer to that of Paul VI. A handful of today's cardinals were in the college in 1978, and others served in the Vatican under Benelli in more junior capacities, or admired him from afar, and may well look for a chance to elect a candidate more like him. (One possible choice along these lines would be Cardinal Giovanni Battista Re, currently head of the Congregation for Bishops, but that's a matter for a later chapter.)

Second, cardinals tend to go into a conclave looking for a candi-date who can correct the flaws of the pope who just died. Even if they agree with 95 percent of what the old pope did, what will likely be on their minds is how to fix the 5 percent that they believe went wrong. In other words, they are looking for a man who can tackle the issues this pope couldn't or wouldn't, and who can correct his excesses. The assumption is that the approach of the current pope has had many years to bear fruit, and now it's time to balance it with another way of doing things. This is almost always a prescription for a different sort of man.

What is John Paul II's unfinished business? In this chapter we will look at five issues most analysts believe to be near the top of the agenda. I call these *voting issues* because the *papabili,* the most likely papal candidates, will be sized up based on where they stand with respect to these issues. Identifying these voting issues is not easy: John Paul II has reigned for twenty-three years, and his record over the course of his ambitious pontificate is complex. Vatican watchers size up the task facing his successor in different ways. Some, for example, insist that the most pressing challenge of the pope is the same in every age—to promote lives of holiness. Of course, this is true, but the forms that challenge takes are constantly changing. Others will object that certain key themes of the John Paul II pontificate, including his vision of a "new evangelization," are absent from this list. But conclaves, as I said above, typically look to fix a pontificate's problems, and thus we concentrate here on the key problems awaiting remedies under a new pope.

Issue 1: Collegiality in the Church

Collegiality is a word that puzzles non-Catholics, and even many Catholics who do not follow church politics closely. The term comes from the word *college,* which is very close to the word *colleague.* Collegiality figured strongly in debates at Vatican II over the relationship that ought to exist between the pope, the Roman Curia, and the world's bishops. If that relationship is collegial, then the bishops, and through them the people of their local churches, should be involved in setting policy—first in their own churches, and even for the universal Catholic Church. Simply put, *collegiality* is a code word for taking power away from the Roman Curia and letting the bishops be bishops. Collegiality also embraces another concept that was given currency at Vatican II: *subsidiarity.* It's a notion that has taken over in many a modern corporation: decisions that can be taken at a lower level should not be kicked up to people who know less about the local situation. At the very least, collegiality calls for more collaborative decision making in the church. This would not make the church a democracy, but it would make it more democratic.

Collegiality is perhaps *the* leading issue heading into the next conclave. Cardinal Godfried Danneels of Belgium said as much at a special consistory of all the world's cardinals in Rome in May 2001: "The theme of collegiality in the church is, whether you like it or not, at the top of the agenda of public opinion in the church and in the media." Danneels could say that because, many loyal Catholics believe, today's Catholic Church is not as collegial as it should be. The fact is that the pope and the papal bureaucracy have never had as much power as they do today, and many observers believe the result is a church that is far too centralized.

This process includes the declaration of papal infallibility at the First Vatican Council, in 1870. We have already seen in Chapter 1 how nineteenth-century popes took the appointment of bishops away from locals and brought it to Rome, a shift formalized in the 1917 Code of Canon Law. This was an enormous boost to papal power, since it means the only route to career advancement within the Catholic hierarchy is fidelity to the pope. Other moves in the last century and a half have been equally decisive. Pius X, pope from 1903 to 1914, beefed up the powers of the Vatican office for doctrine, making it the "supreme" congregation of the Roman Curia and giving it an enhanced degree of control over the intellectual life of the church. Pius XII, pope from 1939 to 1958, acted to curb the influence of lay organizations that offered a counterweight to papal authority. John Paul II has taken the primacy of the pope to entirely new levels, exploiting the platform offered him by modern communications to become, in effect, the bishop of the world. He has also placed restrictions on national bishops' conferences, long seen as too powerful and too independent by the Roman Curia.

The psychological result is that for many Catholics, being Catholic and agreeing with the pope have become virtually the same thing. To the extent one disagrees with the pope, one is that much less Catholic. For some critics, mainly though not exclusively in the church's progressive wing, this papal centrism seems a distortion of church tradition, which offers many examples of leading saints, theologians, and bishops who were fierce critics of the popes of their day. The pope is an important symbol of unity in the church, these critics argue, but he is hardly the only voice that matters. The centralization that has taken place, they say, is a distortion. Bishops, who should be able to set policy for their local churches, have largely been reduced to middle managers, or even altar boys, as some wags put it. They believe Pius XII's famous line has come to describe virtually the entire church. "I don't want collaborators," the pope once said, "only people to execute my orders."

There is, of course, another side to this story. Defenders of a strong papacy argue that historically, efforts to tame the pope have usually created a vacuum that secular powers were only too happy to fill, sometimes to the detriment of the church's independence. In seventeenth-century France, for example, Catholics who began by asserting their independence from Rome ended up as dependents of the king. (In fact, the earliest champions of the doctrine of papal infallibility were liberals, who hoped a strong pope would dislodge European Catholics from their cozy relationship with the ancien régime.) In the modern world, one can point to China, where the Communist government sponsors an official Catholic Church over which the Vatican has no jurisdiction, precisely because the Communists want to keep control. Moreover, defenders say, a strong pope is essential to hold the church together in a time in which centrifugal pressures are constantly pulling it apart. In the welter of languages, cultures, and ideologies created by a globalized world, Catholics should be grateful to have such a formidable agent of unity. These defenders acknowledge that bishops sometimes may have justified complaints about micromanagement or silly decisions from the curia. Yet, they say, the curia, like any bureaucracy, is also a convenient lightning rod for complaint, so that its defects become exaggerated and its many gifts to the church are often minimized or forgotten.

Many people expected the Second Vatican Council to resolve the question of the proper balance between the pope and the bishops. Whereas Vatican I had bolstered the papacy in a critical moment (that is, as it lost the Papal States), Vatican II would bring the bishops back into the picture. In some ways, this has happened. Vatican II gave national conferences of bishops decision-making authority. It assigned the conferences responsibility for translating the Catholic liturgy, up to then celebrated almost exclusively in Latin, into the various vernacular languages. (*Liturgy* is a general word referring to all the rites and sacraments of the church, such as the mass, weddings, and baptisms.) In addition, the council gave birth to a new body called the Synod of Bishops, which was to gather a representative group of bishops from around the world to advise the pope on a regular basis. With national conferences managing many of the affairs of local churches, beginning with liturgical matters, and with the synod advising the pope on the universal level, many thought Vatican II had solved the problem of collegiality.

Critics say things have not worked out that way. To take the synod first, many observers, including many bishops, believe the synod gives only the appearance of consultation. Speeches are delivered in random order with no chance for questions or debate; the contributions of small group discussions are often sanitized before they reach the full body; and the content of the final report is often determined in advance. Moreover, the synod meets only when the pope wants it to meet and discusses only those issues the pope gives it to discuss, and the pope himself issues its conclusions. The synod can make no decisions itself; all it can do is advise the pope. Jesuit theologian Father Aloysius Pieris of Sri Lanka has called the synod "a time-consuming and money-consuming talk-shop with no executive power." Pope Paul VI, who created the synod, once had greater dreams for it. He even entertained the idea that the synod, rather than the College of Cardinals, would elect the pope. Yet Paul was talked out of this change, and the relevance of the synod has been in steady decline. At the May 21–24, 2001, extraordinary consistory in Rome, no topic was mentioned with greater frequency than the need for reforms in the synod. It is possible that some changes will yet be made during the pontificate of John Paul II, but if a major overhaul is to be carried out, it will no doubt be the work of his successor.

As for the bishops' conferences, in some respects they did become a middle layer of authority between the Vatican and the dioceses. In the United States, for example, the National Conference of Catholic Bishops evolved into a major institution, with scores of full-time staff and committees responsible for a wide range of issues. During the 1980s, the U.S. bishops, working collaboratively, managed to issue major teaching documents on two complex and politically sensitive issues. In 1983 they published a letter on modern conflict called *The Gift of Peace,* and their 1986 letter *Economic Justice for All* addressed questions of social and economic morality. Dutch, Italian, and Brazilian episcopal conferences had similarly creative periods. Yet precisely this growth in influence was worrying to Vatican officials, who at times see the bishops' conferences not as companions but as rival sources of authority. They also worried that in some cases the bishops' conferences were issuing documents not fully in conformity with papal teaching. In other cases, Vatican officials felt that the democratic internal structure of the conferences (in which a two-thirds vote decides things) was smothering the voices of bishops in the minority, encouraging a kind of conformism and abandonment of personal responsibility. Thus in 1998, John Paul issued *Apostolos Suos,* a document decreeing that bishops' conferences lack any theological or collegial status. Conferences cannot teach, the pope said, unless their teaching is either unanimously approved (in which case it draws on the authority of each individual bishop, not the conference) or unless they get a prior okay from Rome (in which case it is papal authority that backs up the teaching).

Late in John Paul II's pontificate, the curia has also taken back from the bishops' conferences the powers to regulate the liturgy that Vatican II assigned them. After Vatican II, the English-speaking bishops' conferences of the world set up a joint commission to translate Latin liturgical texts into English. For more than thirty years, the International Commission on English in the Liturgy (ICEL) has been responsible for producing liturgical documents in English, under the supervision of its member episcopal conferences. In the mid-1990s, the Vatican began to express reservations about ICEL's work, especially the use of inclusive language—the word *people,* for example, instead of *man.* Then texts began to be rejected by Rome that had come from the commission, a surprise for many experts since after the council many believed the Vatican's role was not to *review* texts but simply to *confirm* them as to form and juridical status. In March 1999, the Vatican's office on liturgy demanded broad new powers over ICEL, including the right to veto staff and advisers. English-speaking bishops, though divided among themselves, stalled for time. Then in May 2001, the same office issued new rules for translation that granted itself these powers. The rules also insisted that, in the future, texts stick much closer to the Latin originals.

For some, the church's problem with collegiality is even broader than the relationship between the pope and the bishops. There is also the challenge, they believe, of bringing the voice of the laity into church governance. They note that polls routinely indicate that on a number of contested points, whether birth control or married priests, large majorities of Catholics disagree with the current Vatican stand.

A study conducted by the University of Turin found that even in Rome, where 80 percent of the people consider themselves Catholic, more than 70 percent of these Catholics approve of birth control, divorce, cohabitation, and premarital sex. While no one proposes the church put its teachings up for a vote, such a serious disjunction between what church leaders are saying and what the people actually believe suggests, according to some critics, that the leaders and the followers need to be brought into a more fruitful dialogue. While that could mean that many lay Catholics in the Western world need to be jarred out of complacent secularized attitudes, it could also mean that church leaders need to revisit some of their unexamined assumptions.

Collegiality will be on the mind of the cardinals heading into the conclave. Some will be seeking relatively minor changes, like a new set of procedures for the synod. Others will want more sweeping change in the direction of balance between the bishops and the pope. Still others will oppose any change, feeling that the church is already too fractured and fragmented. Some will want a pope who can reach out to constituencies within the church that feel excluded and marginalized. These cardinals will be looking for candidates to represent their views, and the interplay among them will help shape how the voting unfolds.

Issue 2: Ecumenism and Interreligious Dialogue

Within Catholic theology, no issue has been more hotly debated of late than how Catholicism should relate to the other Christian churches and to the non-Christian religions of the world. For analysts looking at the Catholic Church from the outside, trying to understand its policies and priorities, the years from the mid-1990s onward have seemed schizophrenic on this issue. On the one hand, the pope has made many remarkable gestures underlining the wish of the Catholic

Church to pursue unity. He has made well-received journeys to several predominantly Orthodox nations, and he is the first modern pope to go inside an Islamic mosque and a Jewish synagogue. On the other hand, some of the pope's curial lieutenants have published documents and pursued disciplinary measures that have caused many observers to question the seriousness of those papal gestures.

John Paul has said often that he wants the third Christian millennium to be the millennium of reunion (after a first millennium of unity and a second of division). In 1995, the pope published an encyclical, *Ut Unum Sint,* in which he invited theologians and members of other Christian churches to "engage with me in a patient and fraternal dialogue" and to seek "forms in which this [papal] ministry may accomplish a service of love." In effect, the pope seemed to be saying, he was willing to envision a less powerful, less controlling papacy that might be more acceptable to other Christian churches. The pope has reached out to fellow Christians in other important ways. He made respected German theologian Cardinal Walter Kasper the head of the Vatican office for Christian unity in 2001, giving that agency the kind of political and intellectual heavy hitter it needs.

John Paul has made unity with Eastern Orthodox Christians a special priority, and the effort has borne fruit. During his May 1999 trip to Romania, the first to a predominantly Orthodox nation, crowds chanted, "Unity! Unity!" as the pope and Patriarch Teoctist moved down the streets of Bucharest together. (The Romanian patriarch was the first non-Catholic cleric ever to ride in John Paul's popemobile.) In May 2001, John Paul traveled to Athens, one of the nerve centers of the Orthodox world, and delivered a sweeping apology to Archbishop Christodoulos for more than a thousand years of perceived Western offenses against the Orthodox. The apology met with a warm reception. One Athens daily led the next day with the headline "Road Is Now Open for Unity Between the Two Churches," while another declared, "Twelve Centuries of Ice Broken."

Recent years have also seen some powerful steps forward in the

Catholic Church's interreligious relationships. In May 2000, the pope traveled to Israel and visited the Holocaust memorial at Yad Vashem, paying tribute to the millions of Jews who lost their lives. He also went to Jerusalem's Wailing Wall, where, in a traditional Jewish gesture of prayer, he left a note in the wall—expressing regret for centuries of Christian mistreatment of Jews. John Paul has also moved the church's ties with Islam forward. He has met with Muslims more than fifty times over the course of his pontificate. In May 2001 he went to Syria, where he became the first pope to enter a mosque. The sight of John Paul shuffling across the floor of the Omayyad Mosque in Damascus, wearing slippers in accord with Islamic custom, praying respectfully at what is believed to be the tomb of John the Baptist, was broadcast widely across the Islamic world as a signal of friendship.

Despite the pope's contributions, however, there have been many other moments that cut in the opposite direction. John Paul's courageous invitation to a discussion on reform of the papacy, for example, has hardly been sustained in practice. One of the few public figures in the Catholic Church to take the pope at his word was retired archbishop John Quinn of San Francisco, who wrote a book entitled *The Reform of the Papacy: The Costly Call to Christian Unity*, advocating decentralization and curial reform. The response from officialdom has been frosty, and behind the scenes Quinn has been called disloyal. Further down the spectrum from Quinn, Australian Church historian and popular broadcaster Paul Collins, a Sacred Heart priest, published a book on the same subject that quickly became the target of an official investigation by the Congregation for the Doctrine of the Faith. Collins eventually resigned the priesthood rather than put his community into the middle of his dispute. (The final act of Collins's duel with the Vatican, in fact, came in the wake of a July 16, 1999, interview I published in the *National Catholic Reporter*.) Though Collins's *Papal Power* is far more feisty than Quinn's book, the impact of the Vatican crackdown is the same.

Many Catholic thinkers with opinions about reform of the papacy, seeing what happened to Quinn, Collins, and others, have been discouraged from stating them too forcefully. Such chilling of internal conversation has done little to convince other Christian churches that the papacy is serious about turning over a new leaf.

Moreover, the centralizing thrust of recent Vatican policy has alarmed many Christian groups. Two 1998 documents—*Apostolos Suos*, discussed above, and *Ad Tuendam Fidem*, which specified penalties for dissent from noninfallible papal teaching—have been especially worrisome. For many non-Catholic Christians, these documents summoned precisely the images of a dictatorial papacy that most worry them about eventual reunion with Rome. To add insult to injury, in a commentary on *Ad Tuendam Fidem*, Cardinal Joseph Ratzinger offered as an example of a noninfallible but binding Catholic teaching the invalidity of priestly ordinations in the Anglican Communion. Many Anglicans, stung and surprised by the reference, called this a serious blow to ecumenical relations with Rome.

Two other Ratzinger moves have cast even longer shadows. On June 30, 2000, Ratzinger sent a document entitled *Note on the Expression "Sister Churches"* to the presidents of bishops' conferences of the world. It was presented as a correction of ambiguities "in certain publications and in the writings of some theologians," especially the habit of referring to the Catholic Church as a *sister* of some other Christian body. "The one, holy, catholic and apostolic universal Church is not sister but 'mother' of all the particular churches," the document said. "This is not merely a question of terminology, but above all of respecting a basic truth of the Catholic faith: that of the unicity of the Church of Jesus Christ. In fact, there is but a single Church, and therefore the plural term churches can only refer to particular churches." A cover letter from Ratzinger added that use of *sister church* to describe the ties between Roman Catholicism and the Anglican Communion, as well as "non-Catholic ecclesial communities," is also "improper."

Three months later Ratzinger's office issued another document, this time a lengthy theological treatise personally approved by the pope, entitled *Dominus Iesus*. Though directed largely at interreligious dialogue, the document also repeated the ban on use of the phrase *sister churches*. It also suggested that to the extent non-Catholic communities lead people to salvation, that is derived "from the very fullness of grace and truth entrusted to the Catholic Church." Inevitably this kind of language, which seemed to revive the superiority complex of the Catholic Church that Vatican II had softened, produced a wide ecumenical backlash. Even John Paul II himself heard about it when he traveled to Syria in May 2001, where Greek Orthodox patriarch Ignatius IV confronted him publicly during a visit to the Damascus Orthodox cathedral. "Did Cardinal Ratzinger mean that only the Catholic Church is the one true Church?" the patriarch asked the pope. "We believe in all humility that the Church founded by Jesus Christ continues to subsist fully in the Orthodox Church," Ignatius insisted. He wasn't finished. "There is a point that seems crucial to us," he said, "that of the anathemas established by Vatican Council I against those who do not recognize papal infallibility. Are these anathemas addressed at those of us who hold an ecclesiology different from yours?" It was a rare public sign that the pope's overtures of goodwill have to be matched by a different kind of internal policy if he wants to realize new unity between Christians.

The same is true of the Catholic Church's outreach to other religions, and a review of a single week is enough to make the point. When the final history of John Paul II's pontificate is written, it is quite possible that the first week of September 2000 will go down as one of its blackest periods, a time when many of the pope's efforts to advance relations with other religions were damaged or reversed.

On September 3, Pope John Paul II beatified two of his predecessors, John XXIII and Pius IX. Many Jews remember Pius as the pope who kidnapped a Jewish boy and refused to return him to his parents despite an international outcry. Pius also enacted an 1862 law prohibiting Jews from testifying against Christians in civil or criminal proceedings, barring them from owning real estate, and forcing them to pay a tax for upkeep of a house of catechumens whose aim was to convert Jews. He forbade Jews from leaving their quarter of the city after dark. John Paul's decision to elevate Pius IX to the ranks of near saints stunned many Jewish groups, who found the decision nearly impossible to reconcile with the pope's language and gestures in Jerusalem the preceding spring.

Then, on September 4, the Congregation for the Doctrine of the Faith summoned Jesuit theologian Jacques Dupuis and presented him with a sweeping denunciation of his work, which had sought to offer a theological basis for interreligious dialogue. Though his work is complex, essentially Dupuis suggests that Christ as the Word of God could be active in "animating" and "inspiring" religions other than Christianity, and hence in some mysterious sense other religions are part of the divine plan for humanity. The idea is to find a way for Catholics to accept the full theological legitimacy of other religions, without renouncing any of their core principles. It is a project near to the heart of Dupuis, who spent thirty-six years in India as a teacher and scholar before coming to Rome. His experience of religious pluralism in India, where Catholicism is a tiny minority amidst many of humanity's oldest and most noble religious traditions, obviously shaped his outlook. Dupuis refused to accept the denunciation presented to him, and the congregation agreed to take another look. The meeting was a clear signal, however, that Dupuis's line of inquiry is unwelcome in the Catholic Church. Dupuis was later served with a more mild criticism of "potential ambiguities" in his work, but the Vatican had made its point.

Finally, on September 5, the Vatican issued *Dominus Iesus,* a much-anticipated document from Ratzinger's Congregation for the Doctrine of the Faith. It struck the religious world like an asteroid. The document denied that other world religions can offer salvation independent of Christianity and insisted that making converts to

Catholicism is an "urgent duty." While allowing that followers of other religions can be saved (though only in a mysterious fashion and only through the grace of Christ), the document insists they are nevertheless in a "gravely deficient situation" in comparison to Christians, who alone "have the fullness of the means of salvation."

Many Catholic experts on interreligious dialogue were shocked. "The Vatican doesn't have any sense of how dangerous such a document can be," said Father John Prior, who has twenty-seven years' experience as a missionary in Indonesia. "They think they're having a quiet discussion about texts. But when such words are belted out by an Apprentice Boys' March as a prelude to a riot in Northern Ireland, or by Indonesian Christians before their ethnic cleansing in Ambon and Halmahera, exclusivist, 'absolute truth' language becomes not just offensive but dangerous." Despite protests that continued for months, the pope on several occasions publicly associated himself with the content of *Dominus Iesus,* once referring to it as "dear to my heart."

Theologian Paul Knitter of Xavier University in Cincinnati argued in an interview with me in the *National Catholic Reporter* that the pope's own behavior when he meets members of other religions is not consistent with the theological line of *Dominus Iesus.* When John Paul II meets Muslims or Buddhists, said Knitter, there is no talk about the inherent superiority of Catholicism or the "grave deficiencies" of other religions. There is no demand for conversion, no attempt at persuading them that Jesus Christ is the only path to salvation. Instead, Knitter argued, the pope is generous and affirming, always underscoring the great good to be found in their traditions. This is the standard way in which most Catholics conduct themselves in dialogue, Knitter says, and it is entirely proper. But it is not consistent with *Dominus Iesus.* If we really believe Jews or Hindus would be better off as Christians, Knitter said, why would we let good manners stop us from saying it to their faces? In fact, Knitter believes that Catholics have an instinct, a "sense of the faith," that something is wrong with the official formulas generated by the

Congregation for the Doctrine of the Faith during the last years of John Paul's reign.

Of course, not all observers size up the situation in this way. Many see the pope's embrace of *Dominus Iesus* as entirely consistent with his apologies to the Orthodox or his reverence at Yad Vashem. Dialogue, defenders say, requires clarity about one's own identity. The point of dialogue is to find ways to collaborate despite disagreements, not to pretend that disagreements do not exist. Moreover, the Vatican has a practical concern. The gospel calls on Christians to carry the message of Jesus Christ "to the ends of the earth," language that has traditionally been held to require missionary efforts to convert people to the faith. But if Catholics come to believe that other faiths have their own divine revelation and systems that lead to salvation, what's the motive to convert to Catholicism? Why make converts? It is a question progressive missionaries have been asking for decades, and it alarms curial officials.

Cardinals in the next conclave will be evaluating candidates at least in part on the basis of where they stand on Catholicism's relations with the other religions of the world. Three choices seem possible: a pope who will move forward boldly in ecumenical and interfaith relations, without tolerating internal policies that pull in the opposite direction; a pope who will firmly insist on the need to make converts, relegating ecumenism and interreligious dialogue to the status of second-tier priorities; or a pope who can explain to the world how *Dominus Iesus* actually serves the cause of unity. Each position has a constituency within Roman Catholicism, and the tensions between them will consume a good bit of the next pope's attention.

Issue 3: Globalization, Poverty, and Justice

To many people in the Third World, confronted by poverty, oppression, and disease, debates over how the synod works or what doctrine of the Holy Spirit is correct can seem like arguing about the number of angels on the head of a pin. If the new pope is to carry out his mandate of being a spiritual father to all, especially the poor and afflicted, he will have to take up the question of massive global injustice. Sri Lanka's Aloysius Pieris, the Jesuit theologian quoted above, puts the challenge this way:

> Just as the outgoing pope is credited with having assisted at the fall of the Eastern block's inhuman system of domination which oppressed the *civic rights* of its citizens, the next pope will have to speak and act as humanity's voice of conscience and the oppressed majority's voice of protest against the dehumanizing imperialism of the World Bank–IMF complex, through which the rich countries (some of which boast of a Christian heritage), in collaboration with the powerful elite of third-world countries, continually deny the *economic rights* of four fifths of the world's population, driving them into a state of slavery.

As Pieris says, John Paul has been a vigorous human rights champion, defending freedoms of religion, thought, and speech. In so doing the pope capped a remarkable evolution in official Catholic thought, given that from the eighteenth through the early twentieth century popes opposed exactly these same claims of human rights on the grounds that they reflected a secular ideology. (Democracy and human rights were associated by popes with the French Revolution and its assault on all things traditional, including the church.) Yet John Paul II championed the cause, grounding his appeal on the innate dignity of every human person. The pope saw a consistent range of "culture of life" issues that began with abortion and extended to poverty and war, all the way through to legalized euthanasia. His leadership has mobilized other sectors of the church. Today, engagement on issues of justice and social development is incumbent upon Catholic bishops. Up-and-coming leaders speak the language of economic justice as naturally as they do the doctrinal principles of the catechism.

A classic example of the way John Paul has inspired a Catholic commitment for justice came in July 2001, when the leaders of the G-8 nations held a summit in the northern Italian port city of Genoa. Some three thousand Catholics, many of them so-called Papa-boys, young people who had turned out the summer before for a youth gathering with John Paul II in Rome, came to Genoa to protest the growing gap between rich and poor. Two weeks before the G-8 gathering, they presented a "Catholic Manifesto" calling for specific reforms in global economic and political systems, including rules for international trade that allow impoverished nations to offer goods at predictable prices and without barriers; adoption of the Tobin tax (a tax of 0.25 percent on the $2 trillion a day exchanged on global currency markets, designed to discourage speculation and to create funds for international development); cancellation of debt accumulated up to June 1999; assurance that debt payments will be required only after basic needs for health, education, and other essentials are met; a process of arbitration to identify "in terms of justice" the real debt levels of impoverished nations; national and international laws to guarantee a plurality of voices in the media; augmented public funding for medical research, especially for producing drugs to combat diseases that afflict the poor; and efforts to halt the global arms trade, including full disclosure about the flow of weapons, and a halt to public support for manufacturers and distributors. They called themselves "sentinels of the morning," which was what John Paul had asked them to be the summer before in Rome. Their manifesto was blessed by Genoa's Cardinal Dionigi Tettamanzi, himself a candidate to become pope.

The Genoa "Catholic Manifesto," unfortunately obscured by the street violence that came later, was a remarkable moment. Yet for all the advocacy on behalf of justice this pope has inspired, critics question what the passion has produced by way of concrete results. For example, during the great Jubilee Year of 2000, John Paul issued a

call to the governments of the world to forgive the debt of heavily impoverished nations. (In the Old Testament, a jubilee was an occasion
for the forgiveness of debts and the liberty of captives.) The plea was
unveiled to great fanfare in Rome, was widely reported in the media,
and promptly went nowhere. Similarly, John Paul requested an
amnesty for prisoners, a request that similarly fell flat, even in Italy,
where prison overcrowding is a chronically volatile political issue.
The only prisoner that received any sort of papal-related amnesty
during the Jubilee Year was Mehmet Ali Agca, the man who attempted to assassinate John Paul II on May 13, 1981. The pope had
already forgiven Agca, and last year asked the president of Italy, Carlo
Azeglio Ciampi, to formally pardon him in keeping with the request
for amnesty. Ciampi agreed, and Agca was returned to Turkey—
where he was immediately thrown into prison for the murder of a
Turkish journalist.

Moreover, some fault the pope for not backing those within the
church who take up the cause of justice. In Latin America in the
1970s and 1980s, a movement rooted in *liberation theology*, which
sought to combine popular Catholicism with leftist movements for
social change, had been gathering steam. In Nicaragua, Catholics influenced by liberation theology were among the early supporters of
the Sandinista revolution. In Haiti the populist uprising that toppled
the hated Duvalier regime was led by a Catholic priest, Jean-
Bertrand Aristide, inspired by the writings of liberation theologians.
In Chiapas, Mexico, the local bishop, Don Samuel Ruiz, embraced
the indigenous population and criticized the Mexican government.
Many expected John Paul to be sympathetic to these liberationists
because they were attempting to do in Latin America what the
Solidarity movement was doing in Poland, opposing unjust regimes
on the basis of Catholic doctrine. Yet the pope's reaction, organized
largely by his chief deputy, Cardinal Joseph Ratzinger, was precisely
the opposite. He cracked down on the liberation theologians, inves-
tigating their writings, closing their seminaries, and replacing bishops
sympathetic to their work. At times, the actions of the pope and his

diplomats seemed incomprehensible. In a move that still bewilders and shocks many Haitians, for example, the Vatican was the only nation in the world to recognize the military regime that seized power, in a 1991 coup, from Aristide, who had been democratically elected. Supporters of Aristide responded by attacking and burning the papal nuncio's residence, seriously injuring a Zairean priest who was stationed there. In Chiapas, Ruiz was undercut and criticized by Vatican officials, then hustled into retirement.

Meanwhile the pope promoted churchmen to top posts in the Vatican who had a troubled record with respect to human rights. His chief officer for liturgy, Cardinal Jorge Medina Estévez, is a close friend and supporter of Chile's former military ruler Augusto Pinochet. At the peak of the furor over possible extradition of Pinochet from England, Medina revealed that he was personally involved in attempts to win the general's release. "There have been discussions at every level on this affair, and we're hoping that they will have a positive outcome," Medina told a newspaper in January 1999. "I've prayed and prayed for Senator Pinochet as I pray for all people who have suffered." The pope also appointed Colombian Alfonso López Trujillo as head of the Pontifical Council for the Family. During the years of military dictatorship in Latin America, López Trujillo endorsed the national security state. "These military regimes came into existence as a response to social and economic chaos," he wrote. "No society can admit a power vacuum. Faced with tensions and disorders, an appeal to force is inevitable."

Obviously there is another way of reading this record. Many observers believe Latin American liberation theology was far too political and that the pope had to do something to remind his pastors of their primary role as shepherds of souls. A handful of Catholics took up guns in the name of the gospel. Others accepted a crude form of Marxism. Moreover, some of the liberation theologians themselves admit they misdiagnosed their social reality. The ordinary people of Latin America did not want a socialist workers' state, along the model of the Cuban revolution, but a free and open democratic society like developed Western nations. They wanted social justice, but in the form of greater economic opportunity. Hence, to the degree some liberation theologians demonized the free market, they lost touch with the sentiments of the people for whom they claimed to speak.

The next pope will therefore face the deep intellectual challenge of not merely offering verbal support for social justice but finding ways of translating it into concrete proposals for social structures and systems. He will have to move beyond denouncing a gap between rich and poor to promoting credible alternatives. John Paul II has said that the world must globalize not just markets but values, but has left the specifics of that statement vague. What would a more humane, a more just globalized economy look like? As Leo XIII began the process of developing a Catholic counterproposal to the new industrial economy in his encyclical *Rerum Novarum* of 1891, the next pope will have to do much difficult and urgent thinking about a Catholic vision of a globalized economy. His answer will have to be realistic, but at the same time rooted in the gospel imperative to defend the least and most forgotten of the world's peoples.

Issue 4: Bioethics, Sexuality, and the Family

Under this heading comes a bundle of issues both old and new. Questions of sexual and family morality have been with Catholicism for decades: use of artificial birth control, for example, or what to do with Catholics who have divorced and remarried under civil law without seeking official church permission (that is, an annulment of their previous marriage) to do so. These Catholics are supposed to be excluded from the sacraments, though in many parishes they are quietly encouraged to ignore the rules. Other challenges are more recent, some created by technological innovation, such as the moral implications of cloning and the various options for artificial reproduction. Others have been generated by social change, such as the question of marriage rights for homosexuals, an issue that was not on the agenda in most Western societies when Karol Wojtyla was elected pope, in 1978.

John Paul II has worked hard to offer answers. He added an office to the curia, the Pontifical Council for the Family, to respond to the new challenges. (The pope was scheduled to announce its creation on the day he was shot in Saint Peter's Square—May 13, 1981.) In general terms, the pope has sought to identify better and more profound arguments to *defend* the traditional teaching of the church, rather than entertaining proposals to *change* that teaching. He has, for example, refused to permit a relaxation of the rules barring the divorced and remarried from the sacraments. The pope has also reasserted the ban on artificial birth control, elevating it to the status of a near-infallible teaching. On homosexual marriage, the pope has been equally emphatic. He has said: "[Civil unions] between homosexuals are a deplorable distortion of what should be a communion of love and life between a man and a woman in a reciprocal gift open to life."

On the new bioethical questions, positions crafted under John Paul's pontificate have been largely restrictive. The Vatican has said that in vitro fertilization is illicit. For one thing, most forms of it involve the creation and then the destruction of surplus embryos, since more than one embryo is generated by the process and those not used are eventually discarded. The practice, according to Vatican statements, reflects an "abortion mentality." The ban would remain, however, even where the destruction of embryos could be avoided, because in vitro fertilization is "contrary to the unity of marriage, to the dignity of the spouses, to the vocation proper to parents, and to the child's right to be conceived and brought into the world in marriage and from marriage." Artificial insemination is like-wise rejected unless it "helps the conjugal act to reach its natural objectives." The Vatican has said that civil law must prohibit the donation of gametes between unmarried persons, embryo banks, and surrogate motherhood. It has opposed approval of the so-called morning-after pill, which blocks implantation of a fertilized egg cell in the womb, seeing it as a chemical means of abortion. It has opposed research on stem cells, which are cells at primitive stages of development that can be used to treat Alzheimer's disease and a variety of other illnesses, in part because the normal source of stem cells is aborted fetal tissue, in part because growing the cells in a laboratory may involve the creation and subsequent destruction of embryos.

These are complex issues, and many Catholics support the pope's cautious approach. The values the Vatican is striving to defend, above all the right to life, are certainly worth preserving. Yet there are indications that the next pope will face pressure to take a gradually less rigid stance. On the divorce question, for example, pressure for change has been insistent. Approximately 6 million Catholics in the United States and several million more in Europe have remarried without an annulment, creating an immense pastoral challenge. During the 1990s, several bishops have advocated modifications in the church's position. In July 1993, three German prelates—Karl Lehmann of Mainz, Oskar Saier of Freiburg, and Walter Kasper of Rottenburg-Stuttgart—issued a joint pastoral letter offering guidelines for cases in which divorced and remarried persons might be admitted to the sacraments. A 1994 document of the Vatican's doctrine office responded negatively. (Lehmann and Kasper have since become cardinals.) Other bishops, however, have echoed the call for change. In 1998 a group of German bishops proposed that divorced people be allowed full participation in the sacraments after a period of "repentance." At an extraordinary conference October 16–17, 1999, the Italian bishops called for a "Jubilee gesture of reconciliation" toward divorced Catholics. They also affirmed that "divorced people remain full members of the church." Coming from bishops, these calls for new thinking are clear signs of strain on the traditional position.

Many of the bioethical questions will also require an open mind from the new pope, if only because the moral debate will be racing to keep up with the science. Even papal advisers striving to be ultraloyal to tradition have trouble these days. A rare public example broke open in late December 2000 and early January 2001 in the pages of *L'Osservatore Romano,* the official Vatican newspaper, over a method of stem cell research called *somatic cell nuclear transfer.* The idea is to use the genetic material of the patient, rather than fetal tissue or embryos from somebody else, in making stem cells. Some people think the technique avoids creating embryos and hence is acceptable from a Catholic point of view; others disagree. The issue is important because stem cell research could hold the key to treatment of illnesses ranging from heart failure to Alzheimer's disease. Italian theologian Father Gino Concetti, in-house moral expert for *L'Osservatore Romano,* praised the method as "substantially positive" in an article published December 30. But just six days later, a full-page article appeared, coauthored by Juan de Dios Vial Correa, a lay professor and president of the Pontifical Academy for Life, and Archbishop Elio Sgreccia, vice president of the academy. Correa and Sgreccia questioned the assertion that what is created in somatic cell nuclear transfer is not an embryo. In the absence of irrefutable proof that the new cellular fusion could not develop into a human being, they said, somatic cell nuclear transfer is unacceptable.

Obviously, this is a complicated technical question that is a matter not just of moral reflection but of better scientific data. The point, however, is that the next pope will be required to go beyond a "Just say no" policy, to grapple with the profound dilemmas posed by new technical options. In the same way, the next pope will also be called upon to reexamine some teachings in light of evolving social standards. If Western societies decide to allow homosexual couples to marry as a matter of civil right, what will that mean for Catholic ministers who have to operate in those societies? If the gap between church teaching on birth control and the actual practice of Catholics continues to widen, what relevance does the teaching have? These are complex questions that will demand creative responses.

Issue 5: Women and Laity

The word *laity* comes from the Greek term *laos,* meaning simply *the people*. In ordinary usage, it refers to the vast majority of Catholics who are not priests or deacons, brothers or sisters, but ordinary believers. (Technically, brothers and sisters are laity too, but most Catholics don't think of them that way.) English cardinal John Henry Newman once responded in typically wry fashion when asked for his opinion on the laity. "The church would look foolish without them," he said. The Catholic Church invites laity, including women, to participate in the life of the church because of its belief that all children of God have gifts to offer. As a practical matter, the shortage of priests that has beset the church in the West since the Second Vatican Council has also made reliance on laity a necessity. In Europe, secular and religious clergy decreased from 241,379 in 1976 to 217,275 in 1995, while between 1980 and 1995 the number of sisters dropped from 527,707 to 406,065. In France, to take one especially pronounced example, between 1976 and 1995 the number of priests plummeted from 41,163 to 28,694. Meanwhile, the average age of priests in many countries has climbed to sixty-five to seventy years. The situation in the United States is equally alarming. Factoring in resignations, retirements, and deaths, the number of working priests will drop from 23,098 in 1998 to 15,136 by 2010. In order to maintain the current ratio of 1.77 priests to a parish, the church would have to close 6,773 of the country's 19,800 parishes or dramatically increase the number of priestless parishes, already more than 2,000.

In the context of this priest shortage, debate has centered on ways to expand the church's ministerial corps. Some critics argue that the church artificially restricts the number of potential priests by ruling out married men in the Latin rite (there are twenty-one Eastern rite churches in full communion with the pope, and each permits married clergy). Even more explosive, however, is the debate over whether or not the Catholic Church should consider the ordination of women. The firm *no* given to this question by John Paul II, combined with the Vatican's restrictive stance on issues of reproductive rights, has alienated many women in the developed world. Others, however, find the pope's unapologetic defense of traditional values refreshing.

John Paul II has devoted much intellectual energy to articulating his understanding of the dignity and vocation of women. He is, as biographers have noted, the only modern pope who grew up around women. He worked closely with women in various academic roles and has continued to have women friends and collaborators. Thus it is understandable that he should want to speak to the issues facing women in society and in the church. He has condemned machismo and other forms of antifemale bias. He has argued that women are equal in dignity and worth with men, even if they have a different biological constitution. His key theme has been *complementarity*, the notion that men and women were created equal by God but with different qualities that complete each other.

This line of reasoning, among other considerations, led the pope to close the door on discussion of women's ordination as priests in the Catholic Church. On May 22, 1994, John Paul published the letter *Ordinatio Sacerdotalis*, with the theme "On the Reserving of Priestly Ordination to Men Alone." The document was just a few paragraphs long, suggesting the pope wanted his point to be crisp and clear. He wrote: "In order that all doubt may be removed regarding a matter of great importance, a matter which pertains to the Church's divine constitution itself, in virtue of my ministry of confirming the brethren I declare that the Church has no authority whatsoever to confer priestly ordination on women, and that this judgment is to be definitively held by all the Church's faithful." *Ordinatio Sacerdotalis* was interpreted to mean that not only is women's ordination forbidden, but so is advocating it.

Pressure for a reconsideration of this position is intense from activists in the church, and more quietly, from many priests and a handful of bishops. Who knows whether the next pope will be inclined, or even able, to take a new look at the problem? Catholicism takes tradition seriously, and it is clear that the preponderance of more than two thousand years of church tradition is against women priests. That does not mean new developments are impossible, merely that they have to be prepared, that the theological and pastoral groundwork has to be laid carefully over long periods of time. The next pope will have the option of allowing this development to proceed, or he can continue to fight it.

At the same time, the pope will also face continuing pressure to open up to women leadership roles in the church that do not require priestly ordination. In a few dioceses around the world, women now serve as chancellors (that is, second in command after the bishop). Many Catholics are asking why a woman has not been named to head a curial agency inside the Vatican, since there is no theological argument that these positions have to be filled by men. It would make sense for a woman to head the office on religious life, since the majority of vowed religious in the world are women. Or a woman could head the office for the laity. At the moment, there are no women at the level of either prefect or secretary, the two top-level jobs in curia offices. Why not?

Beyond the question of women's ordination, there is a broader debate about the role of laity. Here, too, there have been contradictions under John Paul II. He clearly believes in the mission and importance of laity. One of his closest collaborators is a Spanish layman, papal spokesperson Joaquín Navarro-Valls. Yet the pope is also alarmed by what he sees as "confusion" about the unique identity of the ordained priest in comparison with laypeople. Prior to Vatican II, the distinction between laity and priests was nearly absolute. Priests were set apart, with the unique capacity to channel holiness through the sacraments. After the council, this wall separating priests from laity has largely been torn down. Holiness is now something accessible in a variety of ways, rather than the exclusive property of a clerical caste, and baptism rather than ordination is seen as the sacrament that authorizes people to be ministers.

As a result of this shift in Catholic psychology, laypeople over the last thirty-five years have become collaborators in running parishes, in organizing liturgies, and in delivering various kinds of services that come under the heading of *ministry.* Given the priest shortage, many pastors have welcomed this evolution, seeing it as the only realistic way to keep their churches running. Others, however, feel the priestly identity has been compromised. With laypeople (both men and women) now filling many of the roles traditionally occupied by priests, some worry about confusion over the identity of the ordained priesthood. This fear was captured in a famous phrase reported in an American study in a Catholic parish where a nun leads communion services when no priest is available. "To tell you the truth, I like sister's mass the best," a parishioner said, thereby confirming that some Catholics don't know the difference between a communion service and a mass, and by extension, between what a priest can do and what anyone else can do. Such doctrinal confusion, critics charge, is where lay ministry leads. In a sense, this becomes a recruiting issue: if a young man knows he can do virtually everything a priest does without making the sacrifice of celibacy and lost earnings, why would he enter the priesthood?

Thus in December 1997 the Vatican issued a document attempting to restrict many of the ministerial roles open to laypeople. According to the document, laypeople may not govern parishes, assume titles such as *coordinator* or *chaplain,* deliver homilies, make decisions on parish councils in the absence of a priest, wear stoles or other liturgical garb, or receive training in seminaries. It warned that erosion of the uniqueness of the priesthood may diminish vocations and stated that lay participation in church ministries is a matter of deputation rather than right. Laity were restricted in their ability to lead baptisms or funerals, forbidden to employ liturgical gestures or prayers at mass or to perform anointings with sacred oils. Laity could help administer communion at the mass only when a sufficient number of priests are unavailable. To some extent, these orders have remained in the realm of theory; in many places around the world they have been ignored or diminished. Nevertheless, they reveal the profound concern triggered by the emergence of lay ministry.

Numbers tell the story: there are 29,142 full- or part-time professional lay ministers in the United States today, as compared to 27,155 priests. Many believe the number of lay ministers will only climb, while the number of celibate vocations continues to drop. The new pope will have to find a way to support the laity, without whom the church cannot function, while at the same time protecting the esprit d'corps of the ordained Catholic priesthood. Moreover, it is unlikely that priestly morale can be bolstered by edict. The next pope will have to find other ways to inspire and sustain vocations.

John Paul II has also supported the growth of new lay movements that have grown up in the wake of the Second Vatican Council. On Pentecost 1998, the pope staged a gala gathering of these so-called *new movements* in Saint Peter's Square. It is thought to be the largest single assembly ever held at the Vatican. Despite the papal sponsorship, these movements have been controversial. Some bishops and other Catholics believe these groups, such as Opus Dei, the Neocatechumenate, Communion and Liberation, the lay branch of the Legionaries of Christ, and Focolare, foster a kind of spiritual elitism that threatens to make the church into a sect. In some cases they have divided parishes and dioceses by the question of who's *in* and who's *out*. Certain bishops, such as the late Cardinal Basil Hume of England, placed limits on the ability of some groups to operate in his diocese. Others have been enthusiastic supporters, such as Cardinal Miloslav Vlk in Prague. Most have taken a cautious approach, allowing the groups to function but remaining wary of their methods and aims. Clarifying the status of these groups will be another major challenge of the new pope.

3.

How the Conclave Works

 THE NEXT conclave will attract wall-to-wall coverage on cable TV news networks, in the daily press, and on the Internet, but nonspecialists will probably find the action confusing. Most substantive happenings will be conducted behind closed doors, while the public ceremonies are long and difficult to follow. The rules of the conclave are puzzling, the vocabulary arcane, and the rituals far removed from the ordinary experience of most of the people on earth, even most ordinary Catholic clergy. Few know who the *camerlengo* is or what the cardinals do in a *general congregation,* but when the time comes these terms will be tossed around liberally. In order to make sense of this big event, people need to understand the process—how the days unfold from the death of the pope through the election, who is supposed to do what, and most important, how to interpret what is happening. So let's take a little trip together, moving systematically through the major moments so we can understand what is happening and what it all means.

Technically the conclave begins when the cardinals file into the Sistine Chapel, and it ends the moment the new pope says, after he is elected, "I accept." Public interest, however, will not wait for the entrance procession.

The world will start paying attention the moment news breaks that John Paul II is ill, and will continue through the first major events of the new pope's term, including the *urbi et orbi* blessing—*to the city and to the world*—from the central loggia of Saint Peter's Basilica and his installation mass. Hence the overview in this chapter will cover the entire period of public interest in the papal transition. There is no precise term for this period. It is not the *interregnum,* because that time span begins with the death of the pope and ends the moment a new pope is elected. One could use the language of some TV contracts and call it the *papal death event,* but that has a ghoulish ring. The length of this period, whatever name one chooses for it, is difficult to estimate, since the pope could be ill for an indefinite time. But if the death watch lasts only a few days, we can anticipate that the mass media will be on the story for approximately one month. This would include the funeral and a prescribed period of mourning, the conclave, and the first few days of the new pope's term.

The Death of the Pope

There is an old Roman saying that the pope is never sick until he's dead. The Vatican, like all monarchies, fears instability, and the death of the king is the ultimate unstable moment. In the medieval era, interregnums were associated with plots, invasions, and civil wars. Although today no foreign power is likely to attack the Vatican in its moment of weakness, church leaders are nevertheless heirs to this psychology. They want the transition from one pontiff to the next to be as brief as possible, and this means they want the current pope to be perceived as fully in charge until the very moment of his death. A classic example of this tendency occurred on August 19, 1914, when *L'Osservatore Romano,* the official Vatican newspaper, published a stinging editorial denouncing unnamed commentators who had suggested the previous day that Pope Pius X had a cold. "How dare they?" was the editorial's wounded tone. Less than twenty-four hours later, Pius was dead.

Of course, the fear of transition is not the only factor that explains this reluctance to acknowledge that the pope's health is failing. The people closest to the pope, and hence in the best position to know his true condition, are his most loyal lieutenants. They are protective of his privacy and of his image. Also, when someone speculates the pope may be ill, his confederates often sense an implied criticism. They suspect such comments may be part of a campaign to destabilize the papacy, encouraging people not to pay attention to the current pope in hopes that a new man will soon be on the scene. Of course, these handlers depend upon the pope for their access and power, and some are naturally reluctant to see that pass. All this helps explain why the Vatican is hesitant to tell the world the pope is sick.

Yet popes do become ill and die. Some 263 of them have done so, so there is a pretty good precedent. Sometimes the end can stretch on for some time, as happened with Pope John XXIII. His last public appearance came on May 11, 1963, but he did not succumb until June 3. For much of that time, the world expected his death almost daily. Members of religious communities remember putting out black bunting for mourning, only to take it down again, several times before John XXIII actually died. John Paul I, on the other hand, died suddenly, in September 1978, after only thirty-three days as pope. It is impossible to anticipate how John Paul II's final days will play out, but if I had to guess, I would predict that John Paul II will keep going until the very end. This is a man who has drive. He won't die as a Western movie hero does, with his boots on. He will die with the microphone on. If I am right, we may actually see this pope's passing on television, or hear it on the radio.

On the other hand, John Paul's passion for life notwithstanding, his final illness may take much longer. The Parkinson's disease that causes the pope's hand to tremble and his eyes to take on a glassy, fixed appearance is a slow disorder that does not typically provoke a swift end, especially if the patient gets good medical care. He could be disabled and dependent for months, even years, before a secondary ailment triggers his demise. If John Paul II should become incapacitated, Vatican officials will have to decide at what point to make an announcement. If the pope is unable to carry out routine functions, such as appearing at his balcony window for the recitation of the Sunday Angelus or attending the Wednesday morning general audience in Saint Peter's Square, the world will have a clue that something is wrong, and authorities will have to clarify his condition. If the expectation of imminent death builds over several days, it is likely that a large crowd will gather in Saint Peter's Square for an informal around-the-clock vigil. There is actually a Catholic ritual "For a Sick Pope" that could be enacted in Rome in this period; in 1962 Cardinal Luigi Traglia, then the pope's vicar for the diocese of Rome, celebrated the rite for John XXIII.

If doctors give the pope's aides even a few hours' notice before the end comes, we can predict with some certainty what cast of characters will show up at the deathbed. Cardinal Angelo Sodano, the secretary of state and the number-two man in the Vatican, will be there. So will Cardinal Eduardo Martínez Somalo, the camerlengo, who acts as the interim administrator of the Catholic Church during the period between popes. Cardinal Camillo Ruini, the vicar of Rome, may show. So may Archbishop Leonardo Sandri, the *sostituto* in the Secretariat of State; he is the official responsible for the day-to-day management of church affairs. Bishop Stanislaw Dziwisz, the pope's private secretary, will undoubtedly be the man in charge at the papal bedside and the person most likely to inform the world about the pope's last words. Other possibilities: the pope's physician and his assistants, and perhaps one or more of the Polish nuns who help run the papal quarters.

The pope will probably spend his last hours in his Vatican apartment or at his summer residence at Castel Gondolfo, rather than in a hospital. Although John Paul II has been hospitalized on several occasions, it is still traditional that most papal health care is delivered in his residence. It's a throwback to times when doctors made house calls to the wealthy and powerful, in part because their quarters were likely to be more hygienic and better equipped than a public hospital. Mass will be celebrated for the pope in his apartment, and toward the end he may participate from his bed, as happened in the case of Paul VI. Assuming time and circumstances allow, the pope, like all Catholics, will be given the last rites, including the opportunity to make a confession. In 1962, when John XXIII died, the windows of the papal apartments were illuminated to signify his passing.

The moment of death must be medically certified by an attending physician. Tradition then calls for a few ritual measures from the camerlengo. Martínez Somalo, standing over the pope's body, will call out his baptismal name (Karol) three times to assure that the pope is dead. Protocol says the camerlengo must also strike the pope's forehead with a small silver hammer bearing the papal coat of arms. (Though that gesture may be replaced with the simple placement of a veil over the pope's face.) When the pope does not respond, Martínez Somalo will then pronounce in ritual fashion, "The pope is dead." If the office of camerlengo is vacant when the pope dies, its functions are carried out by the dean of the College of Cardinals, currently African cardinal Bernardin Gantin, until the cardinals elect a new camerlengo. (This last happened after the death of Pius XII. The fifty-five cardinals at the end of Pius's reign elected elderly Roman cardinal Benedetto Aloisi Masella as the camerlengo. There is an office of vice camerlengo, currently held by Archbishop Ettore Cunial, but he does not succeed to the camerlengo's position because he is not a cardinal.)

Rules of procedure specify that the camerlengo must ascertain the pope's death in the presence of the master of papal liturgical celebrations, currently Italian bishop Piero Marini, and the secretary-chancellor and prelates of the Apostolic Camera. The secretary-chancellor is an Italian layman named Enrico Serafini, while the three prelates are currently Monsignors Karel Kasteel, Antonio Macculi, and Vincenzo Ferrara. Kasteel is the dean of the Camera. Serafini will have the responsibility of drawing up the pope's official death certificate. The Apostolic Camera is a department of the curia created in the eleventh century to deal with the financial and administrative affairs of the Papal States; according to a 1967 constitution of Paul VI, the Apostolic Camera manages the financial holdings of the papacy during the interregnum.

The camerlengo will next use the silver hammer to deface, then smash, the *pescatorio,* the "ring of the Fisherman," which signifies papal authority. The custom dates back to the Middle Ages, when papal rings were used to fix a wax seal on official documents. If the ring fell into the wrong hands, all sorts of spurious documents could be issued in the confusion surrounding a change in administrations. (The pope will be buried with his gold episcopal ring, signifying his role as a bishop.) The papal apartments will then be emptied, as Vatican workmen under the direction of the pope's secretary will cart off the private effects of the deceased pope, until their final distribution in accord with the terms of the pope's will. The residence will be sealed with tape and a wax seal, awaiting its next occupant. In a symbolic sense, the camerlengo officially takes possession of the Apostolic Palace, the Lateran Palace at the Church of San Giovanni in Laterano, and the papal summer residence at Castel Gondolfo.

Rules ban any film or video of the dead pope. The camerlengo may allow a trusted person to take photos for documentary purposes, but only after the pope is attired in his pontifical vestments. This provision is the result of a nasty experience after the death of Pius XII, when a series of ghoulish photos were splashed across the pages of Italian newspapers and magazines. They came from Dr. Riccardo Galeazzi-Lisi, one of Pius's physicians, who managed to snap some photos just after Pius had died. For years, Dr. Galeazzi-Lisi had been a paid informant for several news outlets. (Paul Hofmann, former Rome correspondent for the *New York Times,* once confessed that he used to deliver envelopes full of lire to Galeazzi's residence. When Galeazzi had a tip, he would call Hofmann and identify himself as Dick.) Galeazzi also peddled a diary of Pius's final agony to several Italian and foreign papers; one Roman review published its version with an explanation that it had removed some of the most "revolting" details. Galeazzi rounded out the performance by holding a press conference to discuss in detail the procedure followed for embalming Pius.

When the pope dies, all of the cardinals who run curial offices automatically lose their jobs, save three: the camerlengo, the vicar of Rome, and the head of the Apostolic Penitentiary. Even during the interregnum, their three functions must continue: executive decisions on urgent matters must be made, which is the task of the camerlengo; the Rome diocese must keep running; and emergency appeals for absolution in special cases (known as matters of the *internal forum*) must be answered, which is what the Apostolic Penitentiary does. It has a reputation for dealing with supersecret and sometimes bizarre pleas for forgiveness that reach the Vatican. God only knows why a particular case might be so urgent that it could not wait for three weeks, but those on the inside say it can happen. The number-two officials in all the curial departments, the secretaries, stay on to keep the offices running, and report to the College of Cardinals. These jobs are usually held by bishops or archbishops. Two officials in the Secretariat of State also continue in power: the officer for relations with foreign governments, currently French archbishop Jean-Louis Tauran, and the *sostituto,* Italian archbishop Leonardo Sandri, the man responsible for running the daily affairs of the church. The papal nuncios, or ambassadors, likewise remain in their posts.

It is the duty of the camerlengo to notify the vicar for Rome,

Cardinal Camillo Ruini, that the pope is dead, so that Ruini may officially relay the news to the people of Rome. Ruini will likely go on Italian television to make a brief announcement. Meanwhile the prefect of the papal household, currently an American archbishop named James Harvey, will inform the dean of the College of Cardinals, Gantin, who will relay the news to the other cardinals, the ambassadors accredited to the Holy See, and the various heads of state. In reality, everyone will have long since heard the news from instant media reports (Paul VI died at 9:41 P.M. on Sunday evening, August 6, and the first word came from the Associated Press, which moved a flash over their wire at 9:44 P.M. saying simply, POPE DEAD).

In the next few hours, reactions from all over the world will begin to stream into the Vatican. Diplomats and heads of state will cable in their condolences, while ordinary people will also offer various expressions of their feelings. In the first twenty-four hours after the death of Paul VI, in 1978, the Vatican switchboard registered 27,800 phone calls, and one can expect an even greater outpouring of calls, faxes, and e-mails of tribute and mourning for the passing of John Paul II. A crowd will also assemble in Saint Peter's Square expecting some kind of announcement, but there will likely be no official declaration or event in the square until the funeral service. In the meantime, people will spontaneously organize a kind of free-form wake in the square, with rosaries, prayer services, and mourning.

A short while later notes will go out to the cardinals, summoning them to Rome. If form holds, they will be brusque. After the death of Paul VI, the cardinal who served as camerlengo, Frenchman Jean Villot, sent the following telegram: THE POPE IS DEAD. COME AT ONCE. VILLOT.

What Is a Cardinal?

In the first few days after the death of the pope, members of the College of Cardinals will arrive in Rome. They will be the center of the world's attention, because since 1179, the right to elect the pope has been restricted exclusively to them. Cardinals are often referred to as *princes of the church*. Some cardinals are the archbishops of major dioceses, such as New York, London, Paris, and Manila. Others run agencies of the Roman Curia. In either case, the decision to make a man a cardinal is a personal choice of the pope—popes are not bound to make the archbishop of New York, for example, a cardinal, though it would be a change from tradition if any pope chose not to do so. Cardinals are regarded as the closest advisers of the pope, with a special responsibility for the welfare of the universal church, but their prime reason for existence in modern times is to elect a new pope.

Church tradition regards Peter as the first pope, but historians say that neither Peter nor his immediate successors were called *pope*. Nor did they exercise any authority over bishops in other parts of the church. That probably didn't happen until the second or third century. Before 1179, the church selected its leader in a variety of ways. Peter, according to Catholic belief, was chosen by Jesus. Tradition holds that Peter left instructions as to who would be his first three successors: Linus, Cletus, and Clement. This method of passing on the job did not outlast the first generation, though over the course of church history various popes have *tried* to dictate the choice of a successor. Generally speaking, bishops in Rome during the first several centuries were chosen like bishops elsewhere, by the clergy and people of the diocese. Though democratic in spirit, this system could lead to political infighting and paralysis. At times arguments over the papal succession spilled into street violence. Wealthy Roman noble families exercised a strong influence, as did Byzantine emperors. Over time another system emerged. The clergy (no longer the people) of the Rome diocese elected a pope, one acceptable to at least a majority of the nobles, and the selection was confirmed by the emperor. This sequence had the disadvantage of built-in delay, since waiting for an imperial reaction could prolong the interregnum for months.

The Roman clergy generally elected someone from their own ranks, on the theory that the bishop of Rome should come from Rome. It was not until 891 that a bishop of another diocese was elected pope. This change was seen by some as virtually heretical, since bishops were considered "married" to their diocese and hence it was tantamount to an act of infidelity to abandon it. Over time this attitude abated, as electors decided it could be good for a pope to have had the experience of being the administrator of a major diocese before taking over the church's top job. Recently, however, some high-ranking cardinals have called for a return to the traditional understanding of an unbreakable bond between a bishop and his diocese, seeing it as an antidote to careerism.

Over centuries abuses in the electoral system became frequent, as noble families came up with various ploys to capture the papacy. This manipulation did little for the good name of the office. One aristocrat, Sergio di Caere, was actually elected to the papacy twice, once in 897 and the second time in 904, after an exile of seven years forced on him by a rival clan. Sometimes the rivalries proved lethal. Pope John X, elected through the machinations of a famous papal femme fatale named Marozia, was suffocated in prison by hired killers. (They used two pillows on which the pope had attempted to recline.) In 931, the same Marozia stage-managed the election of John XI, who was her son from Pope Sergius III. In 955, John XII, Marozia's grandson through her son Alberic, was elected pope at the age of eighteen.

In an attempt to end these abuses, Pope Nicholas II proposed restricting the election to *cardinals.* The term at the time referred to clergy who had been *incardinated,* or transferred, into a new position, as opposed to the one for which they were originally ordained. Generally when a cleric was incardinated, it meant he had been promoted. These men were responsible for running important Roman parishes, administering diocesan programs, or advising the pope in special capacities. In 1179, Pope Alexander III specified that the papal election was the prerogative of all, and only, the cardinals.

There are three *orders* of cardinals: bishop, priest, and deacon. Originally the deacons were responsible for social services and charity work in Rome, while the priests ran the parishes and the bishops headed the seven dioceses surrounding Rome. Today the distinction is virtually meaningless, except for when protocol calls for a particular ritual function to be carried out by a member of one of the three orders. As of the summer of 2001, there were nine cardinal bishops, 146 cardinal priests, and twenty-eight cardinal deacons. For much of its early history, the College of Cardinals had only a few members, twenty to thirty. Then for another long period, the limit of cardinals was fixed at seventy, based on the number of translators that church tradition claimed had been required to produce the Septuagint, the famous translation of the Old Testament from Hebrew into Greek. John XXIII was the first pope to break this ceiling. The College of Cardinals as we know it today, with well more than 140 members from all five continents and sixty-one nations, is a recent development.

Paul VI was the first pope to exclude members of the college who are eighty or older from the election, a rule confirmed by John Paul II. The move was part of a broader reform by Paul that included a mandatory retirement age for bishops of seventy-five. The idea was to try to build in term limits for leadership positions in the church, ensuring that no group of persons, and hence no one set of ideas, could dominate the church for too long. Cardinals over eighty are eligible to take part in all the preparatory meetings for the conclave. In 1978, the cardinals over eighty were good sources for journalists, since their brother cardinals would often tell them secrets, which they were free to pass on to the press corps, since the older cardinals were not bound by the oath of conclave secrecy. In his new rules, John Paul II has plugged that gap.

Several times over the ten centuries in which cardinals have enjoyed an electoral monopoly, proposals to broaden the process have been made. It actually happened once. In 1417, thirty representatives from the Council of Constance who were not cardinals joined twenty-three cardinals in selecting Martin V. The election ended the Great Western Schism, which had divided the church for some forty years, as three different men claimed to be pope. In that 1417 election, six clergymen representing each of the five great Catholic nations of the day were added to the electoral body. It was an attempt to return to the ancient practice by which the people helped choose the new pope. However, the agreement specified that the electoral system was adopted "only for this time," and the next papal election, of 1431, which produced Pope Eugene IV, was decided by the cardinals alone. That has been the rule ever since.

In the 1970s, Pope Paul VI entertained the idea of transferring responsibility for electing the pope from the College of Cardinals to the Synod of Bishops. The members of the synod are chosen by national conferences of bishops and are arguably more representative of the full range of voices within the church. This idea aroused opposition among some cardinals. Paul produced a scaled-down version of the idea on March 5, 1973, proposing to leave the election in the College of Cardinals but to give voting rights also to fifteen members of the Synod Council, who are elected by their peers. He also contemplated adding some Eastern-rite patriarchs. Cardinal Giuseppe Siri, a leading conservative candidate to become pope at several conclaves in the twentieth century, later reported that he had been the one to talk Paul out of this idea. His winning argument: since bishops have constituencies, they can be pressured, while cardinals are answerable only to the pope. In *Universi Dominici Gregis*, the 1996 document setting new rules for the papal election, John Paul II gives two arguments for having the cardinals as the papal electors. They are in a sense Roman, the pope says, because they are linked by tradition to the churches of Rome, but they also embody the universality of the church because they come from every continent.

The Congregations

GENERAL CONGREGATION

From three or four days after the death of the pope until the beginning of the conclave to elect his successor, all the cardinals who are in Rome will meet in a daily session called the *general congregation*. Those cardinals who are over eighty can be excused "should they prefer," but most who are physically able to do so will participate. It is up to the camerlengo and the senior members in each of the three orders of cardinals (bishop, priest, and deacon) to fix the day of the pope's funeral and also the day on which the first general congregation meets. In 1978, for example, there were nineteen days from the death of Paul to the conclave, and fourteen meetings of the general congregation. Meetings take place in the Apostolic Palace in the Vatican. In 1978, the Sala Bologna was used. The meetings would normally be presided over by the dean of the College of Cardinals, Gantin. Since Gantin became eighty on May 8, 2002, his functions inside the conclave itself will pass to the subdean, German cardinal Joseph Ratzinger. (Gantin can still perform some of the functions of the dean *outside* the conclave, such as celebrating a funeral mass for the deceased pope.) The meetings generally last about an hour, more if there is something important to talk about.

The general congregation is the chief decision-making body during the interregnum, though the rules laid down by John Paul II specify that the general congregation settles only those matters that cannot be delayed. The new pope will make all the important decisions. The primary task of the general congregation is to prepare for the funeral of the dead pope and the election of the new one. Logistics will dictate most of their calls; if there's a question that calls for an interpretation of the rules presented by John Paul in *Universi Dominici*

Gregis, a majority decides, with a secret ballot, if the presiders think it's an important matter. In addition to making decisions, however, the general congregations are also an opportunity for cardinals to air some general concerns about the state of the church. While they do not directly discuss candidates in these meetings, the cardinals can be expected to come up with a formulation of the issues facing the future church. In 1978, for example, cardinals discussed the state of church finances in the wake of a series of scandals that had engulfed the Vatican Bank (technically, the Institute for the Works of Religion). During the first conclave of 1978, they also discussed the tricky question of whether there would be an autopsy of the body of John Paul I, since there were rumors of foul play. In the end, the cardinals consulted medical experts, who were unanimous that the death was ordinary. They decided against an autopsy, fearing that even the most mundane results would be manipulated to keep the story going.

During the first meeting of the general congregation, each cardinal is to be given a copy of John Paul's rules for the papal election. The rules will then be read aloud. The cardinals will be asked to swear an oath to uphold these rules, using the following formula:

> We, the Cardinals of Holy Roman Church, of the order of
> bishops, of priests, and of deacons, promise, pledge, and
> swear, as a body and individually, to observe exactly and faith-
> fully all the norms contained in the Apostolic Constitution
> *Universi Dominici Gregis* of the Supreme Pontiff John Paul II,
> and to maintain rigorous secrecy with regard to all matters in
> any way related to the election of the Roman Pontiff or those
> which, by their very nature, during the vacancy of the
> Apostolic See, call for the same secrecy.

Next, every cardinal will add: "And I, *N.* Cardinal *N.,* so promise, pledge, and swear." Then, placing his hand on the gospels, he will say: "So help me God and these holy gospels which I now touch with my hand."

Every cardinal who arrives on a subsequent day is expected to perform the ritual upon entry.

According to the pope's rules, the general congregation is to tackle the following issues immediately:

- the day, hour, and manner in which the body of the deceased pope will be exposed for the homage of the faithful in Saint Peter's Basilica
- arrangements for the funeral rites, to be celebrated for nine consecutive days (the *novemdiales*), determining when they are to begin, sometime between the fourth and sixth day after death
- getting rooms at the Casa Santa Marta and the Sistine Chapel ready for the conclave
- deciding on two clerics "known for their sound doctrine, wisdom, and moral authority," who will address the cardinals on the state of the church, and fixing the times when these addresses will be given
- approving expenses in connection with the death of the pope
- setting the day and hour for the beginning of the conclave

PARTICULAR CONGREGATION

To handle points of detail, a smaller body, called the *particular congregation,* is formed. It is a four-person group consisting of the camerlengo and a cardinal under eighty from each of the three orders of cardinals, chosen at random. Every three days from the death of the pope until the conclave, a new set of three names is selected. The cardinals who sit on the particular congregation with the camerlengo are called *assistants*. They are to help him in administering the finances of the Holy See and defending its rights during the interregnum. They are also charged with routine decisions under the rules of procedure. For example, article 44 of *Universi Dominici Gregis* assigns to the particular congregation the responsibility of making a decision if a cardinal asks to make a phone call during the conclave. The particular congregation also clears the names of people to be lodged at the Casa Santa Marta during the conclave. These include priests to hear confessions as well as the cooking and cleaning staff.

The Funeral

Regardless of where the pope dies, funeral rites will take place at the Vatican. (Both Pius XII and Paul VI died at Castel Gondolfo, the pope's summer residence in the Alban hills, outside Rome.) The body will lie in state for three days in Saint Peter's Basilica, where the pope will be dressed in his pontifical vestments. After the death of John Paul I, an estimated 750,000 people filed past over the three days of viewing. In June of 2001, the Vatican ran a dress rehearsal for this aspect of the transition period when it put the body of the late John XXIII on display for the first time since his death, in 1963. Tens of thousands of visitors, mostly Italians, crammed Saint Peter's Basilica for a glimpse at the remains of "Good Pope John" while attendants cried out, *"Avanti"—move on—*to keep the crowd flowing. Visitors got no more than a few seconds in front of the casket, long enough to make the sign of the cross, before they had to step away.

Vatican officials will take extra care with the preparation of the pope's body in light of their experience with Paul VI. Expecting that Paul would want a closed casket, aides had instructed the mortician to embalm the body only lightly. Yet the body was put on full public display, first at Castel Gondolfo, and then in Saint Peter's. After forty-eight hours the jaw began to sag, the face became discolored, and the fingernails turned parchment gray. The embalmers were called back repeatedly, but deterioration continued in Rome's humid summer, so that officials had to decide in almost hourly consultations whether to keep the casket open. Martínez Somalo, the camerlengo, may want to call on Dr. Gennaro Goglia, the Roman physician who treated John XXIII with ten liters of a concoction of his own invention after the pope's death in 1963. Goglia, who is still living, did such a good job that when the pope's casket was opened in 2001 the face was perfectly preserved.

The formal funeral mass will be held, weather permitting, in Saint Peter's Square, in order to accommodate the enormous crowd that will want to participate. Until 1978 these funerals were typically held inside the Basilica, but the funerals for both Paul VI and John Paul I were held outdoors, the latter despite two downpours of rain (the second lasting a full twenty minutes). More than seventy-five thousand people filled the square for Paul's mass, while fifty thousand came for the last rites of John Paul I. In addition, tens of millions of people will follow the funeral on television and radio, thanks to a live international satellite feed.

Most members of the College of Cardinals will take part in the funeral mass. For Paul VI, 104 of the 128 cardinals at the time took part, while for John Paul I the number was 92 of 127. The lead celebrant will be the dean of the College of Cardinals, currently Gantin. In 1978, the cardinals wore red vestments and white miters, the two-horned hat that is the sign of the bishop's office. They processed into the mass in order of seniority, and took seats in the sanctuary before the pope's coffin, which was placed atop a rug in front of the altar. The crowd will be full of dignitaries. For Paul's funeral, the 105 VIPs included United Nations secretary general Kurt Waldheim, Zambian president Kenneth Kaunda, Spanish premier Adolfo Suarez, and a dozen other prime ministers and vice presidents. President Jimmy Carter's wife, Rosalynn, headed the U.S. delegation, which included Senator Edward M. Kennedy and New York governor Hugh Carey.

The ceremony lasts almost two and a half hours (Paul VI's took exactly 159 minutes). For the most part it is a conventional funeral mass, though details of uniquely papal ritual will be observed; the Swiss Guards, for example, will kneel for the consecration of the host, dipping their halberds with their right hand and saluting with their left. The mass will end with the pope's coffin being carried into Saint Peter's Basilica by black-suited pallbearers, likely to a crypt below the surface. Only family members and a few selected Vatican associates will be able to observe this procession, which will pass through the "door of death" to the left side of the main altar in the basilica, and then the final interment. As the coffin is carried inside, a ten-ton funeral bell will ring out. During the mass for John Paul I, the sound was almost drowned out by the spontaneous applause from the crowd, a further sign of the popularity "the smiling pope" had so quickly acquired. When John XXIII's body passed by, people in the square cried out, "May you be blessed," "Intercede for us," "Bring us peace," "Thank you because you taught me to pray," "Bless your children," and "Never leave us!"

The pope's coffin will likely be made of wood, and will then be placed in a lead liner weighing almost nine hundred pounds. This in turn will be placed in a more massive oaken casket, with a bronze plaque bearing Latin inscriptions that detail the dates of John Paul's life and reign. If form holds, the coffin will eventually be lowered into a marble sarcophagus and covered with a large stone slab. John Paul II would become the 148th pope buried in the crypt beneath Saint Peter's.

One of the more striking symbols adopted for both of the 1978 funerals was the placement of a book of the gospels atop the coffin, its pages being turned by the wind (though the effect was spoiled by the rain during the funeral of John Paul I). This touch was part of Paul's desire for humility and a return to the papacy's roots in the simple message of the gospel. A large white candle, a symbol of the resurrection, will stand next to the coffin. During the mass, the celebrant will deliver a homily eulogizing the pope. In 1978, Cardinal Carlo Confalonieri described Paul VI as "a great spirit, of keen intelligence . . . a voice speaking out in defense of truth and justice, condemning violence in every form." One month later, Confalonieri said that John Paul I "passed as a meteor which unexpectedly lights up the heavens and then disappears, leaving us amazed and astonished."

The comments were not without political significance. Confalonieri's sympathies were with the conservatives in the College of Cardinals, and both homilies were read by the press corps for signals of how the conservatives were spinning the pontificates of the popes who had just died. When Confalonieri asserted John Paul I would have emphasized "the authenticity and integrity of faith, the perfection of Christian life, the love of great discipline," this was read in many quarters as a kind of preelection platform. Confalonieri also suggested it was society's "general neglect of spiritual values" that pushed the multitudes toward the pope's crowded Wednesday audiences—implicitly, therefore, not his humility and general disregard of papal pomp and circumstance.

The funeral will be seized upon by parties who want to make political points. During Paul's funeral, the walls around Saint Peter's Square were plastered with posters placed by a conservative Roman Catholic organization, Civiltà Cristiana, calling on the cardinals to elect a strict doctrinaire as pope. The organization had frequently criticized Pope Paul and the revisions of the Second Vatican Council as too liberal. There will also be a massive, if discreet, security presence. In 1978, more than seven thousand policemen, antiterrorist agents, and sharpshooters were assigned to the Vatican City to protect the foreign delegations during the funeral, but for the most part they could not be seen by the mourners because many of them blended into the crowd and others were held in reserve blocks away from the square. Helicopters circled overhead a short distance away as the funeral went on without incident, with olive and khaki-uniformed carabinieri strolling nonchalantly around the square talking with tourists.

The Novemdiales *and Conclave Politics*

Rules of procedure set out by John Paul II specify that the conclave must begin no fewer than fifteen days and no more than twenty days after the death of the pope. The official reason John Paul II gave for the fifteen-day delay in *Universi Dominici Gregis* was to allow time for all the cardinals to reach Rome. In the bygone days of steamships and horse-and-buggy travel, it happened that some cardinals, especially the Americans, missed the conclave because they could not arrive in Rome in time. Today, virtually every member of the College of Cardinals could be in Rome within fifteen hours if necessary. The longer time span, however, affords the cardinals time to get organized—both for the logistics of the conclave and for its politics. John Paul II seemed to imply in article 37 of *Universi Dominici Gregis* that the conclave not only can but *should* begin just fifteen days after the pope's death; a delay of up to twenty days was foreseen only for serious reasons. During the days after the death of the pope but before the conclave actually starts, cardinals are free to stay wherever they like in Rome. Some will take rooms at their national colleges (some Americans will probably reside at the North American College, the U.S. seminary in Rome just up the Janiculum Hill near the Vatican), while others will stay in friends' apartments and still others will book hotel rooms.

Within this fifteen-to-twenty-day span is a formal period of mourning for the dead pope called the the *novemdiales,* or *nine days.* The term reaches back to ancient Rome, when the ninth day of the month was considered a day of expiation and a service for the dead called the *novemdiale sacrum* was observed. This is the likely origin of the Catholic custom of saying a *novena,* or nine days of prayer, for the dead, still widespread in many Latin American and southern European countries. At one point in its history the conclave began ten days after the pope's death, so that the *novemdiales* covered the entire interregnum. Today, even though the interregnum runs more than nine days, many still refer to the entire period between the death of the pope and the start of the conclave as the *novemdiales*. (If the pope's funeral were to occur on the sixth day after death, and the conclave began on the fifteenth day, then the *novemdiales* would fit perfectly between the two.)

Each day during the *novemdiales* there will be a funeral rite for the deceased pope. Some are assigned to the personnel of the papal chapel, others to the Roman clergy, the clergy of the major basilicas, the Roman Curia, and members of religious orders. (The order is given in the liturgical text *De Funere Summi Pontificis.*) Cardinals sometimes preach at these liturgies, and their comments are widely followed for hints of what the electors might be thinking. In 1978, it was widely believed that Cardinal Giuseppe Siri was given the task of delivering sermons as a means of promoting his candidacy to become pope. However, Cardinal Basil Hume of England, a leading moderate, preached as well. The homilies will be closely followed in the press, in part for indications of what church leaders are saying about the needs of the church, in part for the simple reason that they will be among the few events during the *novemdiales* not conducted behind closed doors.

Conclave veterans warn against overinterpreting these few meager public clues. Cardinal Franz König of Vienna, in a July 2001 interview, said that virtually all of the real work of the conclave is done in behind-the-scenes meetings of three and four cardinals, perhaps over glasses of wine and cigars, as opposed to any of the formal events. "An external observer would think that nothing is happening," König said. "All the conversation happens in private." Thus despite the commentator's natural temptation to put a lot of weight on what a cardinal may say in a sermon or in a quick television interview, readers and viewers should know very little of this means much. The real action is out of public view.

Theoretically, the cardinals are not supposed to discuss the papal succession, even among themselves, before the *novemdiales*. The ban on talking about the succession before the pope dies dates to the reign of Felix IV (526–30), who had tried to tell the electors how to vote. Boniface III later sponsored a synod that decreed excommunication for anyone who talked about the next pope until three days after the current pope's death. While originally this taboo was meant to preserve the freedom of the electors, today it tends to function in exactly the opposite way. Cardinals who badly need opportunities to discuss issues and candidates are discouraged from finding them because they're not supposed to discuss such things until the time comes. Thus the electors are less free, rather than more, because of the gag order.

In fact, however, discussions do go on despite the rules. Archbishop Keith Michael Patrick O'Brien of Scotland told the press at the European Synod in October 1999 that the bishops were talking about potential popes at that gathering. "Bishops gossip just as much as everyone else," O'Brien said. "I would say to Cardinal [Thomas] Winning, 'Who's so and so, who's that guy down there?' I saw Tettamanzi and I said, 'Who's the wee fat guy?' I know the famous ones, like Martini and so forth. Who's that Spaniard? Rouco Varela. Boy, I wouldn't want him. He talks and talks. But yes, bishops do talk about it. Obviously we'll talk about *the* position."

The *novemdiales* is the peak campaign season, although technically cardinals are forbidden from politics in the usual sense of the term. John Paul's 1996 constitution says: "The cardinal electors shall abstain from any form of pact, agreement, promise or other commitment of any kind. . . . [They are] not to allow themselves to be guided . . . by friendship or aversion, or to be influenced by favor or personal relationships toward anyone, or to be constrained by the interference of persons in authority or by pressure groups, by the suggestions of the mass media, or by force, fear or the pursuit of popularity." Yet the pope also strikes this realistic note: "It is not my intention . . . to forbid, during the period in which the See is vacant, the exchange of views concerning the election."

Sometimes this exchange of views takes the form of one cardinal sounding out a potential candidate on a particularly sensitive issue, then reporting to others. In the *novemdiales* of 1958, for example, curial Cardinal Giuseppe Pizzardo went to visit the patriarch of Venice, Cardinal Angelo Roncalli, on October 17 to ascertain his position on one of the most highly charged issues of that conclave—what the new pope would do about Archbishop Giovanni Battista Montini of Milan, who had been exiled from Pius XII's curia. The curial forces were terrified that Montini might return as secretary of state and clean house. Roncalli, never the political naïf some took him for, gave a reassuring response: "How could a man be secretary of state when he is not desired by the cardinals of the curia?" he said. Roncalli went on to be elected pope, and honored his old friendship with Montini in another way, making Montini his first appointment as a cardinal. Roncalli's diary from the preconclave period records a number of visitors who sought him out at his lodgings at the Domus Mariae on the Via Aurelia, above the Vatican. On October 15, he writes, there had been "a grand movement of butterflies around my poor person."

Cardinal Giuseppe Siri noted in his official biography that during the *novemdiales* leading up to the first 1978 conclave, he was visited by Cardinals Egidio Vagnozzi and Pietro Palazzini to sound him out about becoming pope. "I was asked to express myself with respect to the idea of my candidacy," Siri wrote. "I responded that I was not asking anything of anyone, nor was I denying anything to anyone." In this quintessentially oblique Italian way, Siri made it clear he was available. His green light was communicated by Vagnozzi and Palazzini to Cardinals Josef Höffner of Germany, Terence Cooke of New York, and Avelar Brandão Vilela of Brazil, leaders of the conservative forces.

Sometimes these encounters take place over a typically exquisite Roman dinner. One privileged spot is L'Eau Vive, a French restaurant located behind the Pantheon in the historic center of Rome. It is run by a Belgian order of nuns, and at 10:00 P.M. every evening service is interrupted for night prayer, which involves the guests in singing hymns to the Virgin Mary. It is one of the privileged spots where high-powered clerics gather to talk shop. Other eateries similarly well adapted include the Abruzzi, near the Gregorian University, Rome's premier pontifical university and the alma mater of many a bishop and cardinal, and Roberto's, on the Borgo Pio, near the Vatican. Enterprising journalists will keep tabs on such spots; knowing this, cardinals who dine together at L'Eau Vive or Roberto's will do so because they want to be seen in one another's company. It's another way of testing the winds, seeing how various coalitions might take shape.

Other times these sessions involve several like-minded cardinals who gather in private to form strategies and identify candidates. As reported by veteran Vatican analyst Giancarlo Zizola, on June 18, 1963, two days before the conclave that elected Paul VI, one such session took place at the convent of the Capuchins of Frascati, near Rome. Present were French cardinal Achille Liénart, Dutchman Bernardus Alfrink, Canadian Paul-Emile Léger, Austrian Franz König, Belgian Leo Suenens, German Josef Frings, and Italian Giovanni Battista Montini. They agreed it would be a difficult conclave, for while the progressives had a large vote in the council, the curialists and conservatives certainly remained strong within the College of Cardinals. They recognized that the conclave was a heaven-sent opportunity for these forces to reassert control. Everyone also agreed that the future of the council depended on the selection of the next pope, since the rules specified that if a council is under way when a pope dies, the council is automatically suspended. The new pope chooses when or if to call it back into session.

The meeting at the Capuchin convent decided to support

Montini as the only man who could capture the proconciliar vote yet persuade enough of the conservatives that he would not go too far, too fast, given his own curial background. The other alternative was Cardinal Giacomo Lercaro of Bologna, who had overseen work on the document on liturgical reform, the only text the council had not rejected in its first session. Lercaro had spoken with eloquence about "a church of the poor" that was more spiritual than political. His supporters believed he was the candidate who truly embodied the spirit of John XXIII. Frings, König, and the others, however, felt that Lercaro could never reach the two-thirds consensus necessary to become pope. That did nothing to lessen the esteem in which many held him, including Montini. When the cardinals first approached Paul VI, he said to Lercaro, "So, that is how life goes, Eminence. You should be sitting here instead of me."

The rules of procedure specify that the cardinals meeting in the general congregation select two clerics to address them on the state of the church. These talks are formally entitled *de eligendo pontifice,* or *on electing the pontiff.* The first is to be delivered during one of the meetings of the general congregation. The second occurs the first afternoon of the conclave, after the cardinals have already processed into the Sistine Chapel and the order *"Extra omnes"*—Everyone out— has been given, signifying the formal start of the process. In 1958, for example, the last public act before the veil of secrecy descended over the conclave was the *de eligendo pontifice* speech given by Cardinal Antonio Bacci. He told the assembled cardinals:

> We need a pope gifted with great spiritual strength and ardent charity. . . . He will need to embrace the Eastern and Western church. He will belong to all peoples, and his heart must beat especially for those oppressed by totalitarian persecution and those in great poverty. . . . May the new vicar of Christ form a bridge between all levels of society, between all nations—even those that reject and persecute the Christian religion. Rather than someone who has explored and experienced the subtle

principles belonging to the art and discipline of diplomacy,
we need a pope who is above all holy, so that he may obtain
from God what lies beyond natural gifts. . . . He will freely receive and welcome the bishops "whom the Holy Spirit has
chosen to rule over the church of God" (Acts 20.28). He will
be prepared to give them counsel in their doubts, to listen
and comfort them in their anxieties, and to encourage their
plans.

The speech was a point-by-point description of what Pius XII was
not, and helped steer the conclave toward Angelo Roncalli.

Sometimes these speeches are useful in giving voice to the
loyal opposition. In 1963, for example, one of the *de eligendo pontifice*
addresses was delivered on June 19 by Amleto Tondini, a curial official in charge of Latin letters. Tondini's talk was a clear declaration
of the curial agenda heading into the conclave. He opposed the
optimistic vision of Pope John with a vision of the world that was qua-
siapocalyptic. He insisted that the enthusiasm that had greeted John
XXIII's push for peace with the Soviet bloc was not based on any
moral or religious consideration. "Would he be accused of pessimism
who advances reservations about the meaning of much of that enthusiastic applause directed at the pope of peace, asking himself if it was
truly the expression of souls that feel the true values of the spirit and
believe in Christ or in the dogmatic and moral teachings of the
church?" Tondini asked. He went on to condemn the errors of science, of materialism, and of relativism. He suggested that before the
new pope recalls the council, he should allow some of its questions to
"mature," language that was equivalent to saying the council should
be put on hold. Tondini's speech was, therefore, a pitch for church
governance from the right.

The initial conclave of 1978, which elected John Paul I, was the
first modern conclave in which public opinion was a decisive force in
the preelection debate. Two factors explain this evolution. First, mass

media offered alternative voices the opportunity to make themselves heard on a wide scale. Second, Vatican II had emphasized that the church is the entire people of God, not simply the hierarchy or the curia. Profoundly affected by that shift in thinking, many Catholics felt a new investment in the outcome of the papal election and a right to express their views on it. Thus the period leading up to the conclave was full of press conferences, book releases, manifestos, petitions, and commentaries that provided the cardinals with additional perspectives.

The cardinals themselves became part of this public discourse, accepting invitations to appear on television and radio and to be interviewed by newspapers. They found a new tool for communicating their views to one another—the press. In addition to reports through second- and third-hand channels about what cardinal so-and-so felt, one could also simply open *Il Messaggero* or *La Stampa* or the *New York Times* and read his comments. The press played a role not just in bringing the wider public into the conversation but also in facilitating the preconclave talk between the electors themselves.

Siri, for example, gave an interview to Italian television in which he ostensibly spoke about the needs of the church but in reality offered a summary of what his papacy would be like. "I believe that we have to put things in order in the doctrinal field," Siri said. "The most grave threat that hangs over the church today is that too many talk and do not talk well." Siri's opposite number among the progressives, Cardinal Giovanni Benelli of Florence, was quoted in one of the Roman dailies on August 24 offering an alternative view of papal priorities: "There is no doubt that the bishops have to become coparticipants in the government of the church. The bishops form a college whose head is the pope, and thus the college with the pope as guide must obviously participate in the government of the church." Benelli added that the Synod of Bishops "is an institution that can be modified according to the needs of the times," through "a development that also includes deliberative powers."

Probably the most consequential interview during the first *novemdiales* of 1978 was that given by Cardinal Albino Luciani, the future John Paul I, in response to questions about the English test-tube baby, Louise Brown, who had just been born as Paul VI died. Catholic teaching bans artificial reproduction, and almost every cardinal was asked for a comment. Luciani's stood out. He said: "I send the most heartfelt congratulations to the English baby girl whose conception took place artificially. As far as the parents are concerned, I have no right to condemn them. If they acted with honest intention and in good faith, they could even be deserving of merit before God for what they wanted and asked the doctors to carry out." It was a brilliant response. First, it was positive and affirming of the new life that had been created; second, it avoided harsh moralism about the parents; third, it did not challenge church teaching, but simply said the parents' subjective intention could be worthy of praise. Luciani's masterstroke helped propel him to the papacy.

In the second conclave of 1978, the one that elected Karol Wojtyla as John Paul II, several conservatives in the college gave interviews that stressed the need to resist pressures on the conclave, presumably a reference to demands for a progressive reformer. Joseph Ratzinger of Munich, who would later become John Paul II's chief doctrinal czar, gave a preconclave interview to the *Frankfurter Allgemeine Zeitung*. He warned of "pressure from the forces of the left," seeming to hint that the media and secular governments would be attempting to sway electors to produce a "modern" pope, who would soften the church's traditional doctrinal commitments.

The American cardinals, in general the most media savvy, actually held a press conference before heading into the conclave. "I don't want a political pope," said New York's Terence Cooke. "Paul VI himself was an excellent pope because he was above all a pastor rather than a diplomat." The Jesuits also held a press conference, during which the order's general, Pedro Arrupe, a Basque, said that the next pope should have the interests of the Third World close to his heart.

The most famous preconclave interview was given by Siri in the *novemdiales* leading up to the second conclave of 1978. He had agreed to speak with the Italian newspaper *Gazzetta del Popolo* in the belief that his remarks would not be printed until after the conclave began, on October 15, and hence the other cardinals would not see them until after the election was over. The newspaper published the interview on October 14, however, ostensibly because Siri gave another interview, to a radio station, and so they believed he had lifted his own embargo. Rumors circulated, however, that Benelli, Siri's main rival, induced the *Gazzetta* to publish the interview early, knowing it would damage Siri's chances. It amounted to a frontal assault on Vatican II. Siri explicitly rejected episcopal collegiality and suggested that a particular speech by John Paul I on the subject did not reflect his own thought. "That speech was written for the pope by others," Siri said. "All he did was read it." As for collegiality, Siri said: "I also don't know what the development of episcopal collegiality means. . . . The synod can never become a deliberative institution in the church because it is not contemplated in the divine constitution of the church." Moreover, "to say only the word 'pastor' is to decapitate the figure of the pope. Not humiliate it, but decapitate it. He has to be a pastor, I agree, but he has to also be the one who governs the church. If he does not govern the church, what is he there to do, to let the sheep graze?" König of Austria confirmed that Siri's interview circulated within the conclave. It was probably a fatal blow to his hopes of becoming pope. (Even the mild-mannered König says that Siri had some "strange ideas.")

Among the Catholic groups who made skillful use of the media to involve themselves in the preconclave conversation in 1978 was the U.S.-based Committee for a Responsible Election of the Pope (CREP, a deliberate play on Richard Nixon's famous Committee for the Reelection of the President, or CREEP). Its chief spokesperson was Father Andrew Greeley, the Chicago priest, novelist, and sociologist, who had become famous for saying in public what many liberal Catholics in America thought privately—that Paul VI's encyclical *Humanae Vitae*, which repeated the church's ban on artificial birth control, was a disaster. Greeley demonstrated, using polling data, that the primary cause of the post–Vatican II decline in ordinations, mass attendance, and agreement with key beliefs in the West was not the council but the loss of credibility caused by *Humanae Vitae*. Greeley brought with him to Rome what he called "a contribution of significance to the church and to the cardinal electors." It was a set of criteria for selecting the next pope based on sociological research.

At a well-attended Rome press conference, Greeley said: "At the present critical time in its history, faced with the most acute crisis, perhaps, since the Reformation, and dealing with a world in which both faith and community are desperately sought, the papacy requires a man of holiness, a man of hope, a man of joy; a sociologically oriented job description of the pope, in other words, must conclude that the Catholic Church needs as its leader a holy man who can smile." Press coverage was hostile but enormous, and Greeley could claim vindication from the short-lived pontificate of Albino Luciani, whose happy, upbeat style earned him the nickname "the smiling pope." The CREP group also distributed a book entitled *The Inner Elite* by veteran Catholic journalist Gary MacEoin, which offered biographical sketches of all the members of the College of Cardinals and which some cardinals took with them into the conclave as a kind of voter's guide.

After Vatican II, a professional class of theologians in the church emerged in the public forum as a source of comment upon, and sometimes criticism of, official policies of the hierarchy. During the *novemdiales*, theologians made themselves heard about the kind of pope they felt the church needed. The French Dominican theologian Yves Congar, for example, published a lengthy article in the French newspaper *La Croix* offering his thoughts, which was much read in Rome. He suggested a non-Italian pope, perhaps from the

Third World, and someone who was ecumenical in his outlook. He felt the advocacy of justice for the poor of the earth and the push toward unity between all Christians should be the key priorities of the next pontificate. Congar even suggested some names, those of Cardinals Johannes Willebrands, the secretary of the Pontifical Council for Promoting Christian Unity, and Paulo Evaristo Arns, the Franciscan archbishop of São Paolo in Brazil. On August 16, eight days before the conclave began, a number of newspapers carried a manifesto signed by a group of progressive Vatican II theologians, including Hans Küng of Switzerland, Marie-Dominique Chenu of France, Gustavo Guttiérez of Peru, and Edward Schillebeeckx of Holland, in addition to Congar. They called for the election of a pope "ready to take the risk of sharing his power with the bishops," someone to transform the Synod of Bishops into "a deliberative organ." German theologians Johannes Baptist Metz and Karl Rahner penned an appeal to the cardinals, asking for a pope capable of responding to the aspirations of the poor in the Third World.

Other sectors of public opinion in the church, using the platform provided by the media, likewise made themselves heard. A group of Christian base communities in Rome, for example, appealed for a pope who would renounce the temporal privileges of the papacy and its political functions in order to concentrate on being a spiritual messenger able to address the powers of the earth from a prophetic stance. Another group of progressive lay Catholics in Italy advocated the election of Cardinal Ugo Poletti, the vicar of Rome, in order to return the papacy to its roots as the see of Rome.

The press is more than a passive medium through which players in the conclave process speak to one another; it also exerts an influence of its own through the kinds of coverage it chooses to offer, the content of the analysis it provides, even the choice of which cardinals it profiles as *papabili*. Some observers deny that the media has any such influence, pointing to the election of Karol Wojtyla as John

Paul II in 1978, the first non-Italian in four hundred years, which few people anticipated. Since 1978, a mythology has grown up to the effect that a conclave's logic can be neither fathomed nor influenced. This is simply not true. In 1939, most media outlets correctly anticipated the election of Eugenio Pacelli as Pius XII, and in 1963 most again tapped Giovanni Battista Montini, who became Paul VI. Roncalli made many shortlists in 1958. In 1978, Luciani's election was anticipated by *Time, L'Espresso,* and *Le Monde,* among others. The fact that these media outlets all pointed to Luciani certainly helped create the early consensus that saw him elected after just four ballots.

As a footnote, not everyone in the press corps was blindsided by Wojtyla. The weekly *Blanco y Negro* in Barcelona published an analysis by well-known Vatican analyst José Luis Martin Descalzo just before the conclave. He quoted Cardinal Antonio Samorè: "In August there were two candidates of which the press never spoke. They were Luciani and Wojtyla," Samorè said, ignoring the fact that many press outlets had identified Luciani as a strong *papabile.* Be that as it may, he was right about Wojtyla. "Luciani is dead," Samorè continued. "Therefore . . ."

König told me in summer 2001 that before each of the three conclaves in which he participated, he made a shortlist of possible candidates and then did some brief research on their backgrounds. If he were going into a conclave today, how would he decide whom to put on this list? "If a name never appears in the papers or on TV or radio, then he may be a good bishop, a good cardinal, but he is probably nothing special. But when you feel, look here, his name turns up [in the press]—why? Why is he being mentioned?" In other words, a high media profile is virtually a sine qua non for a serious papal candidate.

The use of the media will be intensified in the next conclave. The progressive We Are Church coalition, for example, will put on a series of roundtable discussions on the papacy and women, the papacy and ecumenism, and the papacy and authority in the church.

High-profile theologians and church personalities will be invited to take part, and the location will be near enough to the Vatican that reporters waiting for conclave news can get there quickly. The media's need for something to feed public interest, at a time when actual news is limited, gives underfunded grassroots groups such as We Are Church a chance to present their ideas to a vast global audience that otherwise would be impossible for them to reach.

Moreover, the advent of twenty-four-hour cable television means that cardinals will have more opportunities to speak to one another and to the Catholic world. Every morning cardinals will appear on the major networks' morning shows, and throughout the day CNN, Fox, and MSNBC will have updates about what was said in that day's general congregation, or what a certain high-profile *papabile* said upon exiting the Abruzzi after lunch. Each day the world's papers will be filled with reporting, comment, analysis, and forecasts. Many specialized news outlets that follow Vatican affairs on a regular basis, such as my newspaper, the *National Catholic Reporter,* will be delivering news as it happens minute by minute via the Internet. The media will be a part of the conclave story as it never was before.

Italian scholar Alberto Melloni, who worked on the historical materials for the beatification of John XXIII, has predicted this. Because the College of Cardinals is far more international than ever, its members do not know one another well. Long gone are the days in which most cardinals were Italian. Gone too are the days when most cardinals could be expected to have worked at least some time in Rome, where they could gain a working knowledge of the people and the process. In such a context, cardinals are largely dependent upon the media to introduce them to one another. What they know about a particular cardinal's opinions, his history and outlook, his strengths and weaknesses, is just as likely to come from the press as it is from their own experience. During the *novemdiales,* one can be sure the world press will be scoured every day for what it is printing and broadcasting about the candidates—and some of the most avid readers will be the cardinals themselves.

Sistine Chapel and Casa Santa Marta

The word *conclave*—from the Latin for *with a key*—reflects the practice of locking the cardinals in a room and refusing to let them come out until they elect a pope. Locking them in was intended to force them to hurry up. In earlier eras of church history, it was not unusual for badly divided cardinals to argue for months, even years, before making a choice. In 1241, for example, it took seventy days for the cardinals to settle on the archbishop of Milan, Goffredo Castiglioni, who took the name Celestine IV. The cardinals had been locked into a room by the Roman noble Matteo Orsini during one of the city's notoriously stifling Augusts. The cardinals left behind diaries complaining of headaches, collapses, even heart attacks. At one point the leading candidate, Cardinal Roberto di Somercotes, died. The new pope himself survived the conclave by only seventeen days! Thirty years later, Pope Gregory X was so concerned about the prospect of the conclave lasting too long that he prescribed a stringent set of dietary provisions. If the conclave could not reach a decision within three days, Gregory wrote, they were to be reduced to one plate only at lunch and dinner instead of the customary Italian two-plate meal, pasta followed by meat. After five days of this, the rations were to be cut again, this time to bread, water, and wine, until the cardinals elected a pope.

Gregory was writing out of his own personal experience. The conclave that made him pope lasted almost three years, and toward the end the people of Viterbo became so impatient that they tore the roof off the building in which the cardinals were lodged and put them on a diet of bread and water. It was the longest conclave in history. (The longest conclave in more recent times was that of 1831, which elected Gregory XVI after fifty-four days. The longest twentieth-century conclave, which elected Pius XI in 1922, lasted only five days.)

The tradition of a lockup has survived into our times. Cardinals are quartered inside the Vatican for the duration of the papal election, cut off from the outside world. Balloting will take place in the Sistine Chapel, named after Pope Sixtus IV (1471–84), for whom it was built. In earlier times, papal elections happened in other venues. For most of the nineteenth century they occurred in Rome's Quirinale Palace, the seat of the pope's civil administration. In the preceding centuries conclaves were often held wherever the pope died. Sometimes the conclave would move to a town that offered a better combination of climate and political stability. (Rome's summers are notoriously awful. Even today the vast majority of Romans desert the city for the *ferragosto,* the holiday period that lasts virtually the entire month.) The last conclave to happen outside of Rome was in 1800, when the cardinals met in Venice to elect a successor to the unfortunate Pius VI, who died as Napoleon's prisoner.

John Paul II specified that the Sistine Chapel is to remain closed during the entire conclave period, hence the normal flood of tourists that washes through every day will be halted. As Paul VI did before him, John Paul ordered that before the conclave begins, a thorough check should be made to ensure that no electronic devices have been secretly installed. (Some experts on electronic surveillance believe this is a futile exercise. They say that today it is unnecessary to have a bug inside the conclave; one can point a powerful antenna at the Sistine Chapel from a nearby rooftop and pick up every sound on the inside. Whether this will happen, and how the world media will respond if it does, will be interesting to watch.)

During previous conclaves, cardinals actually slept inside the Apostolic Palace, the large complex on the north side of Saint Peter's Square that houses the papal apartments and the offices of the Secretariat of State. Whenever a conclave took place, cubicles were

erected with cots and washbasins, providing extremely Spartan ac-
commodations for men ranging from middle-aged to elderly and
generally accustomed to something more refined. England's late
Cardinal Basil Hume once famously complained that the cots must
have come "from a seminary for very short people." Cardinals were
expected to make their own beds, and bathrooms numbered one for
every ten electors. Italian cardinal Silvio Oddi, whose cell was near
one of the bathrooms in 1978, reported awakening in the middle of
the night to the groans of elderly cardinals who had scuffled down
marble hallways for more than seventy meters only to find their
assigned toilet occupied. Concern for secrecy extended to details
such as closing and blacking out all the windows, so that the rest
of the Vatican could neither peer in nor hear. The first conclave of
1978 took place during August, and the ovenlike heat produced the
nearest thing to an open revolt ever witnessed in a twentieth-century
conclave. Siri recalled the episode in a 1992 interview with *La
Stampa*:

> We were dying of heat, asphyxiation seemed to be getting the
> upper hand and I noticed that some cardinals were on the
> verge of collapse. Then I rebelled, and with the authority of a
> member of the supervising committee, I said: "I order you to
> open the windows." Some responded: "Eminence, it is not
> permitted to open the windows. They could hear the applause
> in the Secretariat of State" [when the new pope is elected]. I
> responded: "What if they hear?" They opened the windows.
> Color began to return to the faces of the moribund.

Siri, the conservative's conservative, could get away with such a minor act of dissent.

This time the living conditions for the cardinals will be much improved, since they will be staying in the Casa Santa Marta, a twenty-
million-dollar hotel inside the Vatican grounds constructed by order

of John Paul II. The Santa Marta is just back from the Paul VI audience hall, across from the entrance to the excavations underneath Saint Peter's Basilica. It features 108 guest suites, each with a living room and a bedroom, and twenty-three single rooms. All have private baths. One point not yet clear is what happens if there are more cardinals under eighty than there are rooms available. There were 134 electors in the summer of 2001, so if the conclave had happened then, three cardinals would have been looking for roommates. Inside, the Casa Santa Marta looks like any upscale modern hotel, with a reception desk, meeting rooms, a dining room, a TV lounge, and marble staircases. On the ground level, the only distinctive feature marking it as a Catholic facility is the chapel, a modernistic design of glass and wood. Some Vatican personnel live at the Casa Santa Marta and will have to be vacated when the time comes. Mostly, however, the facility is used to house guests at Vatican events. Cardinals often stay at the Casa Santa Marta when they visit Rome; reporters have found this a good way to contact them, since they tend to pick up the phone in their rooms themselves, momentarily unprotected by their normal layers of bureaucracy.

One logistical issue not yet clarified: how the cardinals will cover the short distance from the Casa Santa Marta to the entrance to the Sistine Chapel for their scheduled twice-a-day vote. The most likely solution seems a short bus ride. *Universi Dominici Gregis* seems to hint at this in article 43, which requires that no one disturb the cardinals "while they are being transported from the Domus Sanctae Marthae to the Apostolic Vatican Palace." Personnel will be under strict orders not to attempt to communicate with the cardinals as they are moving back and forth. John Paul II wanted the cardinals talking to no one but themselves.

John Paul II's rules allow cardinals who are seriously ill to be accompanied by a nurse inside the conclave, even during the period of election. He specifies that a number of priests must be lodged at the Casa Santa Marta for hearing confessions in the different languages, as well as two medical doctors and a "suitable number of persons" for housekeeping and preparing and serving meals. All such personnel are required to swear an oath regarding secrecy, as follows:

> I promise and swear that, unless I should receive a special faculty given expressly by the newly elected Pontiff or by his successors, I will observe absolute and perpetual secrecy with all who are not part of the College of Cardinal electors concerning all matters directly or indirectly related to the ballots cast and their scrutiny for the election of the Supreme Pontiff. I likewise promise and swear to refrain from using any audio or video equipment capable of recording anything which takes place during the period of the election within Vatican City, and in particular anything which in any way, directly or indirectly, is related to the process of the election itself. I declare that I take this oath fully aware that an infraction thereof will make me subject to the spiritual and canonical penalties which the future Supreme Pontiff will see fit to adopt, in accordance with Canon 1399 of the Code of Canon Law. So help me God and these Holy Gospels which I touch with my hand.

While fifteen days should give all the members of the College of Cardinals adequate time to arrive in Rome, a cardinal who for some reason is late may still enter the conclave. However, he joins the event in progress; things do not go back to square one because a new elector has arrived. Once arrived, cardinals cannot leave except for a good reason, presumably serious illness, recognized by a majority of the rest of the cardinals. Another reason one or more cardinals might be sent out of the conclave is to bring back the new pope if he is not a member of the college. This is possible, since in theory any baptized male may be elected pope. Such a development, however, is extremely unlikely. The last noncardinal to be elected was the archbishop of Bari, Bartolomeo Prignano, who became Urban VI in 1378. Superstitious cardinals may see that as an unhappy omen, since Urban triggered the Great Western Schism, which divided the church for decades.

One other point that remains ambiguous is exactly how many cardinals are permitted to enter the conclave. John Paul's 1996 constitution on the papal election, *Universi Dominici Gregis,* seems to set a clear limit: "The maximum number of Cardinal electors must not exceed one hundred and twenty." Yet the pope also says that the right of election of the pope belongs to those cardinals who have not yet reached their eightieth birthday. In article 35 of *Universi Dominici Gregis,* John Paul wrote: "No cardinal elector can be excluded from active or passive voice in the election of the Supreme Pontiff." At present, there are more than 130 such cardinal electors. What then happens to those above the limit of 120? Most canon lawyers take the opinion that the pope, in appointing more electors than anticipated by *Universi Dominici Gregis,* made an exception to his own rules and hence all the cardinals under eighty, regardless of the limit of 120, are eligible to enter the conclave. (Canon lawyers ruefully joke that nobody violates canon law like a pope.) As a political matter, it seems probable that all cardinals under eighty will be admitted regardless of the wording of *Universi Dominici Gregis* because the task of trying to decide who cannot enter could paralyze the process indefinitely.

The Election

The final act of the preconclave period is the mass *Pro Eligendo Papa—for electing the pope.* All the cardinals take part in the mass, which is celebrated in Saint Peter's Basilica the morning of the day the conclave begins. The homily is closely attended, as it is the final signal of what the cardinals may be thinking before they head off to vote. The first event of the conclave occurs that afternoon, when all the cardinals assemble in the Pauline Chapel inside the Apostolic Palace. Less famous than the Sistine Chapel, the Pauline Chapel is nevertheless magnificent in its own right, containing the last two paintings ever by Michelangelo. The cardinals are to sing a Latin hymn, the *Veni Creator,* invoking the guidance of the Holy Spirit, and then are to process from the Pauline Chapel a few yards to the Sistine Chapel. The cardinals will be accompanied by various assistants and junior clerics, and it is possible that the Vatican will permit transmission of television images of the procession.

John Paul's rules of procedure, like those of popes before him, emphasize the need for secrecy. The concern is to protect the independence of the election and to ensure that cardinals are free to vote for the man they consider best suited for the job. The use of any devices to record the conclave is forbidden, whether electronically or in writing. John Paul warns that anyone betraying the conclave's secrets "will be subject to grave penalties according to the judgment of the future pope." Only the new pope has the authority to release the cardinals from their vow of secrecy. Yet it should be noted that many cardinals take a very limited view of what is covered by the requirement of secrecy, holding that it applies only to the actual round-by-round results of the balloting.

For the duration of the conclave, cardinals are forbidden to read newspapers or any other periodicals, or watch television or listen to the radio. *Universi Dominici Gregis* does not mention use of the Internet, but one may presume it too is forbidden. (The cardinal likely to be most frustrated by this provision is Roger Mahony of Los Angeles, the only cardinal with his own entry in the membership directory of America Online.) Here again, the aim is to insulate the cardinals from the pressure of public opinion, political calculations, and so forth, so they can form their own, independent judgment about which candidate would be best.

After the cardinals arrive in the Sistine Chapel, they will take oaths promising to follow the rules of procedure as laid down by John Paul II. The prescribed oath is as follows:

> We, the Cardinal electors present in this election of the Supreme Pontiff, promise, pledge, and swear, as individuals and as a group, to observe faithfully and scrupulously the prescriptions contained in the Apostolic Constitution of the Supreme Pontiff John Paul II, *Universi Dominici Gregis,* published on 22 February 1996. We likewise promise, pledge, and swear that whichever of us by divine disposition is elected Roman Pontiff will commit himself faithfully to carrying out the *munus Petrinum* of Pastor of the Universal Church and will not fail to affirm and defend strenuously the spiritual and temporal rights and the liberty of the Holy See. In a particular way, we promise and swear to observe with the greatest fidelity and with all persons, clerical or lay, secrecy regarding everything that in any way relates to the election of the Roman Pontiff and regarding what occurs in the place of the election, directly or indirectly related to the results of the voting; we promise and swear not to break this secret in any way, either during or after the election of the new Pontiff, unless explicit authorization is granted by the same Pontiff; and never to lend support or favor to any interference, opposition, or any other form of intervention, whereby secular authorities of whatever order and degree or any group of people or individuals might wish to intervene in the election of the Roman Pontiff.

This oath is taken as a group. Then each of the cardinals, in order of seniority, will say individually: "And I, N., do so promise, pledge and swear." Placing his hand on the gospels, he will add: "So help me God and these Holy Gospels which I touch with my hand."

After the last cardinal has recited the oath, the master of papal liturgical ceremonies, Piero Marini, will intone the words

"Extra omnes," or *Everyone out,* and everyone but the cardinals and certain designated individuals must exit the Sistine Chapel. Marini will remain, as will the second cleric chosen by the cardinals in their general congregation to give the *de eligendo pontifice* address. He gives his meditation at this point, and when he is finished, he too will leave. Then the cardinals begin the real work of the conclave. The dean of the College of Cardinals will begin the proceedings by asking whether the election can begin or whether there still remain doubts that need to be clarified concerning the norms and procedures laid down in *Universi Dominici Gregis.* John Paul took pains to emphasize that this was simply a final opportunity to clarify the rules. They may not be changed in any way, even if there is a unanimous consensus, and should the cardinals attempt to make any such changes, the resulting election would be nullified.

If no one expresses any doubts, the election may proceed immediately. If there are doubts, then the cardinals function like a meeting of the general congregation to resolve them. Assuming time permits, one ballot—and only one—is to be held on the afternoon of the first day. For each of the succeeding days of the conclave, there are to be two ballots in the morning and two in the afternoon. Balloting is a complicated and intricate task, regulated down to the last detail by the rules of procedure. According to *Universi Dominici Gregis,* there are three phases to every ballot.

PRESCRUTINY

In this first stage, two or three ballot papers are given to each cardinal elector. These cards are rectangular, with *"Eligo in summum pontificem"* (*I elect as supreme pontiff*) written across the top. A space is left below for writing in the name of a candidate. Each cardinal is to try as much as possible to disguise his handwriting. The ballot is shaped so that it can be folded in half, to further disguise each cardinal's choice (Paul VI is said to have designed the cards himself). After the ballots are distributed, several conclave functions must be filled by drawing names. The junior cardinal deacon under eighty, currently German Cardinal Walter Kasper, will draw three names by lot for the scrutineers, those cardinals who will actually count the ballots; three names for the revisers, cardinals who will check the work of the scrutineers; and three names for the *infirmarii*, cardinals who collect the ballots of any cardinals too sick to vote for themselves. At this stage, before any cardinals begin writing in their selections, the secretary of the College of Cardinals (currently Archbishop Francesco Monterisi, who is also the secretary of the Congregation for Bishops), and Marini must leave the conclave, so that the cardinals are alone. Kasper, as the junior cardinal deacon, will close the door. If it is necessary to allow the *infirmarii* to exit to collect any ballots, Kasper will open and close the door for them.

SCRUTINY PROPER

Each cardinal must write the name of just one candidate on his ballot. If he were to write in more than one name, the ballot would be invalid. After they have finished writing, the cardinals process up to an altar in the Sistine Chapel on which a large chalice has been placed. The cardinals must approach the altar holding their folded ballot so it can be seen. Each cardinal kneels before the altar for a brief moment of prayer, then rises and says in Latin: "I call as my witness Christ the Lord, who will be my judge, that my vote is given to the one who before God I think should be elected."

He then uses a large circular plate, called a paten, to slide his ballot into the chalice. The cardinal bows to the altar and returns to his place. Any cardinal who is present in the chapel but too ill to approach the altar pronounces the oath from his seat and then hands his ballot to one of the scrutineers, who approaches the altar and drops it in the chalice for him. If a cardinal is in the Casa Santa Marta and too sick to be in the chapel, the three *infirmarii* go to him with a box with an opening in the top through which the ballot can be inserted. The box has a lock, and before the *infirmarii* leave the Sistine Chapel the scrutineers open it up and show everyone that it is empty. They lock the box and place the key on the altar. The *infirmarii* take the box and some blank ballots to the Casa Santa Marta, where each sick cardinal is to secretly write in his candidate, take the oath, and place the ballot in the box. If the cardinal is unable to write, one of the *infirmarii*, or another cardinal selected by the sick cardinal, takes an oath of secrecy and then writes in his choice on his behalf. The *infirmarii* take the box back to the Sistine Chapel, where the scrutineers verify that the number of ballots corresponds to the number of sick cardinals. They then add the ballots to the total. The *infirmarii* are permitted to cast their own ballots immediately after the senior cardinal, so they can collect the ballots of the sick cardinals while the others are going through the regular process in the Sistine Chapel.

After the last ballots have been added to the chalice, the first scrutineer shakes it thoroughly. The last scrutineer then begins to take out the ballots, unopened, and counts them, lifting each one in full view and placing it in another receptacle. The number of ballots must correspond to the number of electors. If the numbers do not match, all the ballots are burned immediately, before they are opened. Assuming the numbers do match, the counting begins. The first scrutineer opens the ballot, writes down the name in silence, and passes it to the second scrutineer, who does the same. The third scrutineer pronounces the name on the ballot in a loud voice so that all the cardinals may keep track of the votes on a sheet of paper. After reading out the name, the third scrutineer passes a needle and thread through each ballot, being sure that it passes through the word *Eligo*.

At the end of the count the thread is tied in a knot and the ballots placed on one side of the counting table.

POSTSCRUTINY

The scrutineers are to add up all the votes each individual has received. If no one gets two-thirds, then no pope has been elected. The rules specify that a two-thirds majority of the cardinal electors is necessary to elect a pope. If the number of cardinals cannot be divided evenly into thirds, the requirement becomes two-thirds plus one. Whether a pope is elected or not, the revisers must check both the ballots and the notes made by the scrutineers to be sure that the count has been correct. If the first ballot is inconclusive, a second must be held immediately, except on the afternoon of the first day. The procedure for the second ballot is the same as the first, except that the cardinals do not have to swear their oath again, and new scrutineers, revisers, and *infirmarii* do not have to be chosen. Afterward the ballots are to be burned by the three scrutineers, assisted by a cleric appointed to serve as secretary of the conclave and the master of ceremonies, who have been summoned by Kasper or whoever is the junior cardinal deacon. If a second ballot is to be taken immediately, the ballots from the first and second rounds are to be burned together. Barring special circumstances, there will be dramatic wisps of smoke from the conclave twice a day, once in the late morning and once in the early evening, until the pope is elected. As is well known, black smoke means no pope has been elected; white smoke means that a new pope is in power. The cardinals hand over their notes to the camerlengo or the scrutineers, and these are burned along with the ballots. No cardinal is to save his record of how the balloting goes. This rule has been violated in the past; we know how the voting went in 1914 and 1922, for example, because Cardinal Friedrich Gustav Piffl of Vienna put his records of the balloting in his secret diary, published in 1963. The only authorized record of the voting, however, is to be drawn up by the camerlengo, who gives it to the new pope. John Paul's rules say the record should be kept in an archive in a sealed envelope that can be opened only with the pope's permission.

In 1996, John Paul made an important change in the rules. If the balloting is inconclusive after three days, there will be a pause of one day. During that time, the cardinals pray and engage in informal discussions. They also hear a brief spiritual exhortation from the senior cardinal in the order of deacons who is under eighty, currently Australian cardinal Edward Cassidy. After this pause, voting is to resume. After seven more ballots, if the result is still inconclusive, there is another pause for prayer and discussion. This time the reflection would be given by the senior cardinal in the order of priests, currently Puerto Rican cardinal Luis Aponte Martínez. Another seven ballots are to take place, followed by another pause, this time with remarks from the senior cardinal in the order of bishops, now German cardinal Joseph Ratzinger. Voting is again resumed for another seven ballots. If there is still no winner, the camerlengo is to invite the cardinals to express an opinion on how things should proceed, with the result to be determined by an absolute majority—that is, 50 percent plus one. That majority may decide to proceed to election by majority, or to take the two names with the largest number of votes in the previous round and decide between them by a majority vote. The impact of this new rule is clear: after approximately thirty ballots or twelve days, a majority in the conclave can change the rules and put through a candidate with only 50 percent plus one of the votes.

This change has produced much speculation about the possibility of a protracted conclave, in which a determined majority unable to generate two-thirds support for their candidate simply waits it out until they can change the rules and elect their man. Some have observed that while the College of Cardinals is predominantly conservative, there is a significant moderate-to-progressive minority, especially among European cardinals. Perhaps, some believe, John

Paul wanted to give the conservatives the tool they need to elect a like-minded pope, even if a stubborn minority is not willing to go along. At a meeting of all the world's cardinals in Rome in May 2001, the German-speaking language group requested that the pope reverse this change, perhaps reflecting fear of just such an eventuality. Recent conclave experience, however, seems to make this scenario a long shot. The longest conclave of the twentieth century, the conclave of 1922, which elected Pius XI, lasted only five days and fourteen ballots. It is a considerable stretch from five to twelve days, and from eight to thirty ballots.

Of course, the capacity to change the rules did not exist before, nor did the cardinals have the chance to relax in relative comfort in the Casa Santa Marta. Still, most analysts regard this scenario as unlikely. Since an interregnum is by definition destabilizing for the church, there is enormous psychological pressure to bring it to an end quickly. Moreover, cardinals do not like to create the impression of disunity. Since the Holy Spirit is supposed to be guiding the process, anything that smacks too overtly of bare-knuckled politics is considered poor form. Finally, cardinals realize that if the pope is elected under what some might regard as dubious circumstances, his authority could be weakened. Still, if the conclave lasts more than two or three days, speculation in the press will begin to grow that a majority is holding out for the rule change to kick in.

John Paul added a few final points in *Universi Dominici Gregis*. If simony were to occur inside the conclave—that is, if someone were to try to pay off electors, either for their own candidacy or someone else's—those guilty would incur the penalty of excommuncication. (This is a formal judgment of grave sin that prevents someone from receiving the sacraments.) Yet the election of the new pope would not for that reason be invalid. In other words, even if a man bought the papacy, he is still pope, as long as the election occurred according to the rules of procedure. John Paul also forbade any cardinal from expressing a veto on behalf of a secular government against any papal candidate. This rule is a holdover from previous centuries, when

Catholic powers such as France and Austria claimed the right to veto candidates they found unacceptable. The last time this was attempted was in the conclave of 1903, when the Austrian emperor wished to veto the candidacy of Cardinal Mariano Rampolla as the successor to Leo XIII. The conclave rejected the veto, and then proceeded to elect Giuseppe Sarto as Pius X instead.

Cardinals are forbidden from making deals that would oblige them to give their votes to certain candidates, nor can the candidates themselves make promises to secure votes. This provision harks back to earlier periods in church history in which elaborate *capitulations* would be drawn up during conclaves obliging the future pope to follow certain policies or to make certain appointments. Quite often the new pope would simply disavow the capitulation after he was elected. In *Universi Dominici Gregis,* John Paul II releases his successor in advance from any promises he may have made. (This is another example of how these rules cover all the bases; John Paul forbids the behavior, then makes a provision for what happens if someone does it anyway.)

"Habemus Papam": *We Have a Pope*

Once a cardinal receives two-thirds of the vote (or a simple majority after the rule change described above), applause will burst out in the conclave because a new pope will have been chosen. Kasper as the junior cardinal deacon will summon the secretary of the College of Cardinals, Monterisi, and the master of papal liturgical celebrations, Marini. The acting dean of the College of Cardinals, Ratzinger, will approach the newly elected pope and ask: "Do you accept your canonical election as Supreme Pontiff?" From the moment the new pope utters the word *Accepto (I accept),* as a canonical matter he is the pope. (There is an improbable exception to this rule: if the man elected is not yet a bishop, he must be ordained a bishop first before he can become the pope. This happened in 1831, when a Camaldolese monk who had been named a cardinal was elected as Pope Gregory XVI. Theoretically, the electors in the next conclave might choose one of the Jesuit cardinals, Roberto Tucci or Avery Dulles, who received permission not to be made bishops when they were inducted into the college in 2001. Both are over eighty, however, and very unlikely candidates.)

Some new popes have hesitated when asked if they accepted election, and a few have actually refused. Saint Charles Borromeo (1538–84), for one, turned down the job. König said that when he looked at Albino Luciani's face in 1978, he was convinced that he would not accept. John Paul II in *Universi Dominici Gregis* asks his successor to be bold. "I also ask the one who is elected not to refuse, for fear of its weight, the office to which he has been called, but to submit humbly to the design of the divine will. God, who imposes the burden, will sustain him with his hand, so that he will be able to bear it," he wrote. Marini, as the master of papal liturgical celebrations, and two other masters of ceremonies will draw up a certificate making the election official.

Often the newly elected pope will say a few words just before accepting the job, or just afterward, and these remarks become known quickly. Cardinal Josef Höffner of Cologne, for example, revealed that John Paul I's first words as pope were, "May God forgive you for what you have done!" It was a typically humble gesture from Luciani, who genuinely considered himself unworthy of the job. Obviously, however, the words took on a wholly different significance for many of the electors when the pope died just thirty-three days later. Wojtyla was more traditional. When asked if he accepted his election, he replied: "With obedience in faith to Christ, my Lord, and with trust in the Mother of Christ and the church, in spite of great difficulties, I accept." The one hint about the new pope's personal style came in the reference to the Mother of Christ, since devotion to Mary has become a major hallmark of John Paul II's reign.

The dean will then ask him by what name he wishes to be called. The tradition of popes taking a new name dates from 533, when a priest named Mercury was elected as bishop of Rome. He believed that Mercury was too pagan a name for the pope, and hence took John II. Up to that point, popes had simply been called by their given names. Today the choice of name can be the first signal a new pope gives about the kind of pontificate he intends to have. If the new pope calls himself John Paul III, this will be a sign that he intends to continue the policies of the Wojtyla years: rock-solid discipline inside the church, aggressive evangelization and championing of social justice outside. Were the new pope to take the name Pius XIII, it would be a signal he intends to move to the right of John Paul, to stand in continuity with the pontificates of traditionalists such as Pius IX, X, and XII. If, on the other hand, the new pope calls himself John XXIV, it will be an indication that he wishes to return to the reform-minded spirit of the Second Vatican Council. If the new pope is from the Third World, he may want to take a name not used before that reflects his place of origin—Tochukwu I, for example, or Sugeng I. It would be taken as a message that Catholicism is truly opening itself to the entire world. Just as often, however, popes pick names because they want to honor a family member or a patron saint, so it's important not to overinterpret.

Once these formalities are finished, each of the cardinals approaches the new pope to kneel before him in an act of homage and obedience. In some cases the pope will raise his closest friends and mentors to their feet and embrace them. The new pope is likely to ask the cardinals to stay in the conclave in order to dine with him, as Paul VI, John Paul I, and John Paul II did after their elections. While this is happening, a tailor from Rome's Gammarelli clothing shop will be summoned to the Apostolic Palace to make the final fittings on the new pope's apparel. The pope is taken to the Pauline Chapel, where he dons for the first time the white cassock that will be the external sign of his office from that moment forward. Then the new pope will be led down the Hall of Blessings to the central window of the Basilica of Saint Peter, just above the name of Paul V, the Borgia pope who had the structure rebuilt. It is the same window from which the pope traditionally gives the *urbi et orbi* blessing, that is, a blessing to the city of Rome and to the world, every Easter. Presumably the electrified metal rails that deliver small jolts to ward off pigeons will have been temporarily removed from the balcony so that the speakers may walk outside without fear of being shocked.

Since the seventeenth century, this has been the window from which the new pope offers his first blessing. By this time the senior cardinal deacon, likely to be Cardinal Jan Schotte of Belgium, will have made the announcement for which the world has been waiting. He will step out onto the balcony, illuminated by massive spotlights, and say: *"Annuntio vobis gaudium magnum!"—I announce to you news of great joy.* *"Habemus papam"—we have a pope.* He then will reveal the pope's identity, using the formula *"Eminentissimum ac Reverendissimum Dominum Cardinalem Sanctae Romanae Ecclesiae . . . ,"* and at this point he inserts the name, in Latin. Even if many in the crowd don't recognize it at first, they will explode in cheers. He will finish the sentence by saying, *"qui sibi nomen imposuit,"* followed by the name the new pope has chosen to take.

After a few moments (in October 1978, John Paul II appeared approximately a half hour after he had been announced), the new pope will step forward, accept the cheers, and deliver his first greeting to the people in Saint Peter's Square. The blessing itself is a quick affair:

POPE: Blessed be the name of the Lord.
PEOPLE: Now and forever.
POPE: Our help is in the name of the Lord.
PEOPLE: Who made heaven and earth.

POPE (*tracing the sign of the cross with his arm*): May the
blessing of Almighty God, Father, Son, and Holy Spirit,
descend upon you and remain forever.
PEOPLE: Amen.

The new pope will probably say a few words either before or after
the blessing, and they will be extremely important. Every syllable, every
gesture will be considered significant. If the new pope is a non-Italian,
the Romans will be anxious to hear how well he speaks their language.
John Paul II started off winningly by confessing that he did not speak
"your . . . *our* Italian language well enough." He then invited the crowd
to correct him if he made a mistake. The gesture won him an immediate following among the locals. The rest of the world will likewise
be taking its first offhand measure of the new man. If he appears
stern or distant, all the worst stereotypes about papal arrogance and
the coldness of institutional religion may be revived; if he is too effu-
sive or enthusiastic, he risks being dismissed as less than a serious person.

Not everyone will have the same reaction. In 1978, when John
Paul I appeared at the window, his huge grin and his humble confession that he had neither the "wisdom of heart" of John XXIII nor the
intelligence of Paul VI won sympathy from the crowd. Some figures
in the curia, meanwhile, complained that Luciani was already com-
promising the majesty of the papal office. John Paul II, for his part,
demonstrated the independence he intended to maintain from curial
handlers when, at 7:21 P.M. on October 16, 1978, he flicked aside the
hand of Virgilio Noè, the master of ceremonies, who was trying to tell
him what to do. The pope felt he could decide for himself what came
next.

After the greeting, the new pope is likely to return to the conclave for a meal with the cardinals. In 1963, Paul VI impressed the
cardinals by simply returning to the seat he had been occupying during the conclave meals, rather than claiming a place of honor. John

Paul II delighted the cardinals in 1978 by moving around the room pouring flutes of champagne (he uncorked the first bottle himself). He sang Polish folk songs with Cardinals Stefan Wyszynski of Warsaw and John Krol, another Pole, of Philadelphia. As the festivities unfolded, the new pope found himself pouring champagne for the nuns who had served the conclave meals as he belted out one of the tunes. It was, most observers agreed, a first in the annals of conclave history.

Installation Mass

A few days later (in October 1978 it was six days), the new pope will celebrate a mass that symbolizes the beginning of his ministry. This used to be called the *incoronation* mass on the style of a king taking up his crown, and in fact the new pope would traditionally receive a three-layered crown called the papal *tiara*. The crown was placed on his head by the senior cardinal deacon, the same man who announced the new pope, and in the same spot—the balcony of Saint Peter's Basilica. Paul VI was the last to accept such a tiara, and later had it sold at auction in New York and the proceeds given to the poor. John Paul I refused to be crowned. Instead he took on a bishop's miter as a symbol of his pastoral, rather than worldly, authority. He was thus the first pope to refuse to have an incoronation mass; his ceremony was officially called the "solemn mass to mark the beginning of the pastoral ministry of the supreme pontiff." Instead of all the triumphal papal symbolism of years past, John Paul I's mass had a plain altar with two books in front—the gospels in Latin and in Greek. The new pope entered the square on foot, rather than in the portable papal throne, the *sedia gestatoria*. There were also no trumpets and no procession of Roman nobles, as had been the case in ceremonies past.

This reduction to the essentials included a new key moment to the ceremony, the *imposition of the pallium,* when the pope received a circular band of white wool called a pallium. It has six black silk crosses, and front and back pendants that sometimes hold precious stones; it is placed around the pope's neck by the senior cardinal deacon. Palliums were once worn by Roman emperors but are today regarded as a sign of pastoral authority and also of service to God's people. Every year on June 29, the feast of Saints Peter and Paul, newly appointed archbishops come to Rome to receive their own pallium from the pope. A community of cloistered Benedictine nuns at Rome's Basilica of Saint Cecilia fashions the pallium from the wool of two lambs blessed on January 21, the feast of Saint Agnes (whose name resembles *lamb* in Latin). The two lambs are raised at a Trappist monastery near Rome's Basilica of Saint Paul Outside the Walls. After they are shorn, the lambs are sometimes slaughtered during Holy Week and the meat used for the nuns' Easter Sunday banquet.

The senior cardinal deacon who imposes the pallium on the pope will say in Latin: "Blessed be God who has chosen you to be pastor of the universal church, and who has clothed you with the shining stole of your apostolate. May you reign gloriously through many years of earthly light until, called by your Lord, you will be reclothed with the stole of immortality in the kingdom of heaven. Amen." The cardinals will process up to kiss the pope's ring, and he in turn will embrace them. Later in the mass, the pope will deliver a homily that will be keenly anticipated as one of the first signs of the direction in which he intends to take the Church. This too is a sign of change in the church; Pope John XXIII was the first modern pope to preach at his own coronation mass. Prior to 1958, the custom was that the pope sit mute, regally, while orations are delivered at him and for him. John instead wanted a chance to speak to his people, and each of the succeeding three popes has followed his cue. Prior to the pope's remarks, the senior cardinal deacon will deliver an address of homage.

Conclave Rhythms

Based on the best information available, a breakdown is provided below of how long each twentieth-century conclave lasted in terms of days and ballots. Recall that the cardinals process into the conclave in the afternoon, after the mass *Pro Eligendo Papa* in the morning, and conduct only one ballot that first day. So even if the pope is elected the next morning, less than twenty-four hours after the conclave begins, it will be registered as a conclave of two days. This was in fact the case with Pius XII. In terms of ballots, the exact number is sometimes disputed by historians (there is only one official record of each conclave, and it lies in a sealed envelope in the papal archives). Hence the numbers could be off, but not by much.

1903 (Pius X): 4 days, 7 ballots
1914 (Benedict XV): 3 days, 10 ballots
1922 (Pius XI): 5 days, 14 ballots
1939 (Pius XII): 2 days, 3 ballots
1958 (John XXIII): 4 days, 11 ballots
1963 (Paul VI): 3 days, 6 ballots
1978 (John Paul I): 2 days, 4 ballots
1978 (John Paul II): 3 days, 8 ballots

The shortest conclave of the century was the one that elected Eugenio Pacelli as Pius XII. It is also in some ways the least representative, since it occurred against the backdrop of the beginning of the Second World War. In such a context, the cardinals had a rare degree of unity in what they were looking for—a pope with strong diplomatic skills. Pacelli, who had been the nuncio to Germany and knew the papal ambassadorial corps like the back of his hand, was the only obvious candidate. In some ways the surprise is that he was not elected by acclamation, which owes to the fact that a few curial cardinals who were old enemies of Pacelli held out against him to the bitter end.

To a somewhat lesser extent, Paul VI was the obvious *papabile* in 1963. As the cardinals processed into the conclave, some in the Roman crowd were already hailing Cardinal Montini as *il papa*. He had been the last noncardinal to receive votes to become pope when, in 1958, a few electors wrote in his name despite the fact that he was only the archbishop of Milan, not yet a cardinal. John XXIII had once said he was only keeping the seat warm for his friend Montini. It was obvious to most that Montini was the only Italian cardinal attitudinally and intellectually prepared to finish the work of the Second Vatican Council that John XXIII had started. Yet as with Pius XII, Montini had several curial enemies who were determined to block him. This opposition was even more stiff in 1963, because it was linked to a last-ditch curial offensive against the council itself. This accounts for the six ballots it took for Montini to be elected. In that sense, the dynamic of the 1963 conclave was really whether or not it would be Montini.

More typically, conclaves open with two or more candidates who have strong followings. It is customary that on the first ballot, cardinals will spread their votes around, often voting for friends or respected colleagues who they realize stand little real chance of being elected. Hence the first vote often has a symbolic function, and it is the next morning's task to get down to the serious business of choosing a pope. As one or more names begin to gather steam over the next couple of ballots, the drama is whether one of them will be able to reach the two-thirds majority before his candidacy begins to decline. If not, alternatives will have to be found. This kind of sorting out usually starts in earnest on the second day, which is the first full day of the conclave.

To get a sense of how the dynamics work, we'll examine two twentieth-century conclaves. The first is the conclave of 1922, which elected Cardinal Achille Ratti as Pius XI. It is a useful one to consider because we are very well informed about what happened on the inside. We have the diary of Cardinal Friedrich Gustav Piffl of Vienna, published in 1963, as well as a set of notes from Cardinal Pietro La Fontaine, who was himself a strong candidate. It was also the most protracted conclave of the century, and hence throws some possibly complicating political factors into clear relief. The second will be the conclave of 1978 that elected John Paul I, which probably offers the best parallel to the next conclave. Like the first one of 1978, the next conclave will come at the end of a long, controversial pontificate, and it will be decided by a large and very international College of Cardinals.

The conclave in 1922 opened on February 2, with fifty-three of the sixty cardinals present who had the right to vote. Once again cardinals from the Americas, forced to take steamers across the Atlantic, were unable to arrive in Rome in time. Benedict XV had died after just seven years in office, so he had appointed just twenty-five of the sixty cardinals. The majority were nominees of Pius X. The two popes had very different styles. Pius X was a stern autocrat who had launched a great crackdown on the intellectual life of the church, anathematizing all attempts to harmonize Catholic doctrine with modern thought. He also inflated the power of the Roman Curia, beginning the process of stretching his papal infallibility to cover the decisions of curial congregations, known as the *ordinary magisterium,* that reached full flower under John Paul II. Benedict XV, on the other hand, was consumed more by the tragic war engulfing Europe than he was by inner-church disputes. He put an end to the antimodernism purges of Pius, declaring that it was unnecessary to demand of any Catholic more than acceptance of the basic principles of the faith. "It is enough for each to say, 'Christian is my name, and Catholic my family name.' What matters is to live up to these names in one's life," Benedict said. The politics of the 1922 conclave, therefore, were determined largely by a struggle between those who wanted to return to the firm doctrinal line of Pius X and those who wanted a more open and modern papacy along the lines of Benedict XV.

Piffl records a meeting of the German-speaking cardinals on

January 27, in which the group identified five qualities they wanted in a new pope. He should be (1) a man of profound religious life, (2) a diplomat, (3) a man familiar with science, (4) a man comfortable in the world of politics, (5) someone with a correct position toward the Italian government. Since the Catholic Church still did not officially recognize the Italian government after the fall of the Papal States in 1870, it was taken for granted that the new pope would have to be an Italian to handle the complicated negotiations over church-state relations. (In fact, however, one of the strong candidates, Cardinal Rafael Merry del Val, was Spanish, not Italian, but his many years of service in Rome had convinced most electors to regard him as de facto Italian.) One cardinal, according to Piffl, predicted that the archbishop of Milan, Achille Ratti, could never win because he was "too little a man of principles." However, during the *novemdiales* period, it became clear that a small party of papal diplomats and curial officials was pushing Ratti's candidacy.

Initially the battle in the conclave of 1922 was between two secretaries of state—Pietro Gasparri, who had served Benedict XV, and Merry del Val, who was the chief architect of the papacy of Pius X. (One frequently heard joke was that Merry del Val could never be canonized because then there would be no one to blame for Pius's mistakes.) Merry del Val peaked at 17 votes on the fourth ballot, and by the seventh ballot received no votes. Gasparri stayed alive longer, reaching a peak of 24 votes on the sixth, seventh, eighth, and ninth ballots. Then he too dropped from the running, since it was obvious that he was stalled and would never reach the 36 votes necessary to be elected. The pro–Pius X faction had come prepared with a backup candidate, Cardinal Pietro La Fontaine, the patriarch of Venice, who had been head of the doctrinal office under Pius X. The political hardball played inside the conclave is clear from Piffl's note that La Fontaine's candidacy had a hard time getting off the ground because someone in the College of Cardinals had started a rumor that there was a history of mental instability in his family. Once La

Fontaine had reassured the cardinals on this score, however, he started picking up support, reaching as many as 23 votes on the eleventh ballot.

Ratti, meanwhile, had been steadily attracting between 4 and 6 votes during the first eight ballots. He jumped then to 11 on the ninth ballot, then 14, then 24 on the eleventh. It was the first time he had captured more votes than any of the other candidates. As it was clear that both Gasparri and La Fontaine were blocked, Ratti continued to accelerate, claiming 27 votes in the twelfth round, then 30, and finally winning the papacy with 42. He drew votes from the backers of both Gasparri and Merry del Val, which suggests that he was seen as an acceptable compromise candidate who would not alienate either faction. This more or less held up in his pontificate. Pius XI did not revive the aggressive doctrinal head-hunting of the Pius X years, but he was a firm defender of the institutional rights of the church. He was the pope who negotiated the 1929 Lateran Accords with Mussolini, which restored sovereignty to the Vatican in exchange for recognition of the Italian state. Mussolini also paid a hefty settlement to the Holy See.

As a footnote, the 1922 conclave is the only one of the twentieth century in which someone is believed to have been excommunicated for a breach of the rules. In his memoirs, Gasparri said that two cardinals were secretly excommunicated after the conclave. They were Rafael Merry del Val and Gaetano de Lai, another key figure in the regime of Pius X, who had once accused the young Angelo Roncalli (the future John XXIII) of modernism. The charge against del Val and de Lai was that they had tried to force a capitulation, or electoral agreement, on Ratti in exchange for voting for him. The central point of the deal was that Ratti would not make Gasparri his secretary of state. If so, the excommunication never apparently took effect, because shortly after his death a canonization process was begun for Merry del Val, who is buried in the crypts beneath Saint Peter's Basilica.

In the first conclave of 1978, there was a similar dynamic to that of 1922: two basic choices lay before the cardinals. They could continue the church reform launched by John XXIII's Second Vatican Council and carried forward, albeit with some angst, by Paul VI, or they could move in a more conservative direction, declaring the time of experimentation finished in favor of a new period of conservation and consolidation. Faced with these fundamental options, the 1978 conclave followed the pattern of 1922 in one sense: it rejected high-profile candidates who would have represented a clear victory for one option or the other, and instead found a compromise. It differed from 1922, however, in that there were no hardball politics and extended infighting; it was all over in essentially twenty-four hours, after just four ballots.

The difference was that Cardinal Giovanni Benelli of Florence, who had been Paul VI's right-hand man and who was in many ways the obvious candidate to succeed him, took himself out of the running. He knew his candidacy would be divisive. Instead, he utilized the *novemdiales* period to stump for his preferred *papabile*—Albino Luciani of Venice. Benelli felt that Luciani could be relied upon to continue the reforms associated with Paul VI, but he also knew that Luciani would not be too deeply unsettling to the conservatives. Luciani could count on broad support from the Third World, where he had traveled extensively. He was a good friend of Brazil's Cardinal Paulo Evaristo Arns, who commanded enormous respect among the Third World cardinals and whose own preference would therefore be closely watched.

The conclave began on August 25 with 111 cardinals, of whom only twenty-eight were members of the Roman Curia. For the first time it was truly an international body: twelve cardinals came from Africa, nine from Asia, three from Australia and Oceania, ten from North America, and twenty-one from Latin America. The number of non-Europeans was roughly equal to the number of Europeans for the first time in church history. Another significant point is that of the 111 cardinals, eighty-three either had been or were still the heads of dioceses. All things being equal, these residential cardinals wanted to elect one of their own as opposed to a curial official, on the theory that a residential cardinal has a better sense of the needs of local churches. Here too Luciani fit the bill. König tells the story of accompanying Luciani to give his first *urbi et orbi* blessing in the moments after his election as John Paul I. Afterward, the new pope and König were walking down the Hall of Blessings in Saint Peter's together when Luciani stopped and asked König: "Where do I go for dinner?" The omnipresent Cardinal Jean Villot overheard and volunteered to show the Holy Father to his dining room. It was a sign, König recalled, of how much an outsider to the Vatican Luciani was.

The only other serious candidate in 1978 was Giuseppe Siri, the perennial conservative front-runner. Siri, unlike Benelli, was not hesitant about allowing his name to be put forward as a candidate. Some observers believe that Siri frankly expected to be elected pope in 1978. There were a few other names floated from curial circles, including Sebastiano Baggio and Sergio Pignedoli, but it was clear that Siri was the first choice of those who felt the church needed a break from the reforming spirit of the previous two popes.

The conclave opened on the evening of August 25, but the cardinals did not hold a vote that evening, contenting themselves with taking the prescribed oaths and hearing an exhortation from Villot to the effect that they should think only of the well-being of the universal church. The next morning they celebrated mass in the Sistine Chapel and then had a small breakfast before assembling at 9:30 A.M. for the first ballot. In the first round, the votes were scattered. Siri was in the lead with 25, followed by Luciani with 23. In the second ballot, which followed immediately, there was a dramatic increase in Luciani's total, to 53. Siri, meanwhile, actually dropped one vote, to 24. In a sign of things to come, 4 ballots had the name of Cardinal Karol Wojtyla of Krakow.

After the cardinals broke for lunch, the Hungarian László Lékai reportedly said to Luciani, "Your votes are increasing," to which he responded, "This is only a summer storm." Yet that afternoon, in the third ballot, Luciani attracted 70 votes, just short of the 73 needed for a two-thirds margin. On the fourth ballot, the result was quasi-unanimous—according to one version, Luciani received 101 of the 111 total votes. Höffner told the media there was no need to count the votes, because the only name read out by the scrutineer was Luciani.

Would John Paul I have become the pope Benelli wanted, a cautious reformer in the mold of Paul VI? Would he have been persuaded by the conservative critics of Paul, who wanted a firmer hand on the rudder? Would he have struck out in his own direction? It is impossible to say on the basis of his thirty-three days in office. In some ways John Paul I is like a Rorschach test for Catholics with strong views on church politics—people see in his pontificate what they want to see. People wanting a reformed papacy, reduced in size and power, see in John Paul I's humility and his outsider status a man who might have walked their path. Certainly Luciani was no creature of the Vatican establishment. "I'm a novice here," he told the cardinals at his first audience with them. "The first thing I did was to flip through the *Annuario Pontificio* [the Vatican yearbook] to see who everybody is and how the place works." Doctrinal liberals saw in him a man open to change on some entrenched doctrines, seizing on chance remarks such as his statement at a papal audience that in some sense, God "is father, but even more, mother."

Yet conservatives could also point to certain hints from the new pope, such as a critical attitude toward liberation theology, a new movement in Latin America that sought to align the Catholic Church with progressive movements for social change. On September 20, for example, the pope warned that "it is wrong to say . . . that where is Lenin there is Jerusalem." John Paul I actually dispatched Cardinal Joseph Ratzinger of Munich, already a well-known foe of liberation theology, as a papal legate to a Marian congress in Ecuador in September 1978. There Ratzinger cautioned against Marxist ideologies infiltrating the church. When the cardinals met again to elect another pope in October, Ratzinger urged them to follow the line of John Paul I against the liberationists. In the end, one cannot know what kind of pope Albino Luciani would have been. But his remarkably quick election prompts the question of the next chapter: is there another Albino Luciani out there now, around whom preconclave energies are gathering?

4.

Political Parties in the College of Cardinals

 TOWARD THE end of the fifteen-year reign of Pope Paul VI, Cardinal Jean Villot, the chain-smoking Frenchman who was the pope's secretary of state and his camerlengo, was calling most of the shots. During his last few months, Paul, known as the Hamlet pope because of his agonized decisions, had retreated into his own spiritual preparation for death. Not many weeks before, he had been shaken by the kidnapping of his close friend Italian prime minister Aldo Moro by the left-wing terrorist Red Brigades, and he had grieved openly over the discovery of Moro's body in the trunk of a car on May 9, 1978. Meanwhile, Villot kept the machinery of the church functioning, issuing orders and keeping tabs on compliance in the name of the pope. He was well equipped for the role. The French press referred to Villot—imperious, demanding, and accustomed to command—as "God's de Gaulle." Beyond ecclesiastical power, there seemed to be little else that Villot loved, except his Gauloise cigarettes (he was rumored to smoke forty a day) and the stock of fine wines that filled his Vatican cellar.

On May 18, three months before Paul VI died, Villot sponsored a small luncheon in honor of Cardinal Karol Wojtyla of Krakow, who was in Rome celebrating his fifty-eighth birthday. This Roman spring day, a handful of other prelates found themselves around Villot's table with Wojtyla, who was already a familiar figure. He had been given the red hat by Paul VI at the tender age of forty-seven, and thus had been a cardinal for eleven years. Conversation turned to Paul's successor. Villot pointed at the young Pole and said something the others would later recall as prophetic. Wojtyla, he said, was perhaps the only candidate who could get two-thirds of the vote in a future conclave. Though such speculation could technically be construed as a violation of Pope Boniface III's rule against discussing the succession, Villot wanted to make clear that it had been no mere chance remark. He later sent a note to one of his dining companions, polish Cardinal Andrzej Deskur. "I confirm what I said," Villot wrote emphatically. "It was not a slip of the tongue."

Villot, who died on March 9, 1979, served for a few months as Wojtyla's secretary of state after he became pope, on October 16, 1978. There's no indication that Villot was playing up to a *papabile* at that May luncheon, because at the time there was no clear signal that Paul VI's death was imminent, nor was there a consensus that Wojtyla was on anyone's shortlist as the successor. True, he had been elected to the Council of the Secretary General of the Synod of Bishops in both 1971 and 1977, a sign of respect from his fellow bishops, and he had been selected by Paul VI to preach the Lenten retreat for the Vatican in 1976. Yet these distinctions hardly marked him as a man of destiny, as much as later biographers might want to see them in that light. This was May 1978, when it was still taken for granted that the next pope would be an Italian.

Why did Villot believe Wojtyla was in a privileged position to attract a two-thirds vote? We do not know for sure, because Villot never explained himself. But we can guess that Villot, like most other observers, believed the next conclave was shaping up as a battle between curial conservatives, led by Cardinal Giuseppe Siri, and moderates in the Paul VI tradition, led by Cardinal Giovanni Benelli. The moderates had bigger numbers and the conservatives were more tenacious, but neither could count on a two-thirds majority. They had to find someone who could appeal to both parties—someone, even better, who would come to the conclave as a representative of neither wing. Wojtyla's reputation for being to the left of the senior Polish cardinal, Stefan Wyszynski, might bring some moderates to a Wojtyla candidacy; so would sponsorship by Cardinal Franz König of Vienna, whose conciliar credentials were impeccable. The fact that Wojtyla came from a church that had suffered under the Communists, meanwhile, made him attractive to conservatives who wished to express solidarity with the "church of silence." The fact that Wojtyla was a residential cardinal, not of the curia, would reassure those who feared too much control by Rome. So, in the argot of Western democracies, Wojtyla was a man who could cross party lines.

Villot's prognostication turned out to be wrong, temporarily, because Benelli took himself out of the running in the August conclave and handed the election to Cardinal Albino Luciani of Venice. (Hence there was at least one other man who could receive a two-thirds majority, contrary to Villot's self-assured prognostication.) But the second time around, after the sudden death of John Paul I, Villot was right on the money. Karol Wojtyla became the 264th successor of Saint Peter. Though the media and much of the Catholic world professed to be stunned, at least those few guests at Villot's table were not.

Villot's prediction, and the logic it reflected, illustrates one of the key dynamics of a conclave. Papal elections, like any other kind, are shaped by the interplay of parties—groups of voters organized around a particular set of ideas or interests. However much the cardinals themselves may want to deny it, there are political parties within the College of Cardinals. Of course, they do not issue platform statements, or print buttons or bumper stickers, nor do they have televised conventions. There is no membership roster, and no party apparat. We are better advised to think of these parties as currents of thought, or bodies of opinion, than to look upon them as ecclesiastical equivalents of Democrats or Republicans, or Tories or Labour. Yet their agendas hold the key to the papal election because the game of choosing a pope comes down to finding a man who can attract enough crossover votes from more than one of the tendencies in order to patch together a winning coalition. Candidates and their backers rarely express conclave dynamics in these terms, but conclaves have always been an exercise in what can only be called political debate.

Political Debate

People are sometimes taken aback by the very idea that there is such a thing as political debate among the cardinals. For one thing, the Catholic Church teaches that the Holy Spirit, the third person of the Holy Trinity, watches over the election of a pope. For some pious souls it is difficult to reconcile this belief with the idea that there are candidates, or parties, or political differences in the College of Cardinals, just as it is difficult for others to believe that although the Holy Spirit inspired the writers of the Bible, it nevertheless contains fallible human judgments about history, geography, and science. Some Catholics ask: If God inspires the process, what is there to debate?

No less an authority than Cardinal Joseph Ratzinger, the top doctrinal official for Pope John Paul II, has said this is a misunderstanding of how the Holy Spirit works in the conclave. Ratzinger, who participated in both conclaves of 1978, made his comments in an April 15, 1997, interview on Bavarian television.

> INTERVIEWER: Your Eminence, you are very familiar with
> church history and know well what has happened in papal
> elections. . . . Do you really believe that the Holy Spirit
> plays a role in the election of the pope?
> RATZINGER: I would not say so in the sense that the Holy
> Spirit picks out the pope, because there are too many contrary instances of popes the Holy Spirit would obviously
> not have picked. I would say that the Spirit does not ex-

actly take control of the affair, but rather like a good educator, as it were, leaves us much space, much freedom, without entirely abandoning us. Thus the Spirit's role should be
understood in a much more elastic sense, not that he dictates the candidate for whom one must vote. Probably the
only assurance he offers is that the thing cannot be totally
ruined.

When a cardinal decides whom to vote for, in other words, ideas
do not drop from heaven. He listens to what the candidates have to
say, reflects on their record, consults members of the college whose
judgment he most trusts, and then makes a choice. It is an eminently
political process, the lifeblood of which is debate.

Other observers may be dubious that cardinals have much to
debate. They suppose that, by the time a man receives the red
hat, he must be singing from the same songbook as the rest of the
choir. There is some truth to this view. In fact, the things that unite
most cardinals are far more numerous than those that divide
them. Cardinals believe in the Trinity and the Incarnation, they accept the doctrine of apostolic succession and look forward to a life
after death. They are men who value institutional religion and recognize the need for a chain of command. They go to mass, pray, and ven-
erate angels and saints, even if some of them might understand these
acts differently than others. Hence, whatever disagreements cardinals may have are less fundamental than the differences a cardinal
would have with an atheist, or a pantheist, or a nihilist. Yet precisely
because the cardinals have an intense personal commitment to the
fundamentals of the faith, they often disagree strongly about how
those fundamentals should be expressed or implemented.

Another form of the same misconception is the idea that since
one hallmark of being a cardinal is loyalty to the pope, disagreement
has to be stifled. But sometimes the responsibility of being the pope's
closest advisers *demands* that the cardinals voice dissenting views. In

any event, the expectation of loyal submission is suspended during a conclave, when the very nature of the event demands a critical analysis of what has happened under the pontificate that just ended. Popes can and do make mistakes, and certainly cardinals who watch a pontificate from up close know that better than most. Being human, they will have different takes on the strengths and weaknesses, the good moves and the bad. The same holds true for their overall judgments about the church and its current needs.

No one should be surprised or scandalized by such disagreement. Cardinals are intelligent, strong-willed men who have occupied various leadership positions. Many have led large, complex archdioceses, while others have headed departments of the Roman Curia. They have learned to trust their instincts, to believe that they can make the necessary choices to lead the church forward. In a few cases this lifetime of command can breed arrogance, or make a man heady with power, but mostly it produces healthy self-confidence. Cardinals may respect and even like their colleagues, but this doesn't mean they are prepared to set aside their own vision, or their own considered judgment, about the issues that are most important to the church. The conclave is an act of prayer, but it is also a supremely political act, given shape and direction by cardinals working in coalitions to advance their agendas. Let's look at those groups.

Parties in the College of Cardinals

Because political groupings in the College of Cardinals are informal and undeclared, we have two problems analyzing them. The first is that there is no agreed-upon classification system, no list of parties that all observers would accept. Groupings are fluid, and major events in the life of the church, or simply the passage of time and personalities, can produce markedly different configurations. Second, no cardinal is ever forced to declare that he belongs to group A rather than group B. Because these men are complex figures with conflicting ideas and impulses, few would see themselves fully in any given camp. Most would agree with one body of opinion on some issues, but not on others. In a sense this is no different than in any deliberative body. In the U.S. Senate, for example, John McCain of Arizona is a Republican who is closer to the Democrats on some issues, especially campaign finance reform. Yet at the end of the day, McCain has to register for one party or the other, and hence we can all tell if he is a Republican. Not so within the College of Cardinals, where membership in a given party is always subtle and much harder to pin down.

Some cardinals deny the existence of political alignments within their ranks, thinking that if they don't see themselves working a party line, then no party line must exist. Yet they do exist, at least as ideal types—that is, as a way of looking at a set of issues or of protecting a set of common interests. What follows is my own classification of the political parties I see in the College of Cardinals. The names of the parties are entirely my invention. The list is one way of identifying the currents of opinion, with the understanding that most cardinals occupy more than one niche and few would fully agree in all the particulars with any one.

The Border Patrol Party

Border Patrol cardinals are theological conservatives worried about the impact of relativism and secularization on the Catholic Church. *Relativism* is a word for one of the dominant tendencies in modern thought since the sixteenth century, which is to question humankind's ability to know things as absolutely true, especially in the field of moral truth. Under the impact of relativism, contemporary Western culture is dominated by phrases such as "People are entitled to their opinion" and "This is right *for me.*" To some extent, church leaders worry about relativism because in extreme forms it can lead to moral paralysis in the face of evil; were the Nazis, to take the most obvious example, just doing what was right for them? Were the Allies wrong to stop them? Many Christian thinkers hold that only religious belief can provide an adequate basis for a system of morality capable of standing up to relativism. (Some nonreligious philosophers disagree, but that's another discussion.)

For the Catholic Church, relativism also poses some very practical challenges. In the First World, it contributes to defiance of church authorities among the rank and file. If truth is a matter of subjective judgment, why should Catholics feel bound to obey when the Vatican issues rules on contraception, or divorce, or homosexuality? This is not to say one has to be a relativist to disagree with Vatican pronouncements on these issues, merely that on a popular level relativism has weakened the hold of all sources of authority, including the church. In the Third World, especially in Asia, relativism contributes to a decline in missionary energies. If Hindus and Buddhists and others have just as much claim on the truth as Catholics, why should we bother to try to convert them? For church leaders who believe that Christians are obligated to spread the faith, this too is a worrying phenomenon.

Secularization, meanwhile, refers to the trend toward separating church and state, church and culture. In most parts of the Western world today, laws are passed, books are printed, and goods are produced without any control or approval from religious authorities. The most pronounced example of secularization in the Western world is probably Holland, where, despite several centuries of Catholic heritage, secular authorities have legalized abortion, drugs, prostitution, and euthanasia, all over the strong protests of Catholic leaders. Pope Paul VI once referred to the gap between the gospel and the culture as one of the most problematic aspects of the modern age, and this is at least in part what he meant. Religion becomes more and more a private affair, while social life is constructed on the basis of values that are sometimes foreign to, even hostile to, religious traditions.

Border Patrol cardinals worry that under the psychological and cultural impact of relativism and secularization, members of the church are becoming less and less Catholic, in the sense of having a clear identity, even if they continue to go to church, receive the sacraments, and call themselves believers. All the while, they are increasingly taking on the attitudes, behaviors, and values of the surrounding culture. The principal fear of the Border Patrol party is that in light of these trends, Catholicism will gradually assimilate to the surrounding culture. If so, the church will eventually become indistinct, placing no demands on anyone, making no claims that would too dramatically upset the status quo, and in the end having nothing to offer. These cardinals worry when they hear of pastors who give communion to divorced and remarried Catholics or who bless homosexual unions, in the name of compassion. They see such sentiment as misguided, since in the long run the most compassionate thing you can do for someone, they believe, is tell them the truth. They say that if the teachings of the church are true, then they must be followed; if they are false, then we should all find another line of work.

The remedy for such confusion offered by the Border Patrol faction is doctrinal clarity. Catholicism must have the courage to speak its traditional truths boldly, even—perhaps especially—in the face of a culture that no longer wants to hear them. The price may be controversy, but the church will be more faithful and therefore stronger. Border Patrol cardinals realize that calling a spade a spade, such as calling homosexuality evil or single-parent families undesirable, or saying that Catholics are right and Hindus wrong, makes them controversial. They realize that a church guided by such convictions is unlikely to win popularity contests in a world in which tolerance is the most prized virtue. Yet in their view, fidelity is more important than acceptance. Moreover, they regard acclaim in a secularized and relativistic culture as a false promise. In the end a church that craves popularity will be weakened internally because it no longer will know what it stands for.

The need for a clear identity is a special imperative, given what some in the Border Patrol see as a looming global showdown with Islam, the other monotheistic religion with a global presence. Leaders of the Border Patrol tend to see Islam as an aggressive missionary religion that threatens Christianity on several fronts. They point to voices within Islam saying that Christianity and the West are corrupt and the future belongs to them. They suspect that Muslims are not really interested in peaceful coexistence within a pluralistic culture; rather, they believe Muslims want to reshape society in accord with the dictates of the Koran. These Catholic leaders tend to be wary of calls for dialogue with Islam. They see a long struggle ahead, and why should anyone practice unilateral disarmament? One exponent of this view in the College of Cardinals is Giacomo Biffi of Bologna, who has suggested Italy adopt laws restricting Islamic immigration in order to preserve its Catholic culture.

The leader of the Border Patrol within the college is the man who has been John Paul II's top doctrinal adviser as the head of the Congregation for the Doctrine of the Faith since 1981, German cardinal Joseph Ratzinger. Ratzinger released the Border Patrol's charter document, *Dominus Iesus,* on September 5, 2001. Styled as a clarification of Church teaching on the relationship between Catholicism and other world religions, *Dominus Iesus* clearly rejected religious relativism, insisting that Jesus Christ is the unique and only savior of the world. The document also reasserted Catholicism's claim to be superior to all other religions and Christian churches. Its uncompromising language created an international uproar, and some church leaders criticized both the timing and the tone. Yet for those cardinals worried that the Catholic Church might be losing its edge, *Dominus Iesus* was a welcome call to arms.

The Border Patrol also takes a strong interest in the liturgy, the rites and rituals celebrated by the Catholic Church, especially the mass. Before the Second Vatican Council, in the 1960s, Catholic liturgy was something like the McDonald's of organized religion. No matter where you went in the world, you could find essentially the same celebration—a mass conducted in the same language, Latin, by a priest wearing the same vestments and saying the same words and performing the same gestures. It provided a sense of unity to a far-flung global church. As the winds of change began to blow, however, some critics charged that liturgical uniformity was tantamount to imposing a Roman model on the rest of the world. (Of course it was—that was the point.) If Catholicism was meant for all, these critics argued, it needed to take shape in every one of the world's cultures. Most important, it needed to speak to people in their own living languages. Thus the council decided to move from using Latin to all the languages on the face of the earth. In the postconciliar church, its liturgies would become much more diverse. The mass celebrated in the United States would not look like the mass in Indonesia or Peru.

After thirty years of experimentation with these changes, the Vatican under John Paul II in the mid-1990s began to pull back, fearing the reforms had gone too far. Some Vatican officials and other church leaders believe that the liturgies have been reshaped according to ideological pressures, above all in the English-speaking world. On the one hand, they charge, the mass and other rituals have been *desacralized*—that is, made too simple and ordinary—in order to make them acceptable to Protestant tastes, in the name of ecumenism. On the other hand, the language of the liturgy, these critics believe, has been manipulated under the impact of feminism. Instead of saying *man* some Catholics often say *human being,* and they edit the traditional language of prayer and worship that has referred to God as *he.* In both cases, the Border Patrol believes, the liturgy has to some extent been robbed of its Catholic identity, and hence of its power to nourish and reinforce the faith, out of a misguided desire to make it "relevant." Under the Chilean cardinal Jorge Medina Estévez, the Vatican's office for liturgical affairs has been taking aggressive control of the liturgy from bishops and bishops' conferences. In May 2001, for example, Medina issued new rules for liturgical texts that insisted translators stick as close as possible to the Latin original, rather than adapting the language to make it either more poetic or more accessible to the people in the pews.

The Border Patrol also wants to maintain a clear distinction between the ordained Catholic priesthood and the laity. In December 1997, the Vatican issued a directive, signed by eight curial prefects, ordering an end to certain practices that have become common around the world. Among them: the routine use of laypeople to distribute communion at mass and allowing laypeople to use titles such as *chaplain*, which belongs only to priests. Some felt the document was an exercise in clericalism, but others defended it as a needed corrective; priests were losing their identity by becoming virtually indistinguishable from everyone else. Leaders of the Border Patrol felt priests should "look like priests." They should wear their clerical dress, and maintain a proper distance between themselves and the secular lay culture around them.

Ratzinger's allies in the Border Patrol within the College of Cardinals include Medina, Biffi, Jan Schotte of Belgium, Christoph Schönborn of Vienna, Bernard Law and Francis George of the United States, Johannes Degenhardt of Paderborn, Ivan Dias of Bombay, Desmond Connell of Ireland, Aloysius Matthew Ambrozic of Canada, Marian Jaworski of Ukraine, and Jozef Tomko, a Slovak who has lived in Rome for many years as a curial official.

Where do members of the Border Patrol party disagree among themselves? For one thing, there are differences about the long-range consequences of drawing such sharp boundaries between Catholicism and the rest of the world. Some Border Patrol cardinals, such as Tomko, believe the world will respond positively to a church that is aggressive, self-confident, and conspicuously different from the surrounding culture. Such a church will reap new conversions and will expand to new territories. Others, such as Ratzinger, strike a less optimistic note, saying the church must be prepared to be a mustard seed—to "exist in small, seemingly insignificant groups that nonetheless live an intensive struggle against evil and bring good into the world." Fidelity, according to Ratzinger, will produce a smaller but stronger church. Hence the disagreement boils down to this: what can we expect from the policies we advocate? One faction sees boom times as the message gets out, the other a long winter of social marginalization. One anticipates success as the consequence of clarity; the other, suffering.

The Salt of the Earth Party

In the gospel of Matthew, during the Sermon on the Mount, Jesus tells his disciples, "You are the salt of the earth" (5:13). He does not offer his own exegesis for the metaphor, but generations of Christians have taken it to mean that their faith must have an impact on the world. Salt adds flavor to food, transforms it. Thus Christians should also transform the world in the light of gospel principles. Christian social crusaders and political revolutionaries have always loved the salt-of-the-earth image; it implies a Christianity that is deeply engaged in the actions and passions of the times. The Claretian order in the Catholic Church publishes a magazine called *Salt of the Earth* that has this spirit. The famous opening line from the Second Vatican Council's crowning document, *Gaudium et Spes,* captures the idea: "The joy and hope, the grief and anguish of the people of our time, especially of those who are poor or afflicted in any way, are the joy and hope, the grief and anguish, of the followers of Christ as well."

Salt of the Earth cardinals believe that the people of God should not be hung up primarily on intraecclesiastical theological debates. Their focus is outside, rather than inside, the institutional church. They are more concerned with what they see as the burning issues of the day, such as poverty, abortion, and war, than with ecclesiastical disputes. Arguments over where the tabernacle should go inside a Catholic place of worship, or whether or not a layperson can use the title *chaplain,* or whether one should say, "And also with you," rather than, "And with your spirit," in response to the priest at mass strike these cardinals largely as wastes of time. (Salt of the Earth cardinals may have markedly different views on these questions; what unites them is a sense that they are not top priorities, that the church's energy should be elsewhere.) Unlike Border Patrol cardinals, who want to raise the barriers between the church and the world, the Salt of the Earth party wishes to lower them. For members of this group the fundamental question always is: How is the world different because the church is in it?

At this stage we have to identify two different wings to the Salt of the Earth party, which roughly correspond to the conservative and liberal options in secular politics. On the right wing is an ideology that Latin Americans and Europeans call *integralism,* which is the belief that the politics and culture of a society should be ordered *wholly* according to the teachings of the Catholic Church. In its pure form, this is an ideology that can be sustained only in overwhelmingly Catholic countries such as Italy or Spain, and many nations in Latin America. Historical examples include the symbiosis between church and state during the Franco years in Spain, in which Catholic leaders blessed Franco's government, giving it badly needed legitimacy, while Franco ensured that in certain areas of social life, church teaching was also the law of the land. Spain did not legalize divorce until 1981, for example, because Franco had banned it. He also annulled all the divorces that had been granted under the Second Republic from 1934 to 1936, before he took power. This was also the model of the social order that characterized Latin America for several hundred years, in which the church was given privileges by the state and in turn church leaders encouraged obedience to civil authorities. It was this integralist ideal, for example, that Archbishop Oscar

Romero of El Salvador decided to challenge in the 1970s, a move that triggered his assassination in March 1980.

Cardinals in less numerically Catholic societies such as the United States can also be integralists, to the extent they insist church teaching should almost automatically become civil law, that there is little room for a distinction between what the church proposes and what the state allows. Hence an American or European cardinal who insists that the state must not recognize a civil status for de facto couples because it contradicts church teaching on the sanctity of the family would reflect an integralist point of view. Integralist cardinals are also strong supporters of state funding for churches and church-run institutions. In the United States, for example, this outlook often takes the form of support for vouchers, a system of state funding for private, including religious, schools. The integralist wing of the Salt of the Earth party would wish either to eliminate, or at least weaken, any constitutional separation between church and state.

In Italy, Cardinal Camillo Ruini, the pope's personal choice as vicar of Rome and head of the Italian bishops' conference, exemplifies this wing of the Salt of the Earth party. Many Italian prelates such as Ruini believe that Italy has a special calling to preserve its Catholic heritage in the form of social policies that reflect church teaching. For example, Ruini and other Catholic leaders in Italy vigorously opposed a recent plan by the country's health minister, Umberto Veronesi, to introduce the so-called morning-after pill in pharmacies. The pill, which must be taken within seventy-two hours after unprotected sexual intercourse, can either prevent an egg cell from being fertilized or block a fertilized egg from implanting in the uterus. In the first case, the Vatican considers the result contraception, and in the second, abortion. Ruini and the Italian church fought a bitter, unsuccessful battle to block approval of this pill. Failing that, they asked a special exemption so that Catholic pharmacists not be obliged to sell the pill, even though Italian law requires that pharmacies make available any medication that is legal for a physician to prescribe. The matter is currently unresolved. These efforts brought strong protests from the left, which accused Ruini and the Vatican of forgetting that Italy is a secular state. It is one thing to urge Catholics not to use the morning-after pill, these critics said; it is another to try to deny the pill even to those who do not share Catholic beliefs on this point by making it illegal.

Another cardinal who illustrates the right-wing option within the Salt of the Earth party is Colombian Alfonso López Trujillo, who heads the Pontifical Council for the Family. During the 1970s, López Trujillo, as archbishop of Medellín, in Colombia, was active in opposing leftist forces who sought to change the social order. (See the discussion of López Trujillo in Chapter 2.) In Rome, López Trujillo has been the most visible and aggressive critic of what John Paul II calls the "culture of death" in the West, referring to a range of issues from abortion to low fertility rates to euthanasia. López Trujillo has vigorously denounced these trends and issued strong condemnations of contraception, childless marriages, homosexual marriages, and artificial insemination that takes place outside the context of ordinary sexual intercourse. Like Ruini, López Trujillo believes that on all of these points, the social order should reflect Catholic teaching. He said in 2000: "The orientation of some political communities today of discriminating against marriage by attributing an institutional status to de facto unions that is similar, or even equivalent, to marriage and the family is a serious sign of the contemporary breakdown in the social moral conscience, of 'weak thought' with regard to the common good, when it is not a real and proper ideological imposition exerted by influential pressure groups."

Other cardinals who are part of this conservative, integralist Salt of the Earth axis include Angelo Sodano of Italy, Józef Glemp of Poland, Norberto Rivera Carrera of Mexico, Juan Luis Antonio Cipriani Thorne of Peru, and Antonio María Rouco Varela of Spain. Again, there are differences within the coalition. Some of these cardinals are aggressive champions of Catholic positions, but from within a basic acceptance of democratic political culture. In other words, they lobby hard for the church's positions but do not challenge at the level of principle the state's right to make policy decisions based on the instruments of a democracy—representative assemblies, majority votes, and the like. The former archbishop of Glasgow, Thomas Winning, who died unexpectedly in June 2001, was a good example of a cardinal who fights hard for the church's agenda but also has a basically positive attitude toward the democratic process. Other cardinals, however, take a darker view, seeing the system of majority rule as a prescription for sinking to the lowest common moral denominator. Some might prefer a more authoritarian solution, though no one in today's College of Cardinals wants a return to the fascist states of the early twentieth century. The question is rather the *degree* of democracy that is desirable, with some cardinals leaning to a stronger state firmly guided by Catholic social policies. López Trujillo would embody this option.

On the left wing of the Salt of the Earth party, meanwhile, are cardinals whose interest lies in questions of social and economic justice, such as debt relief, globalization, and racial justice. While the integralists tend to emphasize how the state intervenes in private moral behavior, or how the state supports the administrative and pastoral work of the church, the left-wing Salt of the Earth party is interested in how social systems can promote justice. They want to identify and critique the root causes of poverty, hunger, illiteracy, disease, and racial prejudice, and then work to remedy those causes. While their motivation for pursuing justice is rooted in gospel values, these cardinals tend to be less committed to invoking specifically Catholic arguments for their positions. Instead, they tend to seek coalitions with other movements and forces in society that share similar objectives. Because they want the widest coalition possible, their principles tend to be rooted in the language of human rights and natural law rather than divine revelation. Thus these prelates are more often involved with non-Catholic, and often nonreligious, groups and leaders, seeking to work together with all people of good-will.

One of the emblematic causes for Salt of the Earth liberals is the massive international campaign seeking debt relief for the most heavily impoverished nations of the Third World. Many activists see this as one of the most pressing social justice issues of the day. The overall global debt of all developing countries, according to United Nations statistics, was $567 billion in 1980 and $1.4 trillion in 1992. It is not that more borrowing took place in those twelve years; in fact, Third World nations paid back three times the amount they had originally received. After they had paid back $1.6 trillion by 1992, they still owed $1.4 trillion, or 250 percent more. Many Third World nations spend far more servicing debt each year than they do on health care and education. In Ecuador, for example, debt payments command 45 percent of the country's financial resources, leaving 4 percent for public health and 10 percent for education. Such inequities have sparked an international movement uniting religious and secular groups, with leading participation from some high-profile Catholic prelates. Though the coalition has yet to achieve the systemic change it seeks, it has enjoyed some lesser victories. President Clinton, for example, signed a $435 million debt relief bill into law on November 6, citing the Old Testament ideal of the jubilee year as a partial motive. Catholic leaders such as Cardinal Theodore McCarrick of Washington, D.C., Archbishop Medardo Mazombwe of Lusaka, Zambia, and Cardinal Oscar Rodríguez Maradiaga of Honduras have taken visible leadership roles.

Rodríguez has been especially visible on the debt relief issue. Rodríguez told reporters in a February 2001 interview that he lives in a part of the world where poverty breeds such desperate acts as kidnapping babies at supermarkets and demanding ransom for them from their mothers in exchange for groceries. He has called debt "a tombstone pressing down on us." In June 1999, Rodríguez and rock star Bono, from U2, joined forces at a G-8 meeting to present a petition with 17 million signatures demanding debt relief. Rodríguez has also met with German chancellor Gerhard Schroeder to press the debt relief issue. His willingness to act as the voice of his people on this and other issues has made Rodríguez extremely popular in Honduras. The moral authority he enjoys was evident in 1997, when a commission he chaired recommended the conversion of Honduras's military police into a civilian force. Shortly after the commission finished its work, Rodríguez went to Houston for a minor surgery. When he left the hospital to celebrate mass, he learned by glancing at a newspaper that in his absence parliament had elected him the country's new chief of police. He declined.

A kind of convention for the left wing of the Salt of the Earth party in the Catholic world took place in Genoa July 7–8, 2001, in anticipation of the G-8 summit two weeks later. More than three thousand Catholics (mostly Italian, but smatterings from other places) took part in an assembly to present a "Catholic Manifesto" for social change to the G-8 leaders. It called for a wide range of political and economic reforms, ranging from debt relief to the Tobin tax on currency transactions to a crackdown on the global arms industry. The meeting was attacked from the Catholic right, especially the conservative Communion and Liberation movement, which derided it as naïve flirtation with the "people of Seattle," reminiscent of the way some leftist Catholics had tried to baptize the student radicals in the 1960s. Nevertheless, Genoa's Cardinal Dionigi Tettamanzi spoke at the assembly, offering a ringing endorsement of its aims. "One African child sick with AIDS counts more than the entire universe," Tettamanzi said to thunderous applause. (Tettamanzi, by the way, illustrates the way these party labels don't always fit neatly, since he can sound like an integralist or a Border Patrol cardinal, depending on the topic. When he was briefed about all the work being done by members of religious orders to organize protests in conjunction with the G-8 summit, for example, he responded, "I wonder if they're putting the same energy into generating vocations.")

Cardinals identified with the social justice wing of the Salt of the Earth party, in addition to Rodríguez and the others mentioned above, include Brazilians Paulo Evaristo Arns and Aloísio Lorscheider, Jaime Sin of the Philippines, Julius Riyadi Darmaatmadja of Indonesia, and Wilfrid Fox Napier of South Africa. Here too there are differences. Some of these cardinals would be on the progressive side of many arguments in the church as well as in society, such as Arns and Lorscheider, who were for many years defenders of the liberation theologians in Brazil. These writers and activists addressed themselves to justice issues not only in society but also in the Catholic Church. Meanwhile Sin, on many theological issues, would be much more conservative than the Brazilians, but the political reality of the Philippines has made him every bit as much a prophet for social justice. Other Salt of the Earth cardinals, such as Indonesia's Darmaatmadja, distance themselves from theological disputes, preferring to concentrate on the welfare of their people in the concrete realities of their daily lives.

The Reform Party

To American ears, the name *Reform party* conjures up images of eccentric billionaire–cum–presidential candidate Ross Perot and professional wrestler-turned-governor Jesse Ventura. While there are no figures in the College of Cardinals anywhere near this colorful, the comparison is not entirely misleading. Just as the American Reform Party was born out of a desire for fundamental change in the political system, so the Catholic Reform party places at the top of its agenda internal reform in the church along the lines indicated by the Second Vatican Council. This group favors greater collegiality, or decentralization, a greater tolerance of diversity and experimentation, and a reform of the Roman Curia in order to make the papacy more acceptable ecumenically. They want a Roman Curia that functions as a servant of the local churches, not their master. They conceive the proper role of the curia more in terms of a clearinghouse of information and a resource for pastors, as opposed to the bureaucracy of a centralized government. They would also generally favor greater freedom for local churches to adapt teachings and practices to their own circumstances.

Reform party cardinals might argue, for example, that while the church is not yet ready to make celibacy optional across the board, perhaps certain regions might experiment with the idea. Above all such a policy would make sense in parts of Latin America or in Africa, where celibacy has always been difficult to reconcile with the local culture. Most of these cardinals are not what would conventionally be regarded as theologically liberal. None openly support the ordination of women as Catholic priests, for example, or endorse homosexual marriage. But they are by instinct men who believe debate is a healthy thing, and hence would tend to allow discussion on these issues to unfold in the church, rather than call it to a halt. Their operating philosophy in this regard tends to be that of the Jewish teacher Gamaliel, who persuaded the Sanhedrin not to persecute the earliest apostles. As recounted in the Acts of the Apostles, Gamaliel's argument went like this: If their undertaking is wrong, it will collapse on its own; if it is from God, nothing you can do will stop it.

These cardinals share a belief that the season of reform launched by Vatican II was, for a variety of reasons, prematurely cut short during the pontificate of John Paul II. Whether the theme is adapting the liturgy to local cultures or taking a new look at the role of women, these church leaders feel the Vatican has slowed, and in many cases actually reversed, the council's momentum. One Reform party cardinal said to me privately in a February 2001 conversation, "The pope is always talking about 'new evangelization.' But what kind of church are we evangelizing people *for*? If we don't finish the work of reform, none of this talk about evangelization makes sense to me."

The Reform party group has an instinctive suspicion of the Roman Curia, regarding it as prone to inflating its authority. (This tension is not restricted to Reform party members; many a bishop and archbishop has raised his eyes to heaven when faced with what he considers an unreasonable infringement on his own authority from Rome.)

The Reform party looks upon the 1995 encyclical of John Paul II, *Ut Unum Sint,* as a charter for change. That document invited a "patient and fraternal dialogue" to restructure papal primacy so that it could become more of a "service of love recognized by all concerned." The pope said, "I am convinced that I have a particular responsibility . . . above all in acknowledging the ecumenical aspirations of the majority of Christian communities and in heeding the request made of me to find a way of exercising the primacy which, while in no way renouncing what is essential to its mission, is nonetheless open to a new situation." Readers took the pope to mean that he was open to a papacy reduced in power and in size, offering a ministry not first and foremost of jurisdiction and governance but of moral and spiritual guidance. In the encyclical, John Paul was careful not to use words such as *Holy Father* or *vicar of Christ* to describe the pope, relying instead on humbler terms such as *bishop of Rome* and *servant of the servants of God.* In fact, the Vatican has not always looked kindly on those who took up the pope's challenge and published suggestions for papal reform, but the fact remains that the pope launched the process.

The Reform party supports greater collegiality in the church, a theme discussed in Chapter Two. Here we'll look at one specific application of it—reform of the Congregation for the Doctrine of the Faith, the former Holy Office, whose job it is to oversee the intellectual life of the church. Before the Second Vatican Council, the Holy Office was the most feared organ of the pope's administrative apparatus. It could silence theologians, send them into exile, end careers, cancel publications, and crush entire theological movements. Some of the theologians who ended up having an enormous impact at the council had been investigated and harassed, even silenced, during the 1950s. When members of the Reform party came together during Vatican II (and found they could command 2,000-to-200 votes on most of the planks in their platform), they urged reform of the Holy Office, and even ended up winning the support on this issue of Pope Paul VI.

German Cardinal Josef Frings spoke for many on November 8, 1963, when, discussing the need to keep administrative and legislative roles separate, he said: "This also goes for the Holy Office, whose methods and behavior do not conform at all to the modern era, and are a cause of scandal to the world." Frings was speaking in Latin, but he was perfectly understood, and when he came to the words *cause of scandal,* he was interrupted by long, loud, sustained applause, despite an earlier warning by the council presidency against cheering. "No one," Frings said, "should be judged and condemned without being heard, without knowing what he is accused of, and without having the opportunity to amend what he can reasonably be reproached with." (A young theologian who was assisting Frings at the council drafted these remarks. His name was Ratzinger.)

After the council, Pope Paul VI issued the document *Integrae Servandae,* decreeing certain reforms in the Holy Office, including the name change to the Congregation for the Doctrine of the Faith. He abolished the Index of Forbidden Books and brought the workings of the office out into the open. The pope wanted to transform the doctrinal congregation from a defensive, watchdog agency into a teaching instrument, using persuasion rather than censorship. "Since charity banishes fear," Paul VI wrote,

> it seems more appropriate now to preserve the faith by means of an office for promoting doctrine. Although it will still correct errors and gently recall those in error to moral excellence, new emphasis is to be given to preaching the Gospel. . . .
> Besides, the progress of human civilization, in which the im-

portance of religion cannot be overlooked, is affecting the faithful in such a way that they will follow the Church's lead more fully and more lovingly if they are provided with full explanations for the Church's definitions and laws. Regarding matters of faith and morals, this is evident by the very nature of things.

Some observers believe Ratzinger has faithfully carried out this reform. The congregation publishes a *ratio agendi,* or rules of procedure, with the most recent version dated June 29, 1997. It is available on the Vatican Web site (www.vatican.va). Ratzinger has broken new ground by giving lengthy interviews and publishing theological works while in office, thus allowing the Catholic world to openly debate the reasoning that leads him to his conclusions. He has brought theologians from around the world, including some who are not Catholic, into the Vatican for periodic seminars. The doctrinal congregation prides itself on engaging in a dialogue with theologians, leading them to see problems in their work and helping them to make the necessary corrections. Yet some theologians complain that the congregation's procedures are inadequate in comparison to the norms of modern democratic societies. Preliminary judgments are taken against a theologian before he is even formally notified a process is under way, for example, and theologians do not have access to their case files. Two well-known theologians, Hans Küng and Charles Curran, have requested access to their files since the 1970s, without success.

Moreover, Paul's idea that the office should promote good theological work as its primary task, rather than correct abuses, seems not to have taken root. The case of Jacques Dupuis, a Belgian theologian who taught at Rome's prestigious Gregorian University, is illustrative. He was placed under investigation by the congregation in 1998, summoned for a meeting on September 4, 2000, and his case closed with a "notification" warning of ambiguities in his writings on February 26, 2001. Dupuis told the press that not once during the sixteen years he taught at the Gregorian, the premier pontifical university in the world, had he ever met Ratzinger or his assistant, Archbishop Tarcisio Bertone, before his official interrogation. How, then, he wondered, could the congregation have helped him toward excellence, if its leaders had never even bothered to come across town for a session with the faculty?

Reform party leaders generally agree that change is needed before the congregation can realize the aims of Paul VI's reform. When Ratzinger's office targeted Dupuis, an expert on the theology of world religions, Austrian Cardinal Franz König denounced the move. (König is the only living member of the college created by John XXIII.) He wrote, "I cannot keep silent, for my heart bleeds when I see such obvious harm being done to the common good of God's Church." He suggested that the doctrinal congregation should be able to "find better ways of doing its job to serve the Church effectively." König said that most of the doctrinal congregation members are "very much afraid that interreligious dialogue will reduce all religions to equal rank. . . . But that is the wrong approach for dialogue with the Eastern religions. It is reminiscent of colonialism and smacks of arrogance." While not every Reform party cardinal would agree with König's conclusions, most concur that the procedures and the attitude of the doctrinal office are in need of an overhaul.

Observers might call König a leader of the Reform party, except for the fact that he is ninety-six, and far over the age limit to participate in the next conclave. But the German Cardinals Karl Lehmann and Walter Kasper, who are in their prime, are definitely in the Reform party camp, along with Cardinal Carlo Maria Martini of Milan, Godfried Danneels of Belgium, Roger Mahony of the United States, and Edward Idris Cassidy of Australia. This group too has its disagreements. For example, Martini and Lehmann have spoken publicly about the idea of calling a Third Vatican Council, which would be a meeting of all the bishops of the world, in order to carry out the needed reforms. Yet Danneels has said that he does not believe the time is right for such a move, and Kasper has said merely that he is open to talking about it, although he sees many problems. Hence the strategies that these cardinals advocate for achieving reform differ, but the desire for a more flexible and decentralized church, one that condemns less and experiments more, is common.

5.

The Candidates

 THERE IS a famous saying about conclaves: "He who goes in as a pope comes out a cardinal." Like many Roman witticisms, it's actually nonsense. Eugenio Pacelli was the favorite in 1939; he came out of the conclave as Pius XII. Angelo Roncalli was not really a surprise in 1958 (despite his age, seventy-six, he was elected and took the name John XXIII). Giovanni Battista Montini was the favorite in 1963, and he became Paul VI. Yet it remains true that predicting the next pope can be a tricky business. Father Andrew Greeley, the American priest-sociologist and best-selling novelist, produced a computer simulation purporting to forecast the next pope before the second conclave of 1978. He didn't even have Karol Wojtyla in his top seven:

1. Corrado Ursi of Naples
2. Salvatore Pappalardo of Palermo
3. Johannes Willebrands of Holland, head of the Council for Promoting Christian Unity
4. Sebastiano Baggio of Italy, head of the Congregation for Bishops
5. Basil Hume of Westminster
6. Michele Pellegrino, retired archbishop of Turin
7. Eduardo Pironio of Argentina, head of the Congregation for Religious

Greeley also said the differences between these seven candidates were narrow, making it a "real horserace." But according to most post-election reconstructions of the voting, Greeley was wrong about this too. None of his seven men were even serious contenders. Before the movement to Wojtyla, Benelli and Siri were the big vote getters, as some longtime Vatican watchers had predicted. The same Vatican watchers had information that Wojtyla also might get some votes, because he had already gotten votes in the previous conclave and because he had some important kingmakers in his corner. But they didn't have the courage to put him on their short-lists because they assumed (based on more than four hundred years of history) that no non-Italian had a chance. Guessers in the upcoming papal sweepstakes might take this story as a cautionary tale: they shouldn't allow themselves to trip on their assumptions.

Technically, any one of the cardinals coming to the conclave is a *papabile,* and one can imagine scenarios in which almost any one of them might just scrape home. Odds makers realize this; the good ones are loath to leave anyone off the list. Yet probabilities give some a better chance than others. Hence the odds in July 2001 posted by Paddy Power, a Dublin handicapper, that had Angelo Sodano, current Vatican secretary of state, as a four-to-one favorite and Ratzinger protégé Christoph Schönborn of Vienna at twelve-to-one. (For readers who just can't resist, this particular bookie takes bets on-line at www.paddypower.com.) At the same time, Jackie Dell, a Las Vegas odds maker made famous when he installed Bill Clinton as a favorite for the U.S. presidency before the 1992 election campaign had even begun, had Cardinal Camillo Ruini as his three-to-one front-runner. The lesson here: the farther one is away from Rome, the more improbable his predictions can be. Ruini's poor health (he underwent serious heart surgery in January 2000) probably took him out of contention.

The next conclave will be conditioned by two new factors, one of which makes the outcome more difficult to anticipate, while the other makes it easier. First, the complicating factor: this will be a conclave in which there is no built-in bias toward electing an Italian. After the election of a non-Italian pope for the first time in 456 years, the Italian monopoly on the job has been shattered. Today's cardinals come from sixty-one countries and all five continents, and of the 123 eligible electors as of fall 2001, only twenty-three are Italian (still the largest single bloc, but an all-time low in terms of percentage of the college). The cardinals may opt for an Italian pope for other reasons—because they think the bishop of Rome should be an Italian, or on the theory that only someone who knows the Roman Curia can fix it. But the days in which their choice simply *had* to be an Italian are over. Hence, the field of candidates is wide open, and handicappers have to look not just at the Italians but at everyone. The only probability determined by geography is that the next pope will not be from the United States. The Vatican prizes its diplomatic independence too keenly to risk it by electing a super-power pope.

The other factor, however, narrows the field considerably. Precisely because the College of Cardinals is so international today and because so many of its members neither speak Italian well nor have passed much time in Rome, few cardinals know one another as well as their predecessors did forty-three years ago. In the election of 1958, for example, the choice of Angelo Roncalli may have surprised some commentators, but he was no stranger to the men who elected him. Today what cardinals know about a particular candidate's opinions, his history and outlook, his strengths and weaknesses is as likely to come from the press as it is from their own experience. Those cardinals floated in the press as candidates are more likely, ipso facto, to be can-didates. Hence, while the international nature of the race makes the outcome more unpredictable, the cardinals' dependence on the media means that we can be sure certain names will at least draw con-sideration.

Front-Runners

A famous Italian ambassador, a Sardinian named Mameli, carried out a study of papal elections just before John XXIII was chosen in 1958, concluding that cardinals always ask themselves three questions:

- Where should the new pope come from?
- How old should he be?
- Should he come from the Roman curia or a diocese?

These classic three questions will still be important the next time around. All things being equal, I believe the cardinals would like to elect a pope who fits this profile: he's from the Third World, in his late sixties or early seventies, and has long pastoral experience in a major diocese, though he is not innocent of the ways of the curia. Of course, you can't always get what you want. The cardinals may be willing to settle for someone who meets only one or two of these points, but who has the right ideas about the issues we discussed in Chapter 2. Nevertheless, keep Mameli's three questions in mind as we move through the candidates.

Like a good horseplayer, I make informed observations by taking a number of factors into account. They include the opinions of more seasoned Vatican watchers than I; my own analysis of church history, including recent events; my personal conversations with cardinals; and a careful reading of the candidates' records—what the *Daily Racing Forum* calls "past performances." There are inevitably some debatable selections in my top twenty list that follows. I do not include secretary of state Cardinal Angelo Sodano, for example, since my own hunch is that the pendulum dynamic discussed in Chapter Two makes his candidacy improbable. For the same reason I omit Cardinal Camillo Ruini, the pope's vicar of Rome. Nor do I include the controversial and high-profile Cardinal Joseph Ratzinger, despite having written a fairly sprawling biography of him—*Cardinal Ratzinger: The Vatican's Enforcer of the Faith* (Continuum, 2000). There are a couple of dark horses, such as Wilfrid Fox Napier of South Africa and Cláudio Hummes of Brazil, who do not make most handicappers' lists. The real shocker is Lubomyr Husar of Ukraine, whose candidacy defies, on at least two scores, the conventional wisdom: that the next pope will not come from Eastern Europe, after a long Polish reign, and that he will not be an American. But Husar, in my opinion, is a classic case of the exception that proves the rule. In total, there are two Africans, one Asian, six Latin Americans, eight Western Europeans, and two Eastern Europeans on my list. There are no North Americans (unless one counts Husar, who took U.S. citizenship during his years in exile from Ukraine). There are two converts to Catholicism: Francis Arinze of Nigeria, who practiced the Ibo tribal religion in Nigeria as a youth, and Jean-Marie Lustiger of France, who grew up Jewish. While surprises are always possible, I believe the odds are very strong that the new pope will be one of the twenty men listed here. They are presented in alphabetical order. (Ages are current as of early June 2002.)

FRANCIS ARINZE (NIGERIA)

The prospect of a black pope has long captivated the world media, making Arinze, sixty-nine, a front-runner. He grew up a member of the Ibo tribe in Nigeria and converted to Catholicism at age nine. Would he still be *papabile* without this headline-making factor? Maybe. He runs the curial department on interreligious dialogue, where he has steered a cautious course. He is a charming figure, with a broad smile and an acute sense of humor, but he has not carved out a reputation as an original thinker. His theological views range from moderate to extremely conservative, and in the blunt speech that Africans prize, he pulls few punches. Asked by the London *Times* in 1994 about homosexuality, for example, he said that when he sees young men with ponytails, earrings, and lipstick on

Roman streets, he would like to "wash their heads with holy water." Those who know Arinze say he does have his own ideas, his own vision, but they are sometimes eclipsed by his loyalty to the current pope. Arinze engineered the beatification of Cyprian Michael Iwene Tansi, a Nigerian Cistercian monk who died in 1964 and in 1998 became the first West African candidate for sainthood to reach the penultimate step. It was Tansi who baptized Arinze and encouraged him to become a priest.

DARIO CASTRILLÓN HOYOS (COLOMBIA)

All things being equal, I believe many cardinals would like to elect a Third World pope. It would be a forward-looking statement about where the church is moving, given that more than half of all Catholics today are in the Southern Hemisphere, and this is where the church is growing. Such logic indicates above all a Latin American, where hundreds of years of tradition and a reputation for conservatism would reassure electors worried about radical change. Among the Latin Americans, Castrillón Hoyos, seventy-two and a Colombian, is one of the strongest candidates. Currently head of the Vatican office for clergy, Castrillón Hoyos served as secretary general of CELAM, the Latin American bishops' conference, from 1983 to 1991, which gave him a wide network of contacts across the continent. As a pastor in Colombia, Castrillón Hoyos earned high marks for defense of the poor, including his willingness to challenge the country's notorious drug barons. He is very traditional doctrinally. He was a fierce opponent of liberation theology, an effort among progressive Latin American Catholics to place the church on the side of progressive social movements. Castrillón Hoyos has been elegized by one of the twentieth century's foremost novelists, Colombian Gabriel García Márquez, who described him as "this rustic man with the profile of an eagle." For those seeking omens about what kind of pope Castrillón Hoyos would be, the fact that he sleeps in the deathbed of Pius XII might offer a hint.

GODFRIED DANNEELS (BELGIUM)

Danneels, sixty-nine, is a favorite of the Reform party. A former professor of liturgy at the Catholic University of Louvain, Danneels has a high reputation as both an intellectual and a pastor. During two recent high-profile gatherings in Rome, the European Synod of 1999 and the extraordinary consistory of 2001, Danneels made perhaps the deepest impression of any papal candidate. In 1999, he turned the pessimistic tide that had dominated the beginning of the synod (with hand-wringing about a "continental apostasy" in Europe) by insisting there is much of value in contemporary Western culture. In a talk at the French national church, he argued that regarding remarried divorcees we may need to learn from the Eastern churches, where the sacraments are seen not as a reward for good behavior but as medicine for the soul. At the consistory, Danneels said bluntly that the church must become more collegial. He also ran the best-organized media operation, holding a series of press conferences for different language groups at the Belgian College, seeming like a candidate on the stump. One could expect serious curial reform from a Danneels papacy. He is open to appointing women to run curial agencies. "Why not?" he said in a 1999 interview with me. "In the congregation for laity, for example, it would only make sense." Yet Danneels is no radical. In early 2000, he did not hesitate to suspend Father Rudi Borremans, a Belgian priest who announced he was homosexual and then concelebrated a mass in violation of Danneels's orders. One question mark about Danneels is his health—in late 1997, he had a serious heart attack.

ROGER ETCHEGARAY (FRANCE)

At seventy-nine, Etchegaray is at the upper limit of electability. But if the conclave happens in the next couple of years, he would be a strong candidate. He is French, but of Basque origin. He is gifted as an intellectual, a pastor, and a diplomat, a rare combination. John Paul II has sent him on sensitive missions to Russia and China, and he served as head of the committee for the Jubilee Year of 2000. Yet Etchegaray is no Wojtyla clone. He has argued that Pedro Arrupe, a former Jesuit superior disciplined by the pope for involving priests in social crusades, was "the forerunner of modern evangelism," and also that Matteo Ricci, a sixteenth-century Jesuit denounced by Rome for adapting Christianity to Chinese culture, is a saint. At the May 2001 consistory, Etchegaray turned heads with a speech arguing that if the church is going to speak credibly *about* poverty in the third millennium, it must speak *from* poverty. Etchegaray is a favorite of progressive decentralizers. At a conference in Genoa in 2000 sponsored by the Sant' Egidio Community, he said pointedly that the pope should not function like a "superbishop." His age might reassure more conservative cardinals that he would not be in charge too long.

CLÁUDIO HUMMES (BRAZIL)

Another strong Latin American candidate, Hummes, sixty-seven, is a member of the Franciscan order, like the legendary Cardinal Paulo Evaristo Arns, whom he replaced in São Paulo. Like Arns, Hummes was born in southern Brazil from German parents. As a young bishop, he had a reputation as a progressive, opposing Brazil's military regime and backing workers' strikes. Hummes also allowed famous Brazilian leftist Luiz Inácio Lula da Silva to make political speeches during masses. Under John Paul II, Hummes moved to the right, adopting a more traditional theological stance and distancing himself from political action. In July 2000, when a Brazilian priest suggested that condoms could be justified to fight AIDS, Hummes threatened disciplinary action. Yet he defends the Movimento Sem Terra (landless movement), arguing that people should be encouraged to organize themselves to defend their rights. He reminds government leaders that the church defends private property, but "with social responsibility." Hummes thus could strike some electors as the right mix between doctrinal caution and social engagement.

LUBOMYR HUSAR (UKRAINE)

Husar, sixty-nine, was born in Ukraine in 1933 and fled with his parents in 1944, arriving in the United States in 1949. He studied at Catholic University and Fordham, and was ordained into a Ukranian Catholic eparchy in the United States. In 1973 he joined a Studite monastery in Italy and became its superior. He was secretly consecrated a bishop in April 1977 in Castel Gandolfo by Cardinal Josyf Slipyj, his predecessor as head of the Ukranian Greek Catholic Church, but the act was not recognized by Paul VI's Vatican, anxious not to upset the Russian Orthodox Church or the Soviets. In 2001, Husar was elected archbishop himself of the 6 million Ukranian Greek Catholics. He is a moderate, easily the most articulate and theologically engaged of the Eastern Catholic prelates. He is amiable and humble, and speaks English and Italian with ease. His disadvantages as a papal candidate are considerable. He holds a U.S. passport, though I suspect most electors might exempt him from the informal taboo against a superpower pope since he is actually Ukrainian. More formidably, it would be difficult for many electors to choose another Eastern European after Wojtyla. Yet there is much in Husar's background they might otherwise find attractive: as an Eastern Catholic patriarch he feels in his bones the argument for the independence of local churches; he is pastorally gifted and politically sophisticated; and he is a warm, smiling, slightly chubby prelate who could remind the world of John XXIII. Husar performed brilliantly during John Paul's June 23–27, 2001, trip to Ukraine, and that opportunity to introduce himself to the world's media did not hurt.

WALTER KASPER (GERMANY)

Born in Germany in 1933, Kasper studied at Tübingen, one of the big leagues of the European theological universe. In 1983 he taught as a visiting professor at the Catholic University of America, in Washington. He is a gifted theologian, with a moderate outlook. In 1993, as a diocesan bishop in Rottenburg-Stuttgart, he joined Bishop Karl Lehmann of Mainz and another German prelate in issuing a pastoral letter encouraging divorced and civilly remarried Catholics to return to the sacraments. The letter was rejected by Cardinal Joseph Ratzinger. Kasper served on the official Catholic-Lutheran dialogue since 1994, and in 1999 he came to Rome to take over as secretary of the ecumenical affairs office. There he continued to joust with Ratzinger, publicly criticizing a document in which Ratzinger reasserted the superiority of Catholicism over other religions and Christian churches. He has also repeatedly voiced a desire for decentralization and reform of the curia. Such attitudes have made him popular in Reform party circles, and a reference to a genial American cartoon character (Caspar the friendly ghost) has even suggested a nickname: "Kasper, the friendly cardinal."

KARL LEHMANN (GERMANY)

For thirteen years, Lehmann, sixty-six, was the most famous noncardinal in the Catholic Church. Despite being the president of the German bishops' conference and the head of a diocese whose last bishop was a cardinal, Lehmann had been passed over four times before John Paul II gave him the red hat in February 2001. His positions on several issues have clashed with those of Vatican officials. Examples: Lehmann has suggested that the priest shortage might require a change on celibacy; has allowed divorced and civilly remarried Catholics in his diocese to receive the sacraments; has criticized Vatican restrictions on lay ministry for reflecting "a climate of mistrust"; and has called for more democracy in church structures. He also defended an abortion counseling system in Germany that the Vatican wanted closed, though ultimately he submitted to papal orders. He served from 1964 to 1967 as an assistant to Jesuit Father Karl Rahner, one of the foremost liberal Catholic theologians of the twentieth century and among the architects of the reforms associated with the Second Vatican Council (1962–65). Lehmann was Rahner's likely successor and intellectual heir before he was named bishop of Mainz in 1983. He has a reputation as a superb pastor that reaches across religious boundaries. In the mid-1990s when fundamentalists began displacing moderates in five Islamic mosques in Mainz, moderates turned to Lehmann for assistance in putting up a sixth.

Nicolás de Jesús López Rodriguez (Dominican Republic)

López Rodriguez, sixty-five, organized a meeting of the Latin American bishops held in Santo Domingo in 1992, which was a showcase for his very traditional views, described as "temporalist and pyramidal" by veteran Vatican observer Giancarlo Zizola. Yet López Rodriguez has been willing to confront government and military officials on behalf of his people. In 1998, when a hurricane struck the Dominican Republic, he went public with charges that the army was siphoning off portions of donated relief supplies. In another combination of social vision and doctrinal conservatism, López Rodriguez proposed a global Marshall Plan with aid flowing from north to south at the 1997 Synod on America, but condemned efforts to force Latin Americans into contraception, sterilization, and abortion in return for economic aid. He has integralist leanings; he has insisted that the parliament in the Dominican Republic approve a law instituting the Catholic feast of the Annunciation, March 25, as a national holiday. López Rodriguez could

be an ideal candidate for a coalition between Border Patrol cardinals
and the right wing of the Salt of the Earth faction.

JEAN-MARIE LUSTIGER (FRANCE)

Lustiger, seventy-five, the archbishop of Paris, is an intellectual who
has also had pastoral success, ordaining an above-average number of
new priests—no mean accomplishment in world-weary France,
where some 4 percent of the population is estimated to go to mass on
a weekly basis. In part, the media buzz around Lustiger has to do
with his Jewish background. He is the son of Jewish immigrants from
Poland, and his mother died at Auschwitz. As a child (his given name
is Aaron) he wore the yellow Star of David armband required of Jews
in Nazi territories. He converted to Catholicism at age fifteen, out of
conviction rather than as a means of avoiding arrest, and has long
been active in promoting Jewish-Christian understanding. (Lustiger
has Jewish cousins in Brooklyn.) His chief drawback as a *papabile* is
that he may be too similar to John Paul II. Like Wojtyla, Lustiger em-
phasizes the spiritual and ascetic dimensions of the priestly office;
also like Wojtyla, he is a stickler for orthodoxy and obedience. In one
of his early acts as archbishop of Paris, he pulled his seminarians out
of the Institut Catholique in Paris, calling its theology "too specula-
tive." In 1999, he gave a provocative talk asking: "Why do we no
longer have fruitful Christian thinking?" He said a tight connection
between bishops and theologians is essential to evangelizing a secular world.

CARLO MARIA MARTINI (ITALY)

Martini, seventy-five, has been the great white hope of Catholicism's
liberal wing for more than two decades, and many analysts believe his

moment has come and gone. Ironically, Martini's age may actually help his case; anyone worried that he would be too radical can at least take comfort that he won't be pope too long. A Jesuit and a biblical scholar, Martini is erudite and at times aloof, yet he has built an enormous following among the young in Milan, who flock to his cathedral for Bible study sessions. He is the leading intellectual in the College of Cardinals, with an extensive body of literature (including an exchange of letters with Italy's most famous living novelist, Umberto Eco). At the European Synod in 1999 he called for a decentralized church, and his other priorities included "the position of women in society and the church, the participation of the laity in some ministerial responsibilities, sexuality, the discipline of marriage, the practice of penance, the relationship with the sister Orthodox churches (and in a more generalized manner, the need to revive ecumenical hope), and the need to work out the relationship between democracy and values, between civil laws and moral law." One obstacle is his status as a Jesuit, since members of the order are not supposed to accept ecclesiastical honors (though there are currently eight Jesuit cardinals). His sense of humor helps, especially about the attention as a papal candidate. Once at a cocktail party a fellow Jesuit playing the role of bartender jokingly pointed to the choice of wine and asked Martini, "What will it be, red or white?" (White is the color of the clothes the pope wears, while red is the cardinal's shade, so the Jesuit was in fact playfully asking Martini if he wanted to become pope.) Martini responded: "Red . . . for now."

WILFRID FOX NAPIER (SOUTH AFRICA)

Napier, sixty-one, is a surprising candidate, largely because he is not widely known. I suspect the world will like what it finds. A black South African, Napier would, like Arinze or Rodríguez Maradiaga, symbolize the church's transition to the Third World. He is well trained theologically, having studied at the Catholic University of Louvain in Belgium. His humble Franciscan spirituality is appealing, as is his advocacy of social justice. He grew up on a South African farm with seven brothers and sisters under the country's apartheid regime. In 1988, Napier opposed a papal visit to South Africa on the grounds that it would legitimize the white-dominated government. "Some eighty percent of the two million Catholics in South Africa have black skin," he said, "and they suffer terrible repression by the very security forces which, during an eventual visit, would have to escort the pope." Local observers note, however, that Napier was not among the vanguard of the antiapartheid movement. Inside the church, Napier has spoken strongly on collegiality. At the extraordinary consistory in May 2001, he criticized a Vatican attempt to retake control of liturgical decisions from local bishops. Yet he is also seen as safe on doctrinal questions, and has been a vigorous opponent of abortion. Napier is a charismatic, pastorally effective leader who could be a good compromise candidate.

FRANÇOIS XAVIER NGUYÊN VAN THUÂN (VIETNAM)

Nguyên Van Thuân, seventy-four, runs the Vatican office on justice and peace. He is a quiet-spoken man who spent thirteen years in Vietnamese Communist prisons, nine in solitary confinement. He still wears the simple wooden cross, dangling from electrical wire, that he fashioned behind bars. Nguyên Van Thuân had been appointed coadjutor archbishop of Saigon, later Ho Chi Minh City, in the closing months of the Vietnam War. The communists opposed the appointment, in part because Nguyên Van Thuân is the nephew of Ngo Dinh Diem, who was the first president of the Republic of South Vietnam. He wrote *Prayers of Hope: Thirteen Years in Prison* based on his experiences. He is widely considered humble and sincere. He is not an original thinker, however, and many observers believe he does not have the force of personality needed to take control of a vast international organization such as the Catholic Church (and especially the Roman Curia).

Jaime Lucas Ortega y Alamino (Cuba)

Ortega, sixty-five, and the archbishop of Havana since 1981, has earned respect for his cautious defiance of Cuba's Communist regime. He is seen as a deft conciliator between the notoriously divided Cuban exile community and Cubans who stayed behind after the Communist revolution. He spent 1967 in one of Castro's labor camps during a period of national history Cuban Catholics call "the silencing of God." On most church questions he hews very closely to the Vatican line; he has said that he feels "very close to the pontificate of John Paul II." Like John Paul, Ortega y Alamino has urged his nation not to construct a post-Communist future on the basis of hypercapitalist principles. In 1998, he warned of the insidious influence in Cuba of a "species of American subculture that invades everything: it is a fashion, a conception of life." Some observers believe that fellow Latin American cardinals may promote his candidacy as a way to show support for the Cuban church, though others feel the parallels with Karol Wojtyla and Catholicism behind the Iron Curtain are simply too obvious.

Giovanni Battista Re (Italy)

Re, sixty-eight, served for eleven years as *sostituto,* the official in the Secretariat of State responsible for the day-to-day management of church affairs. The job has often been a springboard to higher office; Giovanni Battista Montini, for example, was the *sostituto* under Pius XII. Re has not shrunk from the role of curial enforcer; when an Italian priest took part in a progay rally in Rome in July 2000, Re phoned his bishop to demand disciplinary action. He also refused permission for Bishop Martinus Muskens of Holland to hold a diocesan synod, fearing that the liberal prelate might let things get out of hand. Yet Re is generally considered a moderate, and has given signals of support for decentralization. When Scotland's late Cardinal Thomas Winning needed advice in 2001 for an appeal against the Congregation for Divine Worship and its attempts to take control away from bishops' conferences on liturgical issues, he got a sympathetic ear from Re. He is a legendary hard worker, often returning calls from his office late on Sunday nights, and has an encyclopedic grasp of the inner workings of the Vatican. Diplomatic officials liked working with Re at the Secretariat of State: "When he said yes, it stuck," one told me in 2000. Re is personal and approachable in a way few curial figures are, especially at his altitude. He has a quick smile and is good at small talk at embassy receptions. If the cardinals are looking for an insider who could reform the curia, Re could be their man. Others, however, may conclude that Re is too much a creature of the system.

NORBERTO RIVERA CARRERA (MEXICO)

Like many other Latin American churchmen, Rivera Carrera, sixty, of Mexico is a strong advocate of social justice. His criticism of globalization and political corruption so annoyed Mexico's Salinas government that it threatened to adopt a law forbidding priests from commenting on politics. Rivera Carrera is also strong-willed and knows how to handle himself in a fight. For example, he won a 1996 showdown with a famous abbot who ran the Basilica of Our Lady of Guadalupe, who had publicly questioned the historical truth of Mary's appearance to Juan Diego. Although the abbot had been appointed for life by John XXIII, Rivera Carrera succeeded in forcing him to resign. The cardinal is a conservative on virtually all church matters. In 1990, as bishop of Tehuacán, he closed a seminary that he charged was teaching Marxist theology. He is also close to the Legionaries of Christ, one of the new right-wing movements in the life of the church that sprung up after the Second Vatican Council. According to journalist Jason Berry, Rivera Carrera called charges of sexual misconduct against Father Marcial Maciel, the founder of the Legionaries, a "plot." A central problem in classifying him with the *papabile* is his youth; Rivera Carrera was not ordained until 1966, a year after Vatican II ended.

Oscar Andrés Rodríguez Maradiaga (Honduras)

Rodríguez Maradiaga, fifty-nine, archbishop of Tegucigalpa, Honduras, is widely seen as a rising star in the Latin American Church. He served as president of CELAM, the federation of Latin American bishops' conferences, until 1999. A Salesian, he speaks near-perfect Italian and English (along with passable French, Portuguese, German, Latin, and Greek), plays the piano, and has taken pilot training. He is ferocious on social justice issues. He was part of a small group that met German chancellor Gerhard Schroeder in Cologne to hand over the Jubilee 2000 petition for debt relief. "Neoliberal capitalism carries injustice and inequality in its genetic code," he said in 1995. Some say his rhetoric, however, is not matched by a command of policy details. His theological training came in the post–Vatican II period. He studied at the Alphonsian Academy in Rome, where he took classes from the legendary liberal moral theologian Bernard Häring, whom Rodríguez calls an "idol." He has a reputation for being unusually open on ecumenical questions for a Latin American bishop, many of whom have little experience in religiously pluralistic settings. Early in his episcopal career he took a positive view of other church groups working in his diocese. Rodríguez has a warm smile and a ready sense of humor. On the other hand, some local observers say Rodríguez is better known on the embassy reception circuit than among the campesinos; one called him a "1930s cardinal" in that regard. He is young, which works against him, since many observers believe the cardinals will not want a repeat of John Paul's long papacy.

CHRISTOPH SCHÖNBORN (AUSTRIA)

Schönborn, fifty-seven, of Vienna, enjoyed a brief period after his appointment as cardinal in 1998 when he appeared on every list of *papabili*. A Dominican, he studied theology under Joseph Ratzinger in Regensburg, Germany, in the 1970s, and later taught at the prestigious Swiss University of Fribourg. He served as general editor of the *Catechism of the Catholic Church*. Schönborn comes from an aristocratic background—some nineteen members of his family have over the centuries been archbishops, bishops, or priests. As cardinal, he won high marks in his first few months in Austria, where the church had been rocked by a sexual misconduct scandal involving his predecessor. As time went on, however, Schönborn committed a series of missteps. He was involved in an ugly clash with the demagogic Bishop Kurt Krenn of Sankt Pölten, and many people preferred Krenn's blunt talk to Schönborn's shifting and evasive comments. Schönborn next carried out a purge of his staff, in one case informing his popular vicar general that he had been fired by leaving a note on his doorstep. These stumbles, combined with Schönborn's youth and his reputation as rigid in his theological views, present obstacles to his election. One Austrian journalist recently professed puzzlement about the international buzz that still surrounds Schönborn as a *papabile*: "If you asked most Austrian Catholics, they would find such talk incredible," he told me. Inside the country, retired Cardinal Franz König, still dynamic at age ninety-six, remains the dominant Catholic figure.

DIONIGI TETTAMANZI (ITALY)

Tettamanzi, sixty-eight, the archbishop of Genoa, has a roly-poly, affable bearing reminiscent of John XXIII. (In a phrase that will surely pass into legend if Tettamanzi is elected pope, Archbishop Keith O'Brien of Edinburgh, Scotland, referred to him at the 1999 European Synod as "that wee fat guy.") Tettamanzi is moderate to conservative on theological issues. A moral theologian, he is rumored to have worked on John Paul's encyclical *Evangelium Vitae*. He is close to the conservative Catholic organization Opus Dei. In 1998, on the group's seventieth anniversary, Tettamanzi published an article praising founder Josemaría Escrivá de Balaguer as comparable to Saints Benedict and Francis of Assisi in terms of launching new movements within the church. In recent months, Tettamanzi has burnished his credentials with traditionalists by writing letters in support of indulgences and church teaching on the devil. At the same time, he added luster to his standing with the Salt of the Earth party by his performance during the G-8 summit in Genoa in July 2001. He embraced much of the antiglobalization protest, delivering a rousing address at a meeting of thousands of young Catholics in which he insisted that "a single African child sick with AIDS counts more than the entire universe." He rejected criticism from conservative Catholics who demanded that church members steer clear of the "people of Seattle." Tettamanzi said that although Christians must reject violence, there is nevertheless much to applaud in the values upheld by the protestors. Tettamanzi is perhaps the only *papabile* to have corporate sponsorship; in 2000, Microsoft put out his new volume on bioethics on-line and on CD.

MILOSLAV VLK (CZECH REPUBLIC)

Vlk, seventy, of Prague, is considered a long shot by many because he's from Eastern Europe, and after Wojtyla the odds of another pope from that part of the world are long. Nevertheless, Vlk enjoys the support of colleagues, as demonstrated by his election to head the Council of European Bishops' Conferences. His life story also commands respect. Under the Communists in Czechoslovakia, Vlk was denied permission to function as a priest and spent several years on the streets as a window washer, spending his nights in the underground church—risking arrest with virtually every mass he said or confession he heard. His 1999 book, *Also avanti!* reveals a thinker deeply in touch with both the Western and the Eastern halves of the continent, and that could be profoundly appealing to electors. He speaks several languages—including Esperanto! Vlk is close to the new movements such as Focolare, Communion and Liberation, and the Neocatechumenate. Vlk first encountered Focolare when he was in the seminary in East Germany in 1964, and he described it as a kind of "paradise." Because some bishops have reservations about the movements, however, Vlk's enthusiasm for them may raise doubts.

The Rest of the Field

This section offers brief remarks on all the eligible cardinals as of spring 2002.

Agnelo, Geraldo Majella (Brazil, 68). An academic who spent most of his career teaching philosophy and theology, Agnelo was consecrated a bishop by Cardinal Paulo Evaristo Arns on the same day, and in the same hour, that Paul VI died. He has a doctoral degree in liturgy from Sant'Anselmo in Rome, and served from 1991 to 1999 as secretary of the Vatican office for worship. He is seen in Brazil as a competent administrator and generally a man of the center.

Agré, Bernard (Ivory Coast, 76). Enjoying a reputation as a charmer, Agré received a degree in canon law from the Urban University in Rome in 1960 and has spent his entire career in his country. He was made a bishop by Paul VI in 1968 and a cardinal by

John Paul II in 2001. Observers report that he is bright, with a warm personality, and generally institutional in his thinking. John Paul II made him one of three co-presidents of the Synod of Bishops in October 2001.

Alvarez Martínez, Francisco (Spain, 76). With a doctorate in canon law, Alvarez Martínez has pursued a career as an ecclesial bureaucrat, serving as a chancellor, vicar, and university rector over the years. He became a bishop in 1973 and has headed four different dioceses. He is the archbishop of Toledo.

Ambrozic, Aloysius Matthew (Canada, 72). A Slovenian by birth, Ambrozic is an uncharacteristically staunch conservative in a moderate Canadian bishops' conference. He has a reputation for being stern and somewhat difficult. At a press conference in San Francisco in 1998, he was asked about Jerry Falwell's allegation that one of the Teletubbies (a band of TV characters in a children's program) embodies a cryptic progay message. Ambrozic launched into a fifteen-minute discourse on faith and modern society. At the end, the befuddled reporter asked if that meant he agreed with Falwell. Ambrozic testily called it an unfair question, even though it was the same one that he had started out to answer.

Antonetti, Lorenzo (Italy, 79). The former head of the Administration of the Patrimony of the Apostolic See, or the business affairs of the Vatican, Antonetti had a long career in the Vatican diplomatic service. One of his postings was in the United States, and he speaks English relatively well. He was papal nuncio in France from 1988 to 1995.

Aponte Martínez, Luis (Puerto Rico, 79). Aponte Martínez was among the youngest bishops in the world when he was first nominated an auxiliary by John XXIII in 1960. As archbishop of San Juan, he acquired a reputation for pastoral engagement and fierce opposition to government plans for birth control and sterilization. He is thus a classic Latin American cardinal, strong on social issues and firm on doctrine. He is the first native Puerto Rican cardinal.

Araújo, Serafim Fernandes de (Brazil, 77). Araújo was extremely young, thirty-four, when John XXIII made him an auxiliary bishop in 1959. In Brazil's divided bishops' conference, Araújo has played the role of a centrist. He has doctoral degrees in theology and canon law from the Gregorian University in Rome.

Bačkis, Audrys Juozas (Lithuania, 65). The Bačkis family moved from Lithuania to France when Audrys was just one year old, and remained there for fifty years, until the fall of the Berlin Wall. Hence Bačkis' education came in the West, first in France and then in Rome. He worked in the papal diplomatic corps, having served as nuncio to the Netherlands, and in the Secretariat of State. He speaks flawless impromptu Italian, and is quite Roman in his outlook and approach. On doctrinal questions he is a conservative, though Lithuanian observers describe him as relatively open.

Baum, William Wakefield (United States, 75). Born in Dallas, Baum grew up in Kansas City, Missouri, and was named the archbishop of Washington, D.C., in 1973. He came to Rome in 1980 to run the Congregation for Catholic Education. In 1990 he became the head of the supersecret Apostolic Penitentiary, which deals with the most difficult requests for pardon presented to the pope. It is one of three cardinal's jobs that does not lapse during the conclave. Baum is considered moderate and pastoral in his outlook. His health has long been weak, and in late 2001 he stepped down as head of the penitentiary.

Bergoglio, Jorge Mario (Argentina, 65). A Jesuit and the archbishop of Buenos Aires, Bergoglio is one of a handful of cardinals whose education was not initially in philosophy or theology. He actually trained as a chemist before deciding to become a priest. He was elected the Jesuit provincial for Argentina in 1973 and held the position for many years. He pursued theological studies in Germany, has published three books, and serves as grand chancellor of the Catholic University in Argentina. He became the relator of the October 2001 Synod of Bishops when Edward Egan of New York returned home to help lead a national day of prayer.

Bevilacqua, Anthony Joseph (United States, 78). An Italian-American born in Brooklyn and a rock-solid doctrinal conservative, Bevilacqua has been the archbishop of Philadelphia since 1988. Within the U.S. bishops' conference, Bevilacqua is known for strong pro-Roman views. He was an aggressive champion, for example, of the pope's constitution on Catholic education, *Ex Corde Ecclesiae*.

Biffi, Giacomo (Italy, 73). Biffi is one of the most colorful personalities in the Italian church. It is ironic that such a strong conservative should be the cardinal of "red Bologna," for decades the nerve center of Italy's Communist vote (it is actually possible in Bologna to find intersections such as Leningrad Street and Workers' Avenue). Biffi made waves in 2000 by proposing that immigration policies in Italy should favor Catholics in order to protect the country's cultural identity. He has taken even more idiosyncratic positions over the years, once arguing that Catholic churches should not play music by Mozart because the Austrian composer was a Mason.

Billé, Louis-Marie (France, 64). The archbishop of Lyons, Billé is a biblical scholar who studied in Rome and Jerusalem. For most of his career he was a teacher and formation director. In 1996, he was elected head of the French bishops' conference. Billé is seen as a moderate on most issues, and is well respected in the Vatican. In 2001, he was appointed to the Ecclesia Dei Commission, responsible for dealing with the Latin mass and the Lefebvrites, along with heavy hitters such as Ratzinger.

Cacciavillan, Agostino (Italy, 75). Consecrated a bishop by legendary secretary of state Jean Villot, Cacciavillan was the pope's ambassador to Kenya, India, and Nepal before being sent to the United States from 1990 to 1998. Though a likable man, he did not dazzle many American Catholics; listening to him speak at a bishops' conference meeting, an observer caustically remarked that "some Italian village is missing its idiot." Upon his return to Rome, John Paul II made him president of the Administration of the Patrimony of the Apostolic See.

Carles Gordó, Ricardo María (Spain, 75). The archbishop of Barcelona, Carles Gordó started out his career working with young people. He acted as spiritual adviser of a group dedicated to the problems of young workers. He created an institute of spiritual theology in Barcelona, and has promoted pastoral initiatives in the city's slums.

Cassidy, Edward Idris (Australia, 77). After a career as a papal diplomat in spots ranging from Taiwan and Burma to the Netherlands, Cassidy was named the *sostituto,* or chief official in the Secretariat of State responsible for the internal management of the church, in March 1988. It was not a job for which Cassidy was suited, and a little more than a year later he was moved over to run the Vatican office for ecumenism. There he was a hit, winning friends for Catholicism in a wide variety of other Christian confessions. Cassidy's humble and accessible personal style make him one of the more popular cardinals in Rome.

Castillo Lara, Rosalio José (Venezuela, 79). Castillo Lara is a member of the Salesian order. His degree in canon law is from the Salesian University in Turin, and he has spent most of his career in various Vatican administrative capacities, including that of president of the Vatican's Administration of the Patrimony of the Apostolic See and of president of the Pontifical Commission for the State of Vatican City. Castillo Lara is also an adviser to the Vatican Bank.

Cé, Marco (Italy, 76). Cé makes many lists of *papabili* because he seems to fit one obvious post–John Paul II profile: a moderate, pastorally minded Italian in his mid-seventies. He is well respected; in 1988, he and Martini had the most votes to be president of the Italian bishops' conference, when John Paul decided to change the rules and appoint Ruini. Cé has steered a moderate course in the thicket of Italian politics. In 1976, he was named adviser to Catholic Action, a group neither as far right as Communion and Liberation nor as far left as Pax Christi. Cé is said to be a good pastor and very popular in

Venice, where he sometimes reminds people of his predecessor Angelo Roncalli, who became John XXIII. In the twentieth century, three patriarchs of Venice became pope.

Cipriani Thorne, Juan Luis (Peru, 58). Cipriani, who led the Peruvian national basketball team to a Latin American title in his youth, studied engineering and worked as an engineer before deciding to pursue ordination as a priest. He is the first member of Opus Dei to become a cardinal. His role in Peruvian politics during his tenure in Lima has been controversial. Some felt he was too closely identified with the regime of Alberto Fujimori, which earned him the nickname "Fujimori's theologian." Others, however, insist that Cipriani criticized Fujimori's abuses. He has made life extremely difficult for famous liberation theologian Gustavo Gutiérrez, who decided to become a Dominican novice in France in order to get out from under Fujimori's control. Cipriani is conservative on theological issues. Many observers find him impressive in person—articulate and attentive.

Clancy, Edward Bede (Australia, 78). Born in Scotland, Clancy was named archbishop of Sydney in 1983. He stepped down in 2001, making way for the very conservative George Pell to become his successor. As head of the Australian bishops' conference, Clancy epitomized the independent, democratic spirit of the Australian church, sometimes to Rome's dismay. In 1997, several Australian bishops were forced to sign a document along with a number of Vatican officials pointing to a "crisis of faith" in the country. Clancy thought the document was offensive and overstated. He also objected to a crackdown from Rome on use of public confession in Australia, complaining that the Vatican action encouraged right-wing pressure groups.

Colasuonno, Francesco (Italy, 77). Born in Grumo Appula in Italy, Colasuonno held the somewhat odd position of apostolic nuncio to Italy (a superfluous job in light of the routine direct contacts between the Vatican and the Italian government). He was made a bishop in 1974 and a cardinal in 1988, and is today retired. He is viewed as very much a creature of the Vatican diplomatic world.

Connell, Desmond (Ireland, 76). Connell studied theology and philosophy at the Catholic University of Louvain in the early 1950s and then held several teaching positions. At the same time, he was spiritual director to three different communities of contemplative nuns. He became the archbishop of Dublin in 1988 and a cardinal in 2001. He is a strong doctrinal conservative, and one of his key advisers, Father Vincent Twomey, is a former graduate student of Ratzinger. He exemplifies the Border Patrol spirit; he once called the reception of communion by Ireland's Catholic president Mary McAleese at an Anglican service "a sham."

da Cruz Policarpo, José (Portugal, 66). The patriarch of Lisbon, da Cruz Policarpo hosted an interreligious conference in Lisbon in September 2000 in which he distanced himself from Ratzinger and *Dominus Iesus*. When da Cruz Policarpo took office, he presided over a church wedding for Portuguese priest Felicidade Alves, who thirty years earlier had been harassed by the hierarchy for his opposition to the Salazar dictatorship. Alves left the priesthood, married civilly, and joined the Communist Party. His wife had long desired a church wedding, but the former patriarch had refused. Alves died one year after da Cruz Policarpo celebrated his wedding. Da Cruz Policarpo is not a liberal on doctrinal questions, but he allows the reform group We Are Church to hold prayer meetings in a Lisbon church.

Daoud, Ignace Moussa I (Syria, 71). Daoud is a member of the Syrian Catholic rite and head of the Congregation for the Oriental Churches. His appointment to that office was a sign of John Paul's esteem for the Eastern churches, but most observers say Daoud is not the equal of his predecessor, Cardinal Achille Silvestrini. Daoud takes a harder line than the pope in relations with Orthodoxy. At the May 2001 extraordinary consistory, which came just after the pope's request for pardon from the Greek Orthodox leadership in Athens, Daoud warned against apologizing too much.

Darmaatmadja, Julius Riyadi (Indonesia, 67). Archbishop of Jakarta and a Jesuit, Darmaatmadja was a parish priest, a seminary rector, and a Jesuit provincial before being made a bishop. In 1984, he was named the ordinary for the Indonesian armed forces. Darmaatmadja does not have a clear track record on theological issues but is a very socially engaged leader, especially on questions of globalization and economic justice. He is also involved in the church's dialogue with Islam.

De Giorgi, Salvatore (Italy, 71). De Giorgi has been a bishop since 1973, and over the course of his career has been assigned to six different dioceses. Today he is the archbishop of Palermo, in Sicily, where he has been since 1996. As a priest he was diocesan chaplain to the Teachers' Movement of Catholic Action, the mainstream Catholic political and social movement in Italy, and in 1990 as a bishop he was named general president of Catholic Action. Lacking curial or international experience, De Giorgi is not *papabile*.

Degenhardt, Johannes Joachim (Germany, 76). Archbishop since 1974, Degenhardt is one of the leaders of the philo-Ratzinger wing of the German Catholic church. In the debate over Germany's abortion counseling system, Degenhardt was among the first to abandon the system as the pope and Ratzinger demanded, while many other bishops under the leadership of Lehmann battled to find a compromise. It was Degenhardt who in the early 1990s took away priest-psychologist Eugen Drewermann's permission to teach Catholic theology and later expelled him from the priesthood. Drewermann, a best-selling author, had denied the historical reality of doctrines such as Jesus' virgin birth.

Deskur, Andrzej Maria (Poland, 78). Deskur is the former head of the Pontifical Council for Social Communications. He is confined to a wheelchair as a consequence of a bad fall he took on the opening day of the conclave of October 1978. He is a priest of the diocese of Krakow who studied in Freiburg and began working in the Secretariat of State in 1952. He was part of the staff for the Second Vatican Council. Since the election of Karol Wojtyla in 1978, Deskur has been one of the pope's most trusted advisers.

Dias, Ivan (India, 66). The archbishop of Bombay, Dias rose up through the Vatican diplomatic corps, with junior postings in Ghana, Togo, and Benin, then stints as the papal nuncio to Korea and to Albania. He is a cosmopolitan, allegedly speaking at least a little of sixteen languages. He is also a rare theological traditionalist among the Indian bishops, who are known for a more moderate stance. At an October 2000 press conference in Rome sponsored by the Legionaries of Christ, Dias dismissed the theology of religious pluralism associated with India, which accepts other religions as part of God's will, as largely a concoction of theologians rather than something accepted by average mass-going Indian Catholics.

do Nascimento, Alexandre (Angola, 77). Angola was a Portuguese colony, and do Nascimento is said to be close to fellow Portuguese-speaking Brazilian bishops on the conservative wing of that country's church. He spent ten years in Portugal, from 1961 to 1971, during a period of civil war in Angola. Do Nascimento has tried to mediate the ongoing conflict between the Angolan government and the UNITA rebel movement. In 1982, he was taken hostage for a month by the rebels, and was rewarded a year later by the pope by being made a cardinal.

dos Santos, Alexandre José Maria (Mozambique, 78). Dos Santos was the first native priest and first native cardinal in his country, which gained its independence from Portugal in 1974. A Franciscan, dos Santos studied philosophy in Portugal with the White Fathers before returning to Mozambique. As archbishop, he created the Women's Union of Piety in 1981. He has taken a balanced stand on Africa's relation with the West. At the 1994 Synod on Africa, he said Africans see the First World as the source of both "the good of the assistance which guarantees our spiritual and material progress and the bad of the weapons and of the bombs which cause our destruction."

Egan, Edward Michael (United States, 70). Perhaps the most Roman of the American cardinals (despite his Irish heritage), Egan spent thirteen years working in the Vatican's judicial system and teaching canon law, from 1972 to 1985. He advised John Paul on the 1983 revision of the Code of Canon Law and obviously made a good impression on the pope. Egan is a Chicago native, but more moderate Cardinal Joseph Bernadin did not want him as an auxiliary bishop, and so he went to New York, then later to Bridgeport as bishop, before taking over from Cardinal John O'Connor in New York on May 11, 2000. In Bridgeport, he earned a reputation as a tough-as-nails administrator.

Errázuriz Ossa, Francisco Javier (Chile, 68). Errázuriz Ossa is a member of the German order of the Schönstatt Fathers. He worked in the Congregation for Institutes of Consecrated Life and Societies of Apostolic Life from 1990 to 1996, before becoming archbishop of Valparaíso, Chile, in September 1996, and then archbishop of Santiago de Chile on April 24, 1998. Seen as a cautious conservative on church issues, Errázuriz Ossa obtained a degree in mathematics at the Catholic University in Chile before turning to philosophy and theology. It was a letter from Errázuriz Ossa while he was at the congregation for religious life that initiated the Vatican's investigation of Sister Lavinia Byrne, an English nun who wrote a book called *Women at the Altar,* seen by the Vatican as too friendly to women's ordination. Byrne eventually left religious life.

Etsou-Nzabi-Bamungwabi, Frédéric (Congo, 71). A member of the same missionary community as Cardinal Jan Schotte, the Scheut Fathers, Etsou-Nzabi-Bamungwabi is a socially engaged pastor and a traditionalist on most doctrinal matters. As a parish priest, he worked hard to implement a pastoral approach called *kinoise,* the goal of which was to involve parishioners in an intense prayer life. He is the second cardinal to come from the Congo, formerly known as Zaire. He studied in France and Belgium, and was a seminary superior before becoming a bishop.

Falcão, José Freire (Brazil, 76). The archbishop of Brasilia, Falcão is one of a number of bishops in Brazil whose advancement under John Paul II was seemingly intended to balance what had been a progressive majority in the country's Catholic Church. Falcão earned a reputation as a chief opponent of liberation theology, expressing his critiques in articles for two Brazilian daily newspapers, *Journal of Brazil* and *Brazilian Courier*. He has also served as the second vice president of CELAM, the Latin American bishops' conference, where he was responsible for sessions on ecumenism.

George, Francis Eugene (United States, 65). A protégé of Cardinal Bernard Law of Boston, George served in Rome as the vicar general of his religious order, the Oblates of Mary, from 1974 to 1986. In 1990, he became bishop of Yakima in Washington, then archbishop of Portland in 1996, and then archbishop of Chicago in 1998. George is a genuine scholar and a traditionalist on most theological issues. He has made a special cause out of the liturgy, creating his own liturgy institute at the archdiocesan seminary in Mundelein and leading criticism within the U.S. bishops' conference against the International Commission on English in the Liturgy, a translation agency accused of overreliance on inclusive language. At the age of thirteen he was stricken for five months with polio, which caused irreparable damage to his legs.

Giordano, Michele (Italy, 71). Giordano has the dubious distinction of being the cardinal who came the closest in modern Italian history to doing jail time. According to prosecutors in Naples, the cardinal sustained a loan-sharking scam run by his brother with money from diocesan coffers. After a three-year investigation and trial, Giordano was acquitted on December 22, 2000, though some Italians believe the result had more to do with the church's status in Italy than a careful evaluation of the evidence. Theologically, Giordano is conservative, with a reputation as a fairly affable pastor.

Glemp, Józef (Poland, 72). Glemp is among the most conservative prelates in the world. He drew harsh international criticism for his diffidence in 1998 when some Catholics planted crosses near the Auschwitz concentration camp in a deliberately provocative gesture. Glemp's strong positions in debates over social policies such as abortion in post-Communist Poland have also been controversial; some accuse him of not having successfully made the transition to life in a democratic society. Born in 1929, Glemp lived through the Nazi occupation of Poland before entering the seminary.

González Zumárraga, Antonio José (Ecuador, 77). González Zumárraga was born in Ecuador in 1925 and studied both in the diocesan seminary in Quito and in the Pontifical Ecclesiastical University in Salamanca, Spain, where he obtained a doctorate in canon law. He has been a bishop in some capacity in Quito since 1969, and archbishop since 1989. He attended the Synod on America in 1997 in Rome. González Zumárraga comes from a large family with seven brothers.

Grocholewski, Zenon (Poland, 62). Currently the head of the Congregation for Catholic Education, Grocholewski is a canon lawyer who has worked in the Vatican since 1972, and was prefect of the Holy See's supreme tribunal, the Apostolic Signatura, from October 1998 to 2000. Before that he served as the tribunal's secretary. He is also a consultant to the Pontifical Council for the Interpretation of Legislative Texts. A conservative, Grocholewski has a keen sense of protocol; in 2001, he was partially responsible for blocking an attempt by Jesuit Father Joseph Fessio to elicit an intervention from the Vatican on behalf of his Ignatius Institute at the University of San Francisco, because Grocholewski felt the appeal had not followed proper channels.

Gulbinowicz, Henryk Roman (Poland, 73). Originally born in Lithuania, Gulbinowicz moved to Poland to complete his training in moral theology at the famous University of Lublin. He stayed in Poland, where he became a professor at the seminary of Warmia. Gulbinowicz is the author of many essays on moral theology and on the formation of the clergy. He also founded the newspaper *Nowe Zycie* (New Life). He is a safe conservative on matters of theology. As archbishop of Wroclaw (in German, Breslau), he has a reputation as a bricks-and-mortar man, building a number of new parishes.

Jaworski, Marian (Ukraine, 75). Perhaps the pope's closest friend among the cardinals, Jaworski is the only one who stays in the papal apartments when he comes to Rome. He and John Paul served together as priests in Poland, and once Jaworski had agreed to substitute for Wojtyla and had taken a train to reach the appointment. There was an accident, and Jaworski lost his left hand, a sacrifice the pope has obviously not forgotten. Today Jaworski is the leader of the tiny Latin rite community in Ukraine, made up largely of Poles. Many people believe that Jaworski is a powerful backdoor conduit to get John Paul's ear; ultraconservative bishop Kurt Krenn of Sänkt Polten in Austria, for example, is a friend of Jaworski.

Keeler, William Henry (United States, 71). Born in San Antonio, Keeler is among the moderate American cardinals, with a long interest in ecumenism and Christian-Jewish relations. He was a *peritus,* or theological expert, during the Second Vatican Council for Bishop George L. Leech of Harrisburg, Pennsylvania. He became archbishop of Baltimore, the oldest episcopal see in the United States, in 1989. As archbishop, Keeler has stressed education, including moral formation, and evangelization. Baltimore parishes have received financial assistance for hiring youth ministers.

Kitbunchu, Michael Michai (Thailand, 73). Kitbunchu, the archbishop of Bangkok, is the first cardinal from Thailand. He studied in Rome at the Urban University, also known as Propaganda Fide. He was a seminary rector before being named archbishop in 1972. He is said to enjoy good relations with his country's Buddhist majority, whom he credits for important insights about peace and tolerance (only 4 percent of Thailand's 60 million people are Catholic). During his tenure, vocations of both diocesan and religious order priests have increased. Besides Thai and Latin he speaks English, Italian, French, and Chinese.

Korec, Ján Chryzostom (Slovakia, 78). The name Korec means *courage,* and it is apt. The Jesuit was among the church leaders who suffered the most during Communist persecutions in Eastern Europe. When it was illegal to be a priest in Czechoslovakia, Korec worked in a factory in Bratislava making products such as floor and shoe polish. He continued to act as a priest in clandestine fashion, and in 1960 he was arrested and spent twelve years in a prison camp. Today he has trouble walking due to injuries suffered during that time. In prison he gave religious instruction by writing it on cigarette papers and delivering it in matchboxes. When he went to Rome in 1968 during the Prague Spring, Korec had no episcopal regalia to wear, so Paul VI gave him his clothes from his time in Milan. When Korec had visitors in his apartment, he asked them to hold a rubber hose to their ear while he spoke into the other end, to avoid eavesdropping. Korec is quite traditional theologically, a very kind and humble man, and an obvious hero of twentieth-century Catholicism.

Law, Bernard Francis (United States, 70). Like Slovakia's Korec, Law is aptly named, since he is very much a law-and-order man. He challenges anything that looks like doctrinal deviation, such as the late Cardinal Joseph Bernadin's effort to find "common ground" in the country's divided Catholic Church (Law said the church already has common ground, in the *Catechism*). He once called the moderate-to-progressive Catholic Theological Society of America "a theological wasteland." Law studied at Harvard before pursuing his priestly vocation. In the 1970s he served as bishop of Springfield—Cape Girardeau, in Missouri, to which he invited all 166 members of a Vietnamese religious order, the Congregation of the Co-Redemptrix Mother, which had been expelled from that Asian country.

López Trujillo, Alfonso (Colombia, 66). López Trujillo is perhaps the most divisive figure in the College of Cardinals. During the 1970s and 80s, as auxiliary bishop of Bogotá and later archbishop of Medellín, López Trujillo battled liberation theology and allied himself with right-wing social forces. He worked closely with a CIA-funded Belgian Jesuit to create anti-liberation-theology projects. In Rome, he runs the Pontifical Council for the Family, where he carries on a fierce cultural war, denouncing birth control, civil unions, gay marriage, low Western fertility rates, and family planning. He is an intelligent, multilingual man and a very competent administrator, but is seen as more political than spiritual.

Lorscheider, Aloísio (Brazil, 77). A Franciscan, Lorscheider is the son of German immigrants to Brazil. He studied Latin, German, and mathematics in Rome, then returned to Brazil to teach in a seminary. In 1958 his superiors called him back to Rome to teach at the Antonianum. He remained until 1962, when, on February 3, he was appointed bishop of Santo Angelo by Pope John XXIII. Lorscheider participated in the Second Vatican Council. He is a strong supporter of liberation theology and is considered part of the progressive wing of the Latin American church. Today he is the archbishop of Aparecida.

Lourdusamy, D. Simon (India, 78). Lourdusamy served as head of the Vatican Congregation for the Oriental Churches until 1991, and before that as secretary in the Congregation for the Evangelization of Peoples. Pope Paul VI named him archbishop of Bangalore in 1968, and John Paul II made him a cardinal in 1985. Previously, Lourdusamy had worked as a scholar and journalist in India; he edited a newspaper in the Tamil language. He is not a serious theologian but has a reputation for commitment to justice issues in the Third World.

Macharski, Franciszek (Poland, 75). Macharski has the distinction of being John Paul II's successor as the archbishop of Krakow. He was born in the diocese in 1927 and worked as a laborer during the Second World War. He then studied at the prestigious University of Fribourg, in Switzerland. He was rector of the Krakow seminary, one of the most important in the country, and then worked in the Secretariat of State and other Vatican offices. As a Vatican official, he was a frequent traveling companion of the pope. John Paul sent him back to Poland in December 1978. Theologically Macharski is very much cut from Wojtyla's cloth.

Mahony, Roger Michael (United States, 66). The most progressive of the U.S. cardinals, Mahony inherited that role from the late Cardinal Joseph Bernadin of Chicago. At times Mahony can be bold; he has issued pastoral letters on the liturgy and lay ministry, affirming post–Vatican II trends sometimes displeasing to Rome. When an American nun named Mother Angelica challenged Mahony's orthodoxy on her television network, Mahony forced her to sign a retraction and a promise not to do it again. (Cardinal John O'Connor of New York, a Mother Angelica supporter, was delegated to personally take it to her in Alabama for a signature.) Yet in other moments Mahony seems to lack the courage of his convictions. At the May 2001 extraordinary consistory in Rome, some cardinals pushed the collegiality issue dear to Mahony's heart, while he instead made an anodyne proposal for a directory of the "new evangelization." For liberal American Catholics, Mahony is a source of both hope and exasperation.

Maida, Adam Joseph (United States, 72). As the son of Polish immigrants, Maida enjoys a good relationship with John Paul II's "Polish mafia." Maida is a canon lawyer, but he also holds a doctorate in civil law from Duquesne University School of Law, in Pittsburgh. He practised law in the state of Pennsylvania and at the U.S. Supreme Court. Maida is theologically in sync with Vatican positions. Maida is also trusted in Rome, where he is often asked to take on sensitive assignments. For example, he chaired an investigation over a period of several years into the work of American Father Robert Nugent and Sister Jeannine Gramick, whose pastoral outreach to homosexuals made them controversial. The Maida commission recommended disciplinary action, and the pair was eventually banned by Rome from this work.

Martínez Somalo, Eduardo (Spain, 75). Martínez Somalo is a career Vatican functionary. He worked in the Secretariat of State from 1958 to 1970, then served as papal ambassador to Great Britain and Colombia. He served as *sostituto,* or the official in the Secretariat of State responsible for day-to-day management of church affairs, from 1979 to 1988. Since 1992, he has headed the Vatican office for religious life. In 2001, the office was rocked by revelations that it had known for several years about cases of sexual abuse of nuns by priests in Africa and elsewhere. Martínez Somalo is John Paul's camerlengo, the official who will administer the affairs of the Holy See during the interregnum.

McCarrick, Theodore Edgar (United States, 71). McCarrick, whose formative ecclesiastical experience was as secretary to New York's Cardinal Terence Cooke, was the archbishop of Newark before taking over in Washington, D.C., in 2001. He is fluent in Spanish and a longtime champion of social justice issues such as debt relief. In Newark, McCarrick was close to the Neo-catechumenate, one of the new movements known for bringing new energy, and a frequently conservative theological outlook, into the church. McCarrick is generally considered a superlative pastor, funny and approachable.

Medina Estévez, Jorge Arturo (Chile, 75). Medina Estévez was a *peritus,* or theological expert, at Vatican II, where he worked on *Gaudium et Spes (The Pastoral Constitution on the Church in the Modern World).* As bishop, he was identified with the pro-Pinochet wing of the Chilean church. In 1998, he came to Pinochet's aide when the former general was detained in England pending possible extradition. In Chile, Medina was known as a staunch social conservative. He led a campaign against pornography in October 1995 and also tried to ban the rock group Iron Maiden from performing, on the grounds of alleged satanic overtones. As head of the Vatican liturgy office, he has led a strong campaign to restore more traditionalist tastes and to take back control of liturgical decision making, which had been largely handed over to bishops' conferences after the council.

Meisner, Joachim (Germany, 68). It was the appointment of the conservative Meisner as archbishop of Cologne in 1989 that triggered the infamous "Cologne Statement," signed by hundreds of

Catholic theologians around the world. It complained of a lack of consultation on bishops' nominations, of a lack of academic freedom, and other issues. Previously Meisner had been the archbishop of Berlin, where he enjoyed fraternal relations on both sides of the city's famous wall. Meisner played an important role in encouraging the Vatican to crack down on Germany's abortion counseling system in 1998 and 1999. He won applause at the October 2001 Synod for his ringing appeal to bishops to be aggressive in their defense of the faith.

Mejía, Jorge María (Argentina, 79). Born in Buenos Aires, Mejía is an impressive scholar. He earned a doctorate in theology from the Pontifical Angelicum University in Rome and another degree, in biblical science, from the Pontifical Biblical Institute. He taught scripture studies, biblical Greek and Hebrew, and archaeology at the Catholic University of Argentina. He undertook further studies at the Ecole Biblique in Jerusalem and was guest professor at the Ecumenical Institute of Higher Theological Studies in Israel. He attended Vatican II as a *peritus* from 1962 to 1965. He worked as secretary of the Pontifical Commission for Religious Relations with Judaism in the secretariat for Christian unity, and in 1998 was made the Vatican's top archivist and librarian. Mejía has an open, moderate outlook and is popular in Rome.

Murphy-O'Connor, Cormac (England, 69). Murphy-O'Connor was born in England and served mostly as a parish priest until his appointment as rector of the English College in Rome from 1971 to 1977. He became a bishop in 1977 and since 1983 he has been cochairman of the Anglican–Roman Catholic International Commission, the main forum for dialogue between Catholicism and the Anglican Church. He was made archbishop of Westminster on February 15, 2000, succeeding the beloved Basil Hume. Murphy-O'Connor has a strong personal commitment to ecumenism; in May 2001, he proposed that the pope convene a summit of all Christian churches to work out better relations. His brother, Jerome Murphy-

O'Connor, is a well-known Carmelite priest and biblical scholar in the United States.

Neves, Lucas Moreira (Brazil, 76). For many years Neves was considered a leading candidate to succeed John Paul II, but today his health is compromised by severe diabetes. A Dominican, Neves was the secretary of the Congregation for Bishops in the 1980s, and was later its prefect, from 1998 to 2000. In between, he was for ten years the archbishop of São Salvador de Bahia in Brazil. During those years he helped steer the Brazilian bishops' conference away from its progressive orientation. When elected president of the conference in May 1995, Neves wasted no time in announcing a shift. "There will be some changes," he said. "The church's principal mission is a religious one." Neves said that from now on the bishops would concentrate on "proclamation" rather than "denunciation."

Obando Bravo, Miguel (Nicaragua, 76). Obando Bravo is a member of the Salesian order and taught math and physics for the order in schools in El Salvador and Nicaragua during the 1950s and 1960s. He became the first native archbishop of Managua on February 16, 1970, and strived to maintain neutrality under both the Somoza regime and also the Sandinistas. In the 1980s, Obando Bravo spoke strongly against the Sandinistas and witnessed the closing by the revolutionary government of the archdiocesan newspaper and radio. He also took a hard line against liberation theology, and suggested that much of the pro-Sandinista energy in Nicaraguan Catholicism was created by foreign members of religious orders. In recent years he has earned a reputation as a good mediator in a badly divided country.

Otunga, Maurice Michael (Kenya, 79). Otunga studied theology in Rome at the Urban University in the late 1940s but then returned to Kenya and made his career there. He was named archbishop of Nairobi in 1971. He is seen as a champion of inculturation and a distinctively African way of being Catholic, and hence would tend to approve the program of the Reform party. He was made an auxiliary bishop in 1957, and attended all four sessions of the Second Vatican Council, from 1962 to 1965. He is seen as the grand old man of the African church. Otunga stepped down as archbishop in 1997, and in 1999 a biography of him appeared, *Cardinal Otunga: A Gift of Grace* by Margaret A. Ogola (Nairobi: Paulines Publications Africa, 1999).

Paskai, László (Hungary, 75). A Franciscan, Paskai has been the archbishop of Esztergom-Budapest since 1988. His clerical career covered most of the socialist era in Hungary, and like many Hungarian priests of his time, Paskai faced a choice between collaboration and resistance. He chose to get along. In 1981, for example, when a Piarist priest and activist named György Bulányi began preaching pacifism, church leaders such as Paskai said conscientious objection was barred under Hungary's constitution, and the church would not sanction disobedience. It supported government action against priests who defied the law. Bulányi today does not mince words. "In this country, the scum rose to the surface," he said in a 1997 interview. Paskai insists, however, that his option was the correct one. "We had to coexist. Here in Hungary we learned to talk rather than fight," he told me in Budapest in 1999. "The point is that the Catholic Church never supported the socialist ideology."

Pengo, Polycarp (Tanzania, 57). Archbishop of Dar-es-Salaam since 1992, Pengo is one of the youngest cardinals in the world. He succeeded Cardinal Laurean Rugambwa, the first native African bishop ever consecrated in his homeland. Pengo completed a doctorate in moral theology in 1977 at the Accademia Alfonsiana in Rome, run by the Redemptorists. Later he served as a seminary rector, but also did pastoral work with laity and the recruitment of vocations. He is known as a defender of human rights and a church leader with a strong ecumenical and interreligious spirit, critically important in a nation with such a strong Muslim majority. In the 1994 Synod on Africa, Pengo called for a balance between proper inculturation and not "baptising the very cultural institutions which caused so much suffering, fear, and anguish of mind in the traditional life of the people."

Piovanelli, Silvano (Italy, 78). If one takes the ancient prophecies of Saint Malachy seriously, the next pope should have the motto "The Glory of the Olive." That would seem to point to one of two men—either Martini (for martini drinkers, an olive has no greater glory than when it is resting at the bottom of a glass of gin) or Piovanelli, the archbishop of Florence, who comes from Mugello in Tuscany, Italy's prime olive-growing territory. Piovanelli shares some ideas with Martini, especially the desire for a more decentralized, less imperial church. But in his simple love for the poor and for immigrants, Piovanelli does not move in the same intellectual circles. He is moderate theologically and seen as a terrific pastor, more a doer than a thinker. His humility is legendary. Once when a Jesuit liturgical expert visited Florence, Piovanelli actually apologized for the design of the famed Duomo, saying he knew it put too much distance between the celebrant and the people. The expert replied: "Your Eminence, your warmth breaks down that distance." Most Florentines would agree.

Poletto, Severino (Italy, 69). Poletto has been bishop of three different Italian dioceses: Fossano, Asti, and most recently Turin. As the archbishop of Turin, he is the keeper of the legendary shroud, believed by devotees to be the burial cloth of Jesus. Poletto did his studies at the Accademia Alfonsiana in Rome in moral theology. In the 1970s, he was active in pastoral work with families, and in 1974 coordinated a Great Urban Mission to celebrate the five-hundredth anniversary of the foundation of his diocese. He does not have a strong reputation on theological debates and has generally stayed out of the spotlight, though he did make headlines in 2001 when he publicly criticized Italy's state-owned TV system for paying controversial rap star Eminem to play at the San Remo Festival. "This is not a question of censorship," he said. "We have to help young people decide between good and evil."

Pompedda, Mario Francesco (Italy, 73). A canon lawyer, Pompedda was made dean of the Roman Rota in 1993. He has been president of the Disciplinary Commission of the Roman Curia and president of the matrimonial tribunal of Vatican City State. Today he serves as prefect of the church's supreme tribunal, the Apostolic Signatura, a position akin to chief justice of the U.S. Supreme Court. At the extraordinary consistory of May 2001, Pompedda impressed many observers by not only calling in a general way for curial reform but specifically suggesting that local churches should have a greater say in the selection of bishops. Behind the scenes, Pompedda has sometimes come to the defense of fellow churchmen under siege. When controversial American TV nun Mother Angelica questioned the orthodoxy of Cardinal Roger Mahony of Los Angeles in 1997, Pompedda volunteered to bypass all other layers of jurisdiction in order to immediately consider a request by Mahony for disciplinary action (Mahony declined).

Poupard, Paul (France, 71). The pope's minister of culture, Poupard holds doctorate degrees in theology and history from the Sorbonne in Paris. From 1959 to 1972 he worked in the Secretariat of State, then returned to France to run the Catholic Institute in Paris. He has been awarded the Cardinal Grente grand prize from the Académie Française, and is a knight of the Légion d'honneur. Poupard is seen as a man of vision and depth, though also a loyal papal soldier. At the 1999 European Synod, for example, several participants spoke of feeling hemmed in by curial rules and pressure. Poupard appeared at a press conference and rejected such suggestions. "I have breathed the air of freedom and fraternity" at the synod, Poupard said. Saying he had been in five working groups, Poupard said, "In none did I see any tension between the curia and bishops with pastoral responsibilities."

Pujats, Jānis (Latvia, 71). Pujats studied at the seminary in Riga, Latvia, until 1951, when Soviet persecution intensified and the decision was made to ordain, in secret, all seminarians with three years and up in the system. A liturgical expert, Pujats published the first missal for the mass in the Latvian language. His appointment as a cardinal was carried out *in pectore,* or secretly, in 1998, and revealed in February 2001. Appointed archbishop after the fall of the Berlin Wall, Pujats has taken on a prominent public role. In 2000, for example, he led a number of religious leaders in refusing to take part in Latvia's National Day because of the government's adoption of a liberal abortion law and its refusal to crack down on child sexual abuse. Some analysts believe the Latvian Catholic Church is stuck in largely pre–Vatican II modes of thought and behavior, while the country's Lutherans have had better luck modernizing and developing a dynamic presence among families and the young.

Puljić, Vinco (Bosnia, 56). The youngest cardinal in the world, Puljić is the archbishop of Sarajevo. His nomination as a cardinal in 1994 was largely seen as a symbol of papal support during the time of the war in Bosnia-Herzegovina. He is the sixth archbishop of Bosnia, after four hundred years of Turkish domination. Puljić faces the challenge of rebuilding his diocese almost from the ground up after the devastation of war, raising funds from around the world to refurnish schools, hospitals, and churches. Puljić supported the Western intervention in Bosnia and argued that a more rapid response in Kosovo could have prevented bloodshed. Given his overwhelming preoccupations on the ground, Puljić has not expressed himself on many theological questions.

Ratzinger, Joseph (Germany, 75). Probably the best-known cardinal in the world, Ratzinger has served for twenty years as John Paul II's chief theological adviser. As a young priest he was on the progressive side of theological debates, and served at Vatican II as a *peritus* for reform-minded Cardinal Josef Frings. After the student revolutions of 1968, however, Ratzinger shifted to the right. In the Vatican, he has been the driving force behind crackdowns on liberation theology, religious pluralism, challenges to traditional moral teachings on issues such as homosexuality, and dissent on issues such as women's ordination. He is, however, a shy and gentle soul, and he is widely acknowledged as an excellent theologian. Former students speak of him as one of the best-prepared and most caring professors they ever encountered. He is the subject of my biography *Cardinal Ratzinger: The Vatican's Enforcer of the Faith* (Continuum, 2000).

Razafindratandra, Armand Gaétan (Madagascar, 76). Razafindratandra comes from a noble family that converted to Christianity in the ancient world. He studied at the Catholic Institute in Paris and then carried out pastoral work in Madagascar, working especially in catechetics and in the seminaries. He founded an ecumenical group that has played an important role in the country's democratic evolution. Razafindratandra is close in spirit to his fellow French-speaking church leaders, for example Etchegaray.

Rouco Varela, Antonio María (Spain, 65). Rouco Varela became a bishop in 1976 and took over as archbishop of Madrid in 1994. For ten years before that he was the director of the medieval pilgrimage center of San Juan Compostella, where he organized a youth extravaganza for John Paul II and captured the pope's interest. As a *papabile*, Rouco Varela was handed a major international forum in October 1999 when the pope made him the chairman of the European Synod. Most people believe he fumbled the opportunity, depressing the assembly with much Sturm und Drang pessimism about the "de-Christianization" of Europe.

Rubiano Sáenz, Pedro (Colombia, 69). Rubiano Sáenz was made a bishop in 1971, and has been the archbishop of Bogotá and primate of Colombia since 1994. His studies took place outside the country, at the University of Laval in Québec in theology, and at the Catholic University of America in Washington, D.C., in catechetics. He also became exposed to new currents in Catholic social teaching at the ILADES center in Santiago, Chile. He was a pastor, chaplain, educator, and administrator in the years before becoming a bishop. He is seen as cautious on doctrinal issues, with a priority on pastoral work.

Ruini, Camillo (Italy, 71). Ruini is the most powerful Italian cardinal, having been named vicar of Rome and president of the Italian bishops' conference by John Paul II in 1991. He comes from Reggio Emilia, long a breeding ground of ecclesiastical nobility. He is traditional in his theological approach, and is essentially an optimist—he believes that despite all its problems, Catholicism is well rooted in the West, especially among the young, and has a bright future. As head of the Italian bishops, Ruini plays an undefined but hugely important role in the country's politics. Since the collapse of the governing Christian Democrat coalition in 1992, Ruini has encouraged the growth of right-wing movements. In regional elections in 2000, for example, he quietly encouraged priests and nuns in and around Rome to support the neofascist candidate for governor. Ruini's agenda includes blocking change in social policy on homosexuality, birth control, and abortion, and seeking public funding for Catholic schools.

Saldarini, Giovanni (Italy, 77). Saldarini is a scripture scholar with a degree from the Pontifical Biblical Institute in Rome. He taught in a seminary for fifteen years, until Martini picked him as vicar for one of Milan's pastoral regions. Saldarini became an auxiliary bishop under Martini and eventually was named the archbishop of Turin in 1989. The pope asked him to preach the annual Lenten exercises in 1994, a sign of favor. Although Saldarini worked under Martini, he is not as progressive; he is generally regarded as somewhere between Martini and Ruini on most church debates.

Sandoval Iñiguez, Juan (Mexico, 69). Since 1994 the archbishop of Guadalajara, Sandoval Iñiguez entered the minor seminary in Mexico when he was twelve years old. He studied at the Gregorian University in Rome, then returned to Mexico, where he became a seminary instructor and rector before becoming a bishop in 1988. He is a prototypical John Paul II–style Latin American bishop, conservative on theological questions but a ferocious critic of social injustice. He took over from Cardinal Posadas Ocampo, assassinated in May 1993, and pushed for an investigation even against the wishes of the papal nuncio in Mexico. He was one of the chairs at the 1997 Synod on America, where several bishops remarked that they found him "very impressive."

Saraiva Martins, José (Portugal, 70). A Claretian, Saraiva Martins studied at Louvain in Belgium and also holds a doctorate in philosophy. He then taught at the Urban and Lateran Universities in Rome during most of the 1960s, 1970s, and 1980s. In 1998 he was named as the secretary for the Congregation for Catholic Education. Since May 1998, he has been the head of the Vatican's Congregation for the Causes of Saints, where he has helped preside over John Paul II's unprecedented burst of saint making. It was on Saraiva Martins's watch that the fateful decision was made to beatify Pope Pius IX over the objections of Jews, Italians, and many Catholics around the world. In 1990, Saraiva Martins helped craft a Vatican letter that urged seminaries to teach more Latin, Greek, church fathers, and traditional theology, and less history and sociology.

Schotte, Jan Pieter (Belgium, 74). A Scheut missionary, Schotte has run the Synod of Bishops since 1985. Initially this prominent position landed him on some lists of *papabili,* but over time his autocratic manner has diminished his popularity. Today a growing chorus of bishops is frustrated with the secrecy, lack of real exchange, and censorship that characterize the process. Schotte has bristled at most criticisms. In a June 2001 press conference, for example, Schotte rejected suggestions that the Vatican had an obligation to provide information to journalists, who had no more business inside the synod than they might have in a meeting of the board of directors of Coca-Cola. Schotte is also a strong conservative on theological matters; he once asked a missionary member of his own order who said that he believed in "evangelization by presence," rather than explicit appeals for conversion, when he was going to grow up.

Schwery, Henri (Switzerland, 69). Schwery was born near Sion in Switzerland, and after he became a priest he taught and served as chaplain for the Catholic Student Movement in the city. He became bishop of Sion in 1977, and became a cardinal in 1991. Schwery steered a moderate, pro–Vatican II course in a diocese that has been one of the nerve centers for the Saint Pius X movement launched by rebel French archbishop Marcel Lefebvre, a fierce critic of the council's reforms. He also found himself playing the mediator when ultraconservative bishop Wolfgang Haas alienated Catholics in the Swiss diocese of Chur; ultimately a new archdiocese had to be carved out for Haas in Liechtenstein.

Sebastiani, Sergio (Italy, 71). A graduate of the Pontifical Ecclesiastical Academy, Sebastiani worked in papal nunciatures in Peru, Chile, and Brazil in the 1970s, then came back to Rome to work in the Secretariat of State. He then returned to fieldwork, serving in nunciatures in France, Madagascar, and Turkey. Sebastiani was named president of the Prefecture for the Economic Affairs of the Holy See in 1997. Under his leadership, the Vatican has operated in the black, and Sebastiani for the first time in 1997 presented a consolidated financial statement with the costs and revenues of the seven administrations of the Holy See: the Administration of the Patrimony of the Apostolic See, the Congregation for the Evangelization of Peoples, the Apostolic Camera, Vatican Radio, the Tipografia Vaticana and *L'Osservatore Romano,* and the Vatican Television Center. He is a nuts-and-bolts administrator and a talented diplomat, with little track record on theological issues. He got into mild hot water in July 2001 when he told a press conference he thought the pope received a monthly stipend; spokesman Joaquín Navarro-Valls quickly denied it, saying that all the pope's expenses are paid for out of regular Vatican operating funds.

Sepe, Crescenzio (Italy, 59). Sepe is one of the rising stars on the Vatican scene. He first came to prominence as secretary of the Congregation for Clergy in 1996, when he organized a massively successful celebration of the fiftieth anniversary of John Paul's ordination to the priesthood. He then was placed in charge of the Jubilee 2000 effort, and managed to successfully orchestrate a yearlong cal-

endar full of conferences, ceremonies, and spectacles in Saint Peter's
Square that exhausted even battle-hardened Romans. His reward
was swift in coming; in February 2001 he became a cardinal and the
new head of the Congregation for the Evangelization of Peoples, the
Vatican office that oversees missionary efforts. Though seen largely
as an administrator, Sepe possesses a secular doctoral degree in philosophy from Rome's Sapienza University.

Shan Kui-hsi, Paul (Taiwan, 78). A Jesuit, Shan Kui-hsi is
the archbishop of Kao-hsiung in Taiwan. As a young priest he studied in the Philippines and in Rome. Besides Mandarin, his first language, Shan Kui-hsi speaks Latin, English, French, Italian, Spanish,
and Portuguese. He worked in education and Jesuit formation
in Taiwan until his nomination as a bishop in 1979. A strong advocate of inculturation, or allowing Catholicism to take shape in Asian
ways, he made the point clearly at the 1998 Asian Synod. "The
Catholic faith will not be intelligible or attractive to the peoples of
Asia if it continues to be a carbon copy of the Catholic Church in
the West," he said. He also said that if the Catholic Church truly believes that the Spirit of God is at work in the world, then it must "recognize the profound rays of truth and grace" present in other
religions.

Shirayanagi, Peter Seiichi (Japan, 73). Shirayanagi holds doc-
torates in philosophy from the Jesuit-run Sophia University in Japan
and in canon law from the Urban University in Rome. He did pastoral work in Japan in the 1950s and 1960s, and became the archbishop of Tokyo in 1970, a position he held for thirty years until his
retirement on February 17, 2000. Shirayanagi was for many years a
participant in the Federation of Asian Bishops' Conferences, and
shared its commitment to dialogue and inculturation.

Silvestrini, Achille (Italy, 78). Another genuine intellectual in
the college, Silvestrini holds a doctorate in classical philology from
the University of Bologna. Silvestrini has played almost every role the
Vatican bureaucracy has to offer, from a papal diplomat under former

secretary of state Agostino Casaroli (he took part in negotiations for the Helsinki accords in 1977) to prefect of the Congregation for the Oriental Churches from 1991 to 2000. He is moderate to liberal on theological questions in the tradition of the Second Vatican Council, and a churchman unafraid of modern culture. He celebrated a funeral mass for filmmaker Federico Fellini, calling him a "lord of images," despite Fellini's tempestuous relationship with the Vatican over the years. Collaborators say Silvestrini is a man with a keen grasp of details and a respect for talent wherever he finds it.

Simonis, Adrianus Johannes (The Netherlands, 70). Simonis, the archbishop of Utrecht, is symbolic of the change in the Dutch church since the late 1970s. In the years immediately after Vatican II, it was the most progressive and most vibrant Catholic community in the world. Rome became alarmed that things were getting out of control, especially when a wildly popular Dutch national catechism appeared to call into question central Christian teachings such as the historical character of Christ's resurrection. Simonis, a Rome-educated scripture scholar, was sent to Utrecht in 1983 to clean things up. He has drawn the Dutch church into a more Roman orbit, though some believe at the price of eroding its validity.

Sin, Jaime L. (The Philippines, 73). Sin has the distinction of having been instrumental in bringing down two Filipino governments. He was a hero of the Rosary Revolution in 1986 that toppled President Ferdinand Marcos, and in 2001 he insisted that President Joseph Estrada, accused of plundering the national treasury, was no longer fit to govern. Both men were replaced by populist women closely connected to the church, Corazón Aquino and Gloria Macapagal Arroyo. Because of his political engagement, Sin has a high profile (his improbable name, Cardinal Sin, doesn't hurt his exposure). Sin also impressed the Catholic world by turning out 4 million people in Manila for the January 1995 visit of John Paul II for World Youth Day. Sin is a traditionalist on theological questions but is not seen as rigid or inquisitorial.

Sodano, Angelo (Italy, 74). Sodano, a native of Asti in Italy, was born into politics, as his father was a member of the Italian parliament. He had a long career in the Vatican diplomatic corps, including a stint in Chile during the Pinochet years in which he developed a friendly relationship with the general. In 1987 he engineered John Paul's trip to Chile, when the pope appeared with Pinochet on the balcony of Moneda Palace to the cheers of supporters. Sodano became secretary of state in 1991, and has pushed Vatican foreign policy to support political leaders most likely to translate church teaching into public policy. He has also brought a group of like-minded conservative Latin Americans into the curia. Though conservative, Sodano has taken pains to keep lines of communication open. In 1998, he complimented the writings of dissident theologian Hans Küng, saying they are full of "beautiful pages dedicated to the Christian mystery." In 2001, when progressive German cardinal Karl Lehmann got his red hat, Sodano gave him a bear hug and said, "Karl, you don't know how many friends you have here."

Stafford, James Francis (United States, 69). The former archbishop of Denver, Stafford runs the Pontifical Council for the Laity. He is a keen, scholarly man, and conservative theologically; he once wrote to a liturgical translation agency raising objections to their decision not to use the word *man*, for example, in their version of certain Old Testament texts. Yet he is open to debate and thought to be very fair in his personal judgments. Close associates say he struggled in pastoral settings, often preferring work in his study or debates on points of theology or church practice to working crowds at a social gathering. His great success in Denver was organizing the 1993 World Youth Day, which dramatically exceeded expectations in terms of turnout and clearly pleased John Paul. As head of the laity office, Stafford has been an enthusiastic backer of the new movements, such as Focolare, the Neocatechumenate, and the Legionaries of Christ.

Sterzinsky, Georg Maximilian (Germany, 66). A Pole by birth, Sterzinsky's family moved to Germany after World War II. He was incardinated into the diocese of Erfurt-Meiningen, where he did pastoral work and taught in the major seminary. He became the bishop of Berlin in 1989 and was made a cardinal in 1991. (Sterzinsky became an archbishop, however, only in 1994, because prior to that date Berlin was not a metropolitan see.) Sterzinsky forms part of the conservative bloc in the German bishops' conference. He resisted efforts to find a compromise on his country's abortion counseling debate in 1999, for example, pushing instead for abandoning the system, as had been demanded by Rome.

Suárez Rivera, Adolfo Antonio (Mexico, 75). Suárez Rivera was born in San Cristóbal de las Casas in Mexico and studied in Rome, the United States, and Chile. He worked largely in various diocesan offices until he was made a bishop in 1971, and moved through two dioceses before eventually becoming the archbishop of Monterey in 1983. He has a reputation as a relative moderate in Mexico's traditionally quite conservative episcopal conference. He has spoken strongly on issues of globalization, defense of local cultures, and the debt crisis, and as president of the Mexican bishops' conference often clashed with the papal nuncio over the right of the local bishops to make their own decisions.

Szoka, Edmund Casimir (United States, 74). Szoka, the son of a Polish immigrant family in Grand Rapids, Michigan, rose to become the archbishop of Detroit from 1981 to 1990. Szoka was then called to Rome, at the age of seventy, to take on the thankless task of reorganizing Vatican finances in the wake of several banking scandals and years of red ink. Szoka got the job done, and the Holy See has been in the black since. Szoka is also the prelate who actually runs the administration of Vatican City State. He is a bedrock conservative theologically. In Detroit, he engaged in a public struggle with Sister Agnes Mary Mansour, a Mercy nun who directed the state Department of Social Services, which dispensed

Medicaid abortion funding. Szoka told her she had to quit. She resisted, but the struggle ended in Mansour leaving her religious order.

Taofinu'u, Pio (Samoa, 78). Taofinu'u, a member of the Marist order, grew up in Samoa and did his studies in New Zealand and the United States. He was a diocesan official during the 1960s, was made a bishop in 1968, and has been a cardinal since 1973. He was Samoa's first native prelate. One of his pastoral goals has been to build on the indigenous tradition to bolster Samoa's family life. Taofinu'u is also a champion of inculturation. He appears in a video by Chicago-based liturgical publisher Gia that shows a Fijian liturgy with a male dancer in a presentation dance, which rivets the worshiper's attention to a most holy moment as the chalice is offered in a ritual directly lifted from the local culture. Many of the liturgical adaptations were scripted by Taofinu'u.

Terrazas Sandoval, Julio (Bolivia, 66). Terrazas Sandoval, the archbishop of La Paz, is a Redemptorist who studied in Argentina and in France before returning to Bolivia. He is Bolivia's first cardinal. He has a reputation as an excellent pastor, a courageous advocate of social justice, and a theological moderate open to experimentation. At the 1985 meeting of the Synod of Bishops devoted to a review of Vatican II, he laid some issues on the line. "We submit to the synod some considerations: that there be faith in the relative autonomy of the local church; that the urgency of instituting ministers of the Eucharist to serve our communities be understood; that the role of faith and justice in today's world be articulated with greater precision."

Tomko, Jozef (Slovakia, 78). Tomko, a hard-nosed Vatican traditionalist of the old school, started his Vatican career unapologetically censoring books for the Holy Office. He served as head of the Congregation for the Evangelization of Peoples from 1985 to 2000 and pushed for Catholicism to recapture its missionary zeal. He clashed with theologians such as Belgian Jesuit Father Jacques Dupuis, who wanted to say that there may be room for other religions too in God's saving plan. His last shot before retiring in May 2001 was a document insisting that missionary priests who come to Europe and the United States go home, where they're needed, and that First World bishops should stop using them to compensate for priest shortages.

Tumi, Christian Wiyghan (Cameroon, 71). Tumi, the archbishop of Garoua, is a very well educated man, having studied at the University of Lyons in France and Fribourg in Switzerland (he holds a doctorate in philosophy from Fribourg). He did pastoral work and taught in seminaries until being made a bishop in 1979. He has been the head of the Garoua archdiocese since 1982. He is a native French speaker and a theological conservative. He is proud of the growth of the church in Africa. At the Synod on Africa in 1994, he described the change as one from "the status of a church of mission to a church in the mission."

Turcotte, Jean-Claude (Canada, 65). Turcotte, a native French speaker, holds a degree in social pastoral work from the Catholic Faculty in Lille, France. He held a variety of administrative positions in the archdiocesan bureaucracy before becoming the auxiliary bishop of Montreal in 1982. He took over the top job in 1990, and became a cardinal in 1994. One Canadian observer describes him as a diamond in the rough, a potentially magnificent leader who is still finding his way. He is a theological moderate, having allowed his archdiocesan synod in 1998 to adopt positions supporting the ordination of women as priests and deacons and calling for married priests, a greater lay role in decision making, and a new approach to divorce. He once described the post–Vatican II era of Catholic history this way: "From the idea of an authoritarian, hierarchical church, we are moving toward a church of the people of God. An extraordinary hope, a great change."

Velasco García, Ignacio Antonio (Venezuela, 73). Velasco García is a member of the Salesian order, with degrees in philosophy and pedagogy from the Salesian University in Turin and in theology from the Gregorian University in Rome. He worked mostly as a seminary instructor and rector until his nomination as a bishop in 1989. He took over as the archbishop of Caracas in 1995. He has been un-afraid to confront political figures he believes abuse their office. In March 2000, when President Hugo Chávez proposed a constitu-tional change that would expand his own power, Velasco García ac-cused him of "provoking the wrath of God" and thereby triggering mud slides that had devastated several hillside communities days be-fore. He also has not been bashful about pushing the idea of a Latin American pope. Speaking with reporters in February 2001 in Rome, he said, "I think it's likely. It's just a guess, because in a conclave many things happen. There certainly will be some votes," Velasco García said, raising his hand to indicate he could be among those vot-ing for a Latin American.

Vidal, Ricardo J. (The Philippines, 71). Since 1982, Vidal has been archbishop of Cebu, and he functions as something of a coun-terpoint to Sin, in Manila. Where Sin is omnipresent in the media, Vidal is more withdrawn; where Sin is the ultimate populist, Vidal is more hierarchical and Roman in his approach. Quietly, officials from the Secretariat of State have occasionally approached reporters who cover Catholic affairs to ask them to play up Vidal more and Sin less in the Philippines, usually with few results. Vidal is said to be mod-est, deeply spiritual, and very safe on doctrinal issues.

Vithayathil, Varkey (India, 75). Another Redemptorist cardinal, Vithayathil has a reputation as a fix-it man, going where people need him to solve problems or resolve conflicts. Vithayathil is a member of the Syro-Malabar rite and did his doctoral work at the Angelicum University in Rome on Origen and the development of the Syro-Malabar hierarchy. He taught for twenty-five years in the Redemptorist seminary in Bangalore, India. From 1990 to 1996 he had the odd as-signment of apostolic administrator of the Benedictine monastery of Asirvanam, Bangalore, because the monastery was badly divided and in need of external help. He became a bishop in 1996 and a cardinal in 2001. He is seen as a talented administrator and a decisive leader, very loyal to the Vatican authorities.

Wamala, Emmanuel (Uganda, 75). The archbishop of Kampala since 1990, Wamala, an English speaker, studied at the Urban and the Gregorian Universities in Rome and then at the University of Notre Dame in the United States. He has taken the positions expected of a Catholic cardinal on cultural issues, attacking family planning and abortion programs, and has tried to promote peace in Africa's Great Lakes region. He is a routine participant in political debates in Uganda, arguing for reforms in electoral systems. Wamala has not been isolated from the poverty and violence that afflict his country. In February 1996, Wamala was held in his residence for several hours by an armed gunman, who killed himself when he realized he had no way out. On a personal level, Wamala is shy, at times soft-spoken, and can be quite funny.

Wetter, Friedrich (Germany, 74). Wetter is the successor of Joseph Ratzinger in Munich, and is himself a vigorous conservative on theological matters. In February 1998, he instructed the Bavarian culture minister to deny a license to teach to Catholic theologian Perry Schmidt-Luekel, who holds that *pluralism,* the notion that other religions offer salvation on their own terms, should be an option. He is capable of blunt, at times divisive talk; he once compared abortion to the sexual abuse and murder of a six-year-old girl in Munich, causing the girl's father to complain of "poor taste." He also led protests in the wake of a Bavarian supreme court decision that mandated the removal of crucifixes from public school classrooms, calling it an "edict of intolerance." Wetter did his theological studies in Rome and Munich and taught theology before becoming a bishop in 1968.

Williams, Thomas Stafford (New Zealand, 72). The archbishop of Wellington since 1979, Williams did his studies in Rome, at the Urban University, and in Dublin. He is an expert on the Pacific Islands surrounding New Zealand, having long reached out to the scattered peoples there. Williams was one of the copresidents at the 1998 Synod on Oceania, where he suggested taking another look at the church policy that excludes divorced and civilly remarried Catholics from the sacraments. Yet on most doctrinal matters he is no innovator. He took a strong line in 1996 when Victoria University's religious studies lecturer Jim Veitch argued that the divinity of Jesus was a concept introduced by the early church. Denying that Jesus was the Son of God is the "worst form of Scrooge-ism," Cardinal Williams said. "Sadly, there always have been those who, under the guise of scholarly research, regurgitate ancient heresies and long-discredited hypotheses."

Wu Cheng-chung, John Baptist (Hong Kong, 77). Wu Cheng-chung is the archbishop of Hong Kong, and he holds a doctorate in canon law from Rome's Urban University. He also studied in the United States during a period of exile. He became the head of the church in Hong Kong in 1975, and a cardinal in 1988. In 1986, for the first time in forty years, the Chinese authorities allowed Wu Cheng-chung to visit his relatives on the mainland. In his relations with the Communist government of mainland China, Wu Cheng-chung has played a delicate balancing act, not wanting to make things worse for believers but wishing to pressure the state to reform. Hence Wu Cheng-chung has criticized attempts to crack down on the Falun Gong movement and expressed reservations about cooperating with the British handover of Hong Kong to China. His theological views are traditional, but his preoccupation has long been the precarious condition of the Chinese church.

Glossary

Antipope. An antipope is a pope elected in opposition to the pope rightfully chosen under church law. When there is an antipope, at least two men are claiming to be the true leader of the Catholic Church. Often antipopes are obscure figures who have no following (there are at least six antipopes challenging John Paul II's legitimacy, but none seriously). In other cases, antipopes can be greatly destabilizing. In April 1378, Urban VI was elected under suspect circumstances, and shortly afterward the cardinals regrouped and elected Clement VII. The result was the Great Western Schism, a period of some forty years in which the Catholic Church was split in half.

Apostolic succession. Catholic theology holds that the bishops stand in an unbroken line of succession from the twelve apostles, who were Jesus' closest followers. The idea—contested by some historians—is that Jesus chose the apostles, and they chose their successors, and so on, so that today's bishop of Dallas or Denver is part of a chain that reaches back to the foundation of the church.

Bishop. Theologically, bishop is the highest office in the Catholic Church. An archbishop, who is the head of a major diocese, and a cardinal, who is one of the pope's closest collaborators, are simply higher grades of bishops (in fact, some cardinals are not bishops). In ancient Christianity, a bishop was the leader of a local church, the one whose word was most authoritative on matters of faith and morals. Today a bishop is still fundamentally the pastor, or guide, of a local church, so the bishop of Duluth in Minnesota is the leader of Catholics there. However, some bishops hold other jobs. Some, called *auxiliary bishops,* are helpers of a bishop in running a diocese that is especially large or complex. Bishops may also be called upon to work in administrative capacities, such as in the Roman Curia. Every bishop, however, must have a diocese, and so auxiliary bishops and curial bishops are assigned *titular* dioceses, so called because they exist in name only.

Camerlengo. The camerlengo, or chamberlain, is the most important official in the period between the death of a pope and the election of a new one. He administers the property and the finances of the Holy See during the interregnum. In earlier periods the camerlengo could make some decisions for the pope when he was out of Rome, but modern communications technologies have rendered this aspect of the job superfluous.

Capitulation. An agreement drawn up during a conclave, or before, by which papal candidates agree to follow certain policies if elected. The conclave that elected Pius II in 1458, for example, drew up a capitulation in which the new pope promised to continue a war against the Turks, to reform the Roman Curia, and to submit his policies to an annual examination by the College of Cardinals. Often the new pope promptly disavowed the capitulation. In 1562 Pius IV forbade such pacts, and current rules state that even if the new pope swore to follow certain policies during the conclave, once elected he is not bound to do so.

Cardinal. Cardinals are the *princes of the church.* They are the closest advisers of the pope and are normally either archbishops of major dioceses (for example, New York) or heads of offices in the Roman Curia (for example, the Congregation for the Doctrine of the Faith). The pope, however, can make any Catholic he chooses a cardinal, and John Paul has elevated several nonbishops to honor distinguished theological careers (though in virtually every case the honorees were already over eighty and hence ineligible to vote for the next pope). Cardinals wear red as a sign of their being willing to shed their blood for the church. The word comes from the Latin *cardo*, which means *hinge*, and today suggests the cardinal's role of being a connection between the pope and the rest of the church. (The word *cardinal* is often placed in the middle of the man's name, said by some to signify this hinge function: hence *Christoph Cardinal Schönborn* and so on.) There are three kinds of cardinals: cardinal deacons, cardinal priests, and cardinal bishops. Originally the deacons took care of the social work in the diocese of Rome, while the priests ran Roman parishes. The bishops, who governed sees outside of Rome, were the senior members of the college and the closest advisers to the pope. Today these distinctions are largely meaningless; the vast majority of cardinals are cardinal priests.

Casa Santa Marta. A twenty-million-dollar hotel-like residence constructed within the Vatican under John Paul II. It has 108 two-room suites and twenty-three individual rooms, each with an individual bath, and it is where the cardinals will stay during the conclave. Telephone, fax, and e-mail services will be disconnected during the conclave.

College of Cardinals. All the cardinals together form a *college*, whose most important function is the election of the pope. In the eleventh and twelfth centuries, the College of Cardinals emerged as the most important consultative body to the pope. Eventually the issues facing the church became too complex for all the cardinals to deal with them collectively, and subgroups, or congregations, were formed, which developed into the offices of the Roman Curia. In the sixteenth and seventeenth centuries, as papal absolutism took hold, the role of the College of Cardinals was diminished until it became largely ceremonial, except for the right to the papal election. John Paul II somewhat revitalized the cardinals' role, inviting them to Rome to give advice and turning to them for help on especially difficult matters.

Conclave. The secret meeting of cardinals in which a new pope is elected. The word comes from two Latin terms meaning *with key,* referring to the custom that cardinals are locked up for the duration of the balloting. Rules adopted by John Paul II in 1996 require that a pope be elected by a two-thirds vote, although he added a provision that after approximately twelve days and perhaps as many as thirty ballots, the cardinals may decide by an absolute majority to elect the pope by only an absolute majority. They may also decide to go to a majority vote between the two candidates with the most votes in the preceeding ballot.

Consistory. A meeting of the College of Cardinals. There are two kinds. An ordinary consistory is one in which new members of the College of Cardinals are inducted by the pope. An extraordinary consistory occurs when the pope calls the cardinals together to advise him on some topic. John Paul II has done this six times, most recently May 21–24, 2001, when he solicited ideas from the cardinals for taking the church into the third millennium.

Curia. The papal bureaucracy in Rome. The curia includes three types of departments. *Congregations* are older offices with decision-making responsibility for areas of church life such as faith, liturgy, saints, religious communities, and clergy. *Councils* are post–Vatican II offices designed to promote certain goals, such as Christian unity, interreligious dialogue, and peace and justice. Typically they are thought of as less important within the curia because they lack jurisdictional authority. *Tribunals* are the courts of the Catholic Church, which hear appeals of marriage cases, disciplinary actions against priests and nuns, and all other matters arising from canon law.

Dean. The dean of the College of Cardinals, who convokes meetings of cardinals and presides over them, is elected by and from the cardinal bishops. Currently the job belongs to African cardinal Bernardin Gantin, former head of the Congregation for Bishops. It will be the dean who formally informs the cardinals of the death of the pope and who will preside over their meetings during the period between the pope's death and the election of a successor.

Dicastery. A catchall term for the offices of the Roman Curia. Congregations, councils, and tribunals are thus all dicasteries. An *interdicasterial commission* is a special working group composed of members of several curial offices to deal with a specific problem or issue.

Ecumenical council. A gathering of all the bishops to make major decisions about doctrine and the policies of the church. The last ecumenical council was the Second Vatican Council (1962–65).

General congregation. From a few days after the death of the pope until the election of a successor, the cardinals meet in a session called the general congregation. The general congregation cannot decide to change the rules for electing the pope, cannot appoint new cardinals, and cannot make any decisions that would be binding on the new pope. The dean of the college presides over the general congregation. Its meetings are open to all cardinals, including those over eighty.

Holy See. The technical term for the Vatican as a global diplomatic entity, with sovereign status and the capacity to enter into formal relations with other states. Governments do not send ambassadors to the Vatican but to the Holy See, since the pope is not just the governor of Vatican City State but also the spiritual head of the Catholic Church worldwide.

Infirmarii. Inside the conclave, the least senior cardinal deacon will draw three names of cardinals to collect ballots from any cardinals who are present but too sick to physically cast their own ballots. These three cardinals are called the *infirmarii.*

Interregnum. The entire period from the death of the pope to the election of a successor. The term comes from two Latin words, *inter,* meaning *between,* and *regnum,* meaning *reign.*

Novemdiales. Rules for the papal election specify that the conclave must take place no fewer than fifteen days and no more than twenty days after the death of the pope. Within that fifteen-to-twenty-day span is a nine-day period of official mourning called the *novemdiales.* The *novemdiales* period is the peak campaign season for the conclave.

Papabile. An Italian word literally meaning *popeable,* the word *papabile* is applied to a man thought to have a serious chance to become the next pope. Roman newspapers are forever full of lists of *papabili,* sometimes based on inside analysis, often on informed guesses.

Particular congregation. A group of three cardinals chosen by lot, plus the camerlengo, that deals with matters of less importance during the period between the death of the pope and the conclave. One cardinal under eighty from each of the three orders (cardinal bishop, cardinal priest, and cardinal deacon) is chosen to assist the camerlengo. Every three days from the death of the pope until the conclave, a new set of three cardinals is selected.

Revisers. During the conclave, the least senior cardinal deacon, currently Cardinal Crescenzio Sepe, will draw three names of cardinals to serve as revisers, whose function it is to confirm that the vote tallies of each ballot are correct. After the revisers have finished their work, the ballots are burned unless another vote is to take place immediately.

Scrutineers. During the conclave, the least senior cardinal deacon will draw three names of cardinals to serve as scrutineers, who have the job of counting the votes after each ballot. The scrutineers make sure their tallies agree, and their work is then checked by the revisers.

Scrutiny. The technical term in a conclave for election of the pope by secret ballot; each round of balloting is called a scrutiny. In 1996, John Paul II abolished the other two modes of papal election that used to be on the books. One was *acclamation,* by which all the cardinals suddenly and spontaneously proclaim one man as the next pope. Such acclamation had to be unanimous to be valid. The other method was *delegation,* by which the cardinals would empower a subgroup, not to exceed nine, to choose the pope on their behalf. They had to agree unanimously to use this method, and to agree unanimously as to the group's rules of procedure. Today, however, only the scrutiny method may be used.

Sede vacante. Latin for *when the seat is empty.* It refers to the period between the death of one pope and the election of another.

Universi Dominici Gregis. Each pope typically sets out the rules of procedure for electing his successor, usually largely confirming the previous rules but adding a few new twists. John Paul did this in 1996 with *Universi Dominici Gregis,* which, unless the pope issues another document, establishes the rules the conclave is bound to follow. The two major innovations were abolishing all the methods of electing a pope other than scrutiny, and creating a provision by which a pope could be elected by a simple majority after attempts to reach a two-thirds consensus have failed for approximately twelve days or thirty ballots.

Vatican II. The last ecumenical council of the Catholic Church, the Second Vatican Council (1962–65), or Vatican II as it is commonly known, was the only ecumenical council not called to deal with a specific heresy or crisis. Instead it sought a general modernizing of the Catholic Church, referred to by the Italian word *aggiornamento*. The church was to be less condemning, less monarchical, working more in partnership with the modern world. Debate over the legacy of Vatican II will certainly help shape how the cardinals in the conclave go about selecting the next pope.

White smoke. After a round of voting is completed inside the conclave, the ballots are burned and the smoke released through a chimney atop the Sistine Chapel. Before 1550, the voting papers were burned in a *focune,* the touchhole of a gun, which was lit inside the Sistine Chapel. Pope Julius III, however, an art lover, worried that the smoke might damage the frescoes. He ordered that a stove be installed with its chimney clear of the building. Black smoke means the ballot was inconclusive, while white means there is a new pope. Special chemicals are added to achieve the desired color. In 1978, however, the smoke came out a confusing gray.

Index

John L. Allen, Jr., is the Vatican correspondent for the *National Catholic Reporter*, an independent Catholic weekly in the United States. His controversial 2000 biography of Cardinal Joseph Ratzinger, *Cardinal Ratzinger: The Vatican's Enforcer of the Faith* (Continuum), was widely reviewed. His work has appeared in a variety of American and European publications, including the *Miami Herald*, the *Nation*, the *Irish Examiner*, the *Tablet*, *Public Forum*, and *Commonweal*. His reporting has been honored by the Catholic Press Association. During the next conclave Allen will be an expert analyst for the Fox News Channel. He lives in Rome with his wife, Shannon.